Selected Plays

A Note on the Translations

This collection includes new translations of all the plays except *Miss Julie*, translated by Evert Sprinchorn (San Francisco: Chandler, 1961).

A Note on Stage Directions

The stage directions in these translations follow the nineteenth-century Scandinavian custom of indicating left and right from the point of view of the audience, not the actor.

Selected Plays

VOLUME 1
The Pre-Inferno Period

August Strindberg

Translated and Introduced by Evert Sprinchorn

University of Minnesota Press □ Minneapolis

Published by the University of Minnesota Press
2037 University Avenue Southeast, Minneapolis MN 55414.
Published simultaneously in Canada
by Fitzhenry & Whiteside Limited, Markham.
Printed in the United States of America.

Library of Congress Cataloging-in-Publication Data

Strindberg, August, 1849–1912.
  Selected plays.

  Contents: v. 1. The pre-Inferno period – v. 2. The post-Inferno
period.
  1. Strindberg, August, 1849–1912 – Translations,
English. I. Sprinchorn, Evert. II. Title.
PT9811.A3S635   1986   839.7'26   85-30224
ISBN 0-8166-1338-9 (pbk. : v. 1)
ISBN 0-8166-1339-7 (pbk. : v. 2)

The University of Minnesota
is an equal-opportunity
educator and employer.

With two actors I could create
a little world; and with three,
move it.

August Strindberg

Contents

Plays contained in Volume 2: *To Damascus* (I), *Crimes and Crimes, The Dance of Death* (I), *A Dream Play, The Ghost Sonata,* and *The Pelican.*

Introduction

Strindberg's dramatic writings are as remarkable for their variety as for their quantity. The plays in this collection are meant to serve as an introduction to them by representing the different phases in Strindberg's career and the different styles and forms he either adopted or invented.

Although Strindberg began his creative career as a dramatist, he achieved his first unqualified success with the public and critics as a novelist when he published *The Red Room* in 1879. In his native Sweden, Strindberg is equally esteemed as novelist and dramatist. He is also Sweden's greatest social satirist. He differs from all the other truly great dramatists in that he was productive in nearly every form and genre of literature. In addition to his fifty or sixty plays (the number varies depending on whether one includes uncompleted works and how one counts double dramas and trilogies) and four novels, his collected works consist of two volumes of poetry, nine volumes of short stories, three volumes of cultural history, ten volumes of autobiography, and fifteen volumes of articles, essays, and sketches on every conceivable subject. If these writings are regrouped and arranged strictly in the order in which he wrote them, a significant pattern emerges: in each of the four major phases of his career the drama became the vehicle for his deepest thought and most daring techniques.

In the first phase, spanning the 1870s, Strindberg appears as a social critic rebelling against the establishment. In the 1880s the social rebel immerses himself in psychological studies. In his third phase, which links the nineteenth and twentieth centuries, the psychologist plunges into the depths of the soul and there discovers forces larger than social or psychological ones. A few years later the mystic attempts to describe and analyze the great comprehensive design formed out of individual destinies. In passing through these phases the young romantic writer becomes successively a realist, a symbolist, an expressionist, and a surrealist.

This dazzling variety has blinded many students, critics, and casual readers to Strindberg's accomplishments as a spokesman for his time and as a thinker for the ages, while many critics who are willing to accept him as a remarkable chronicler reprobate him for being the spokesman for reactionary and unsavory ideas.

An eminent professor of literature at one of America's larger universities once opined at a cocktail party that Strindberg could not be placed among the truly great creative artists because there was too much hatred in him. Pressed for evidence of this, the professor admitted he had read only *The Father* and *Miss Julie*, and those long ago. His point was that Strindberg's reputation reposed mainly on these plays and that they were filled with a venomous hatred of women. The young students who had formed an adoring circle around their mentor were left to infer how different Strindberg was from Ibsen and Shakespeare in his attitude toward women. Shakespeare had given us such adorable creatures as Juliet, Mariana, Desdemona, Beatrice, and Portia; and Ibsen had spearheaded the feminist movement in the latter half of the nineteenth century by writing *A Doll's House*. Nothing was said about Lady Macbeth as the incarnation of evil, or about Lear's anathemas denouncing the female sex, or about the revulsion against womankind expressed in the sonnets. No one noted the number of times that Ibsen allows women to offer up themselves on the altar of male genius. No one pointed out that the woman in one of Ibsen's earlier plays who calmly accepts the fact that her lot in life is to love, to sacrifice all, and then be forgotten is only one of many such women in the plays of the Norwegian "feminist." No one remarked that Ibsen himself disclaimed the honor of having worked for women's rights and that he was quite unclear about what those rights were. He was very clear, however, concerning women's function in the advancement of civilization: they were to be mothers, first of all, entrusted with the task of breeding and rearing, educating and disciplining children.

Except for the emphasis on discipline, Strindberg agreed
with Ibsen that a woman's primary role in society was to be
a mother. Coming from Strindberg, however, the thought
always seemed antifeminist. Yet it was Strindberg, not Ibsen, who drew up a platform of women's rights (in his preface to a collection of short stories, *Getting Married*) in
which he advocated that boys and girls should be allowed
to mix more freely in school, that women should be given
the franchise as soon as possible, and that separate
bedrooms should be the rule in marriages to ensure women
the right to possess their own bodies. Ibsen prudently left
the idea of women's independence as a vague concept and
won the adoration of the feminists. Strindberg was explicit
and won their hatred.

Why? One answer can be found in Strindberg's short
story "A Doll's House," a riposte to Ibsen's play. Strindberg
regarded Ibsen's Nora with all her talk about miracles and
sacrifices as a hysterical type, an unnatural woman who dis-
liked physical sex. To Strindberg she was the product of a
social class that was overcultured, and consequently she
was of interest only to others of her class.

Strindberg himself said that his misogyny was largely
theoretical, by which he meant that it was his contribution
to the feminist question, a heatedly debated issue in the
1880s, just as it was to be three-quarters of a century later
in America. (To the student of social history the feminist
movement in the 1960s and 1970s seems like a repetition
of events in Scandinavia.) His stand on the subject was intended to complement what he considered to be the narrow
views of Ibsen.

Refusing to be identified with the feminist movement,
Ibsen averred that his task had been the description of humanity. Strindberg would have said the same about himself. He would never have prosecuted the women's rights
movement if he had not been passionately interested in the
behavior of human beings. He first approached the matter
as a sociologist might, but when he was drawn into a bitter
conflict with the feminists, he began to see the whole question in the light of psychology, a subject that was coming
into its own during those years. The feminist question

provided the means by which he could enter certain unexplored areas of the human soul. Out of these investigations came, among other things, a five-volume autobiography and the penetrating psychological dramas *The Father* and *Miss Julie.*

He called his autobiography *The Son of a Servant* and gave it the subtitle "The Story of the Evolution of a Human Soul." The title indicated that his political sympathies were with the lower classes, and the subtitle suggested that he had aligned himself with the French naturalists, who believed that creative writers should adopt the experimental method of scientists, discounting the ideal and concerning themselves exclusively with physical reality. Writing as a scientist who had shed all social and religious prejudices and preconceptions and who believed he was studying the world objectively, Strindberg argued that parents were inevitably tyrannical, that the family was a prison, that children should be allowed to escape from it as soon as possible, that the natural instincts should be given full expression, and that masturbation would not lead to nervous debility but that sexual abstinence might. For espousing these advanced ideas, which only during the height of the Victorian age were deemed particularly dangerous, Strindberg was disowned by the young liberals and ostracized by virtually everybody. By the late 1880s Strindberg, who thought of himself as a great emancipator, was the most hated man in Sweden.

He closed his shop in Stockholm, moved to Berlin and then to Paris, where he occupied himself with alchemical experiments, hoping to prove that the so-called elements could be reduced further and that they could be transmuted one into another. For about five years the investigating scientist usurped the place of the creative writer. When he returned to writing, it became apparent that those years of scientific research had indeed effected a transmutation – not of the elements, however, but of Strindberg himself. The political agitator who had given currency to the term "the lower classes," the aggressive polemicist, the social satirist who had lampooned well-known and recognizable figures and institutions, the atheistic naturalist who had portrayed human beings as animals driven by their instincts, had been transformed into a religious thinker for whom the only reality was that of the spirit. To most of his countrymen the emergence of this new Strindberg was as deplorable an event as the appearance of the first Strindberg had been, but it confirmed them in their view that Strindberg had been quite mad all along. The dangerous radical who had overreached himself in his endeavors to undermine society had now suffered the just consequences: social and mental alienation.

Strindberg's active participation in political and sexual controversies was and still is an impediment to a proper appreciation and understanding of his accomplishments as a creative artist. To most critics he remains a rather unpleasant eccentric at best, a misogynistic madman at worst, an antifeminist pamphleteer with some genuine insight into human behavior, and a mentally unbalanced artist capable of some strokes of genius. It should be apparent now, so many years after his death, that he was a consummate artist, a comprehensive chronicler of the times in which he lived, a perceptive analyst of human nature, and, like all great writers, a profound moral philosopher.

His more severe critics always judged him from their own moral and political positions, which was how Strindberg wanted it. If it was difficult at times to see the artist's technical mastery because politics obscured the view, it was never difficult to see where Strindberg stood on the major social issues. The conflict between those who were for Strindberg and those who were against him embroiled the whole of Sweden near the end of his life, when he deliberately sought a confrontation, challenging his critics to come out of their aesthetic lairs. The resulting public debate, known as the Strindberg controversy, revealed that the judgments pronounced on the moral and artistic value of his works and the diagnoses made of his mental health had been made primarily on social and political grounds. At the time of the controversy the combatants were most readily identified as either pro- or anti-Strindberg, which meant pro- or anti-establishment, pro- or anti-militarism. If the battle had lasted longer, and in a very real sense it did, other labels would have been applied. Not surprisingly, those who ranged themselves against Strindberg in 1910 and who lived on into the 1920s and 1930s revealed themselves with amazing consistency as Fascists and Nazis, while those who had sided with Strindberg came out as supporters of the democracies and the free world.

A late and instructive example of the sort of thinking that characterized the anti-Strindbergian forces is provided by the English critic F. L. Lucas, who in his book *Ibsen and Strindberg* (1962) writes perspicaciously on the former and obtusely on the latter. He sees Strindberg, like Dostoyevsky, as embodying "the assault of chaos and madness on all that is most valuable in western civilization" and finds that the climax of Strindberg's novelette *Chandala* is "worthy, indeed, of a Nazi imagination." But, unable to change his spots, Lucas says elsewhere in the same book that the characters in Tennessee Williams's *Cat on a Hot Tin Roof* "make me feel only that the best thing for the lot of them would be a humane and efficient gas-chamber."

If class conflicts and sexual politics do not get in the reader's way, Strindberg's theatrical techniques probably do. With most dramatists the word carries nearly the entire burden of the play, and even when dramatists such as Shakespeare and Ibsen make exciting use of the stage medium, readers of their plays feel that the message lies exclusively in the words. Strindberg's plays—this is especially true of those he wrote after 1897—exist on the page as unfinished works that have to be brought to completion by directors and designers. In this sense many of Strindberg's plays resemble movie scripts, and in plays like *To Damascus, A Dream Play,* and *The Ghost Sonata* what one sees is sometimes more significant than what one hears. Strindberg had an actor's personality and a painter's eye. He knew that the theater was a collaborative art. He expected actors and designers to embellish his scripts, which he never considered sacrosanct. Readers who have not worked in the theater do not expect to be called on to add "business" to a scene when they peruse a playscript, or to construct sets out of the scanty descriptions Strindberg gives. Those who do work in the theater, however, enjoy the offer Strindberg extends to them to participate in a creative enterprise.

Strindberg theatricalized the theater, drawing on all its resources and trying to discover new ones when he felt he had exhausted the means of expression offered by the realistic drama. Like Ibsen, he was compelled by the theatrical standards of his time to write plays that were supposed to produce a photographic likeness on stage of the streets and parlors and people that could be seen outside the theater. Both Ibsen and Strindberg chafed under the severe restrictions of the realistic theater, not because they found it difficult to give a convincing representation of real life using the cardboard conventions of the theater (that is what troubled the Goncourt brothers, masters of the realistic novel) but because the reality that they became increasingly interested in lay not in the streets and parlors outside the theater but within people. They wanted to portray the life of the soul. Ibsen accommodated himself to the realistic theater by filling it with symbols. Strindberg felt he had to go even further. He broke up the form of the realistic play and converted form into symbol. Conventional ideas could be expressed in the conventional form, but Strindberg's investigations of the subconscious or unconscious life of the human being demanded new forms. The idea determined the form, and for each new idea came a new form. To readers familiar with the standard play of the time, the well-made play, Strindberg's experiments with form were bewildering. It was as if he asked them to put aside *David Copperfield* and turn to *Ulysses*. And, as with Joyce's novel, readers are likely to lose their way unless they have a guide.

Another obstacle to a full appreciation of Strindberg's genius is the difficulty of rendering his prose in another language and another time. During his lifetime he was praised even by his most implacable enemies as a master stylist. He energized the Swedish language, modernized it, and gave it a flexibility that no one had thought it capable of. Now, however, much of Strindberg's prose seems old-fashioned and obscure, since the Swedish language has changed almost as much in the last eighty years as the English language did between Shakespeare and Dryden. To convey the original excitement of Strindberg's prose, a translator would have to reinvent his or her own language.

Strindberg's style is characterized by its spontaneity, by a strong, irresistible rhythmic drive, by the introduction of new words, usually drawn from the sciences, by frequent glances at familiar sayings and old adages, by allusions to the Bible (which everyone read in Strindberg's time), and by the use of submerged metaphors, as in Shakespeare. All this makes Strindberg more difficult to translate and to understand than the Ibsen who wrote realistic plays. Ibsen's dialogue transmits a vast amount of information, and as long as the translation conveys that information, the play makes sense, even though subtleties of characterization and emotional shadings may be lost. Strindberg's dialogue, in contrast, often conveys a good deal of background information that may have only a slight basis in fact, material that the characters invent or embroider because it suits them to do so. As in real life, the way something is said becomes much more significant than what is said.

Adding to the difficulty is the poverty of stage directions in Strindberg's plays. Playwrights generally wrote for actors, not readers. Ibsen was the first dramatist in modern times who created a large reading public for plays, and he made it possible for dramatists like Shaw and O'Neill to publish plays with detailed character sketches that one usually finds in novels and with elaborate instructions that actors often ignore. Strindberg expected his actors to find the right tone and inflection as they worked with one another and to adjust lines if a change was needed to build rhythm, to cover a movement, or to get someone on or off stage. Strindberg's scripts are not novels in the form of dialogues.

Selected Plays

Introduction
to
Master Olof

Strindberg's first efforts as a fledgling playwright reflect his religious upbringing, his growing skepticism, his desire to commit himself to a life in art, and his alienation from his businessman-father. Away from home, as a student at the University of Uppsala, Strindberg came upon the writings of Søren Kierkegaard and read the impassioned speeches of Ibsen's Brand. Coming just then, when Strindberg was trying to resolve his own conflicts and to chart his course through life, they made a tremendous impact. Both believed that the pure heart of the solitary individual weighed more in the scales of salvation than the daily experience and common sense of the multitude. Both made absolute commitment to an ideal or a cause the highest purpose of human existence. "All or nothing" was Brand's motto, and for the sake of his calling he sacrificed his child, his wife, his earthly happiness, only to find at the end of his struggles that he stood alone, scorned by his former followers, apparently having accomplished nothing by way of reforming the paltering, equivocating, and materialistic society in which he lived. Yet he had no regrets. If he could have lived his life over, he would still have pursued the unattainable ideal.

The combined voices of Kierkegaard and Ibsen proved irresistible to the young Strindberg. In the summer of 1872, when he was twenty-three, he went to an island in the Stockholm archipelago, populated only by fishermen, where nothing would disturb his concentration. Within two months he wrote *Master Olof*. Ostensibly it was a chronicle play about the efforts of a Lutheran churchman to introduce the Reformation into Sweden and presented the inevitable clash of religion and politics, of priest and king, at a time when nations were contesting the power of the Catholic church.

Strindberg's chief model was Shakespeare, especially *Henry IV*. Having read an essay by the Danish critic Georg Brandes on how the English dramatist blended homely and insignificant details of character with mighty actions, Strindberg determined to do the same, to show his historical figures both at home and on public display, to lift them from the dead pages of the history books and make them as real and vivid as possible, even if that meant that they would be speaking like nineteenth-century Swedes. Shakespeare employed both prose and verse, which allowed him to move easily from tavern to court. Strindberg stuck to prose, thereby violating a principal rule of the conventional history play of his time. But he gave his characters two kinds of prose to speak: one, common and everyday, the other, exalted and biblical.

As far as theme was concerned, Strindberg intended his play as a reply to the vague and ethereal idealism of Ibsen's *Brand*. Although Brand built himself a church, it is never made clear what the dogmas and tenets of his church are, apart from the paradoxical exhortation that anything worth living for is worth sacrificing one's life for. By giving his hero a specific program and by setting his play in a time when there was a radical transformation of thought in Europe, Strindberg could raise some questions about the moral validity of Brand's teachings. The English historian Henry Thomas Buckle had treated political and social ideals not as eternally true but as ever-changing. He tried to describe the social process of making ideas in the same way that Darwin had described the process of evolution in the realm of biology. "What is truth?" Pontius Pilate had asked, without staying for an answer. Strindberg thought of using Pilate's skeptical question as the title for his play. Why sacrifice one's happiness and that of others for the sake of some truth when there is no truth but only a succession of illusory ideals? Why devote one's life to a cause if today's "ism" is destined to be tomorrow's "wasm." Better to seize the day and its pleasures. Yet when Strindberg wrote *Master Olof*, he temporarily resolved all doubts by choosing the side of total commitment if the cause was a worthy one. For the uncommitted life was not worth living, and only the committed life was worth examining.

Ibsen's *Brand* is a landmark in the history of ideas, not simply in the history of drama, because it was the first literary work to present the existential doctrine that individuals create their own systems of values. Even Kierkegaard had kept the Christian God as final arbiter in matters of the spirit, as Maker Unmade. Ibsen took the final step and made the heroic individual God the

Creator. In writing *Master Olof*, Strindberg turned from philosophy to politics. If the new element in Ibsen's epic drama was existential thought, the new element in Strindberg's historical drama was socialism. Although most of the major events in *Master Olof* are drawn from the historical record, Strindberg invented the character of Gert the Printer, who becomes the pivotal figure in the play. *Master Olof* was composed shortly after the rise and fall of the Paris Commune had exhilarated the political radicals throughout Europe and had alarmed the conservatives. The rousing speeches of Gert, the introduction of the revolutionary Anabaptists into Stockholm against the historical record, and the repeated references to Pentecost, a day that had special meaning to political radicals since it was on that day (May 28, 1871) that the French government soldiers massacred thousands of the Communards, all suggest that the play should be read as a study of the intrusion of the third force into the political life of Europe.

Strindberg's youthful and revolutionary ardor imbue the play with dramatic life, and that is what has kept it alive. The theater in Sweden, not surprisingly, would not stage it at first. Twice Strindberg rewrote it entirely in an effort to make it conform with the dramatic conventions and political attitudes of the established theater. However, the dictum that good plays are not written but rewritten does not hold true for *Master Olof*. Interesting as the other two versions are as a record of Strindberg's five-year struggle to come to terms with everything he was fighting against, the first version, in spite of its unwieldiness, its over-long speeches, and its romantic pathos, is the one that still holds the stage.

Master Olof

(1872 version)

A Play in Five Acts

CHARACTERS

MASTER OLOF
GERT THE PRINTER
GUSTAV VASA, King of Sweden
HANS BRASK, Bishop of Linköping
MAGNUS SOMMAR, Bishop of Strängnäs
NATIONAL MARSHAL OF SWEDEN, Lars Siggeson, Lord High Constable
LARS ANDERSSON, Archdeacon in Strängnäs, later Chancellor to King Gustav
LARS PEDERSSON, Olof's younger brother
HANS WINDRANK, sea captain
THE FARMER FROM SMÅLAND
THE GERMAN
THE DANE
FRIAR MARTIN, a Dominican
FRIAR NILS, a Dominican
THE INNKEEPER
WILLIAM, a student at the abbey school
PETER, another student
THE SEXTON (Bengt) of the Great Church in Stockholm
CATHERINE, the sexton's wife
OLOF'S MOTHER
CHRISTINA, Gert's daughter
THE PROSTITUTE
A NOBLEMAN, young
CITIZEN OF STRÄNGNÄS
CITIZEN'S WIFE
THE SERVANT at Gustav's court, elderly
FOREMAN OF THE WORK CREW
THE DRAYMAN, a young man
MINOR CHARACTERS

The play takes place in Sweden in the first half of the sixteenth century.

ACT I

In Strängnäs, a town some forty miles from Stockholm.

The arcade of the monastery; behind it, the cloister garth with tree-shaded walks. The side chapel in the distance. To the right, the main portal of the cathedral. At the back, a low wall over the top of which fruit trees in bloom are visible. It is late afternoon.

Master Olof is sitting on a stone bench, listening to two students, William and Peter, who are reciting their parts from "The Comedy of Tobias," a play that Olof has written.

PETER:
> "Are we children of Israel never to be free?
> Must we abide in Babylon in captivity?"

WILLIAM:
> "Alas, dear brother, why raise your voice to complain?
> In this foreign land we must forever remain.
> Our foe has taken all we had: our flocks, our land.
> This is now home, this vale of tears where we stand.
> Did I not long ago prophesy our lot?
> The covenant of Abraham is long forgot."

LARS ANDERSSON (*has entered during the last speech. He is about twenty-five years older than Olof*): What are you doing?

OLOF: Playing.

LARS ANDERSSON: Playing!!

OLOF: Yes. A little play about the children of Israel and the Babylonian captivity. I wrote it, and now we are—

LARS ANDERSSON: Have you nothing better to do? Great deeds need doing, and you're the man to do them.

OLOF: No, I'm not. I'm too young.

LARS ANDERSSON: Too young! Say not you're too young.

OLOF: It's true, I shouldn't. Too many use that excuse.

LARS ANDERSSON: (*produces a scroll, unrolls it, stares hard at Olof, and then reads from it*): "Then the word of the Lord came unto me" — Jeremiah — "saying, 'Before I formed thee in the belly I knew thee; and before thou camest forth out of the womb I sanctified thee, and I ordained thee a prophet unto the nations.'

"Then said I, 'Ah, Lord God! behold, I cannot speak: *for I am a child.*'

"But the Lord said unto me, 'Say not, *I am a child:* for thou shalt go to all that I shall send thee, and whatsoever I command thee thou shalt speak. . . . '

"'For, behold, I have made thee this day a defenced city, and an iron pillar, and brasen walls against the whole land, against the kings of Judah, against the princes thereof, against the priests thereof, and against the people of the land.'

"'And they shall fight against thee; but they shall not prevail against thee; for I am with thee,' said the Lord, 'to deliver thee.'"

OLOF (*jumping to his feet*): Did the Lord say that?

LARS ANDERSSON (*reading on*): "'Thou therefore gird up thy loins, and arise, and speak unto them all that I command thee.'"

OLOF: You're a coward.

LARS ANDERSSON: Perhaps. I don't have the strength to be a hero. You do. Now may God give you the faith!

OLOF: Oh, indeed, indeed. There was a time I had the faith, and its fire burned brightly. But a brigade of monks came and doused it with their holy water. They wanted to exorcise the devil from my body.

LARS ANDERSSON: That was only a fire in a haystack. It was meant to fizzle out. Now the Lord will build you a real fire, a fire of great logs, that will burn and consume the Philistines, even to their seed. . . . What do you want out of life?

OLOF: I don't know. I only know that I feel I am suffocating when I think of our poor people, whose souls are gasping for freedom. They're crying out for water, the living water, but no one has any to give.

LARS ANDERSSON: Tear down that rotten old building, Olof. That's the first thing. You can do it. The Lord Himself will build them a new one.

OLOF: They would have no roof over their heads, not for a long while.

LARS ANDERSSON: At least they would have fresh air.

OLOF: To take away the faith from a whole people – they would be driven to despair.

LARS ANDERSSON: Exactly: they would be *driven* to despair.

OLOF: They will revile me, call down curses on me, and drag me before the authorities.

LARS ANDERSSON: Are you afraid?

OLOF: No, it's just that I'd die provoking – instead of –

LARS ANDERSSON: Olof, you were born to be a provocation. You were born to fight. Somebody will get hurt, but the Lord will heal.

OLOF: I can feel the current drawing me. I still have hold of the gate of the dam. If I let go, I'll be swept away.

LARS ANDERSSON: Let go of it, Olof. Others will hold the gate.

OLOF: Will you reach out to me if I get caught in the maelstrom?

LARS ANDERSSON: That isn't in my power. You have to go into the maelstrom even if you perish.

OLOF: You've stirred up a storm in my soul. There I sat in the shade of the tree and played. It was the eve of Pentecost. It was spring, and I was at peace. And now –? Why aren't the trees shaking in the storm; why aren't the heavens dark? Put your hand on my forehead. Can't you feel my blood beating, my pulse pounding? Don't leave me, Lars. I can see an angel coming toward me, with a chalice. She's walking on the rays of the setting sun; her path is blood red; and she's carrying a cross in her hands. —No, Lars, I cannot do it. I'm going back to my peaceful valley. Let others fight; I'll watch. . . . No, I'll follow the troops and heal the wounded. I'll whisper "Peace be with you" in the ears of the dying. Peace. . . . No, not that either. I want to join in the fighting. . . . But I'll take my place in the last ranks. Why should I be in the front?

LARS ANDERSSON: Because you are the boldest.

OLOF: Not the strongest?

LARS ANDERSSON: The strong will be behind you. And the strongest of all will be at your side. He is the one who exhorts you to do battle.

OLOF: Oh, God in heaven, help me! . . . Very well. I'll do it.

LARS ANDERSSON: Amen.

OLOF: And you'll go with me?

LARS ANDERSSON: You must go alone—with God.

OLOF: Why do you draw back?

LARS ANDERSSON: I wasn't born to fight. But I'll make your armor. The pure words of God shall be your weapons. But I'll fashion them, and you'll put them in the hands of the people. The door to the pope's armory has been broken in, and now everyone who calls himself a human being shall fight for the freedom of his own soul.

OLOF: Fight against whom? I'm lusting to do battle, but I don't see my enemies.

LARS ANDERSSON: You won't have to issue a challenge. They'll come. Godspeed, Olof. Begin whenever you feel like it. God go with you!

OLOF: Don't go! I need to talk to you.

LARS ANDERSSON: Here comes the vanguard. Arm yourself! (*He leaves.*)

> *A group of citizens, men, women, and children, approach the church on the right. They stop in front of the door, take off their hats, and cross themselves.*

*Among the group is Gert the Printer, who has disguised
himself as one of the citizens.*

GERT: They haven't rung the bells for vespers. And this is the
eve of Pentecost. Most unusual!

CITIZEN: The door is shut. The church is closed! Could the
priest be sick?

GERT: Perhaps he hasn't risen yet.

CITIZEN: What is that supposed to mean?

GERT: I mean he's sick, that's all.

CITIZEN: I don't understand it. He's got plenty of acolytes. One
of them could conduct Mass.

GERT: All busy, obviously.

CITIZEN: Doing what, I'd like to know.

GERT: Wouldn't we all!

CITIZEN: Take care, my good man. None of that Luther talk.
I happen to know that Bishop Brask—he's the bishop in Linköping—is in town. And so is the king himself.

GERT: Bishop Brask here?

CITIZEN: As God is my word. —Shouldn't we try that door
again?

GERT (*runs up the steps of the church and pounds on the door*):
The house of the Lord is closed this Saturday, this eve of Pentecost. The reverend priests will not grant you an audience with
God this evening. You praiseworthy citizens will have to go
home and to bed without your evening mass. Look, good people,
look at this door! A wooden door, a simple wooden door. But
lined with copper. Look at it! If I tell you that God dwells
within—it is, after all, His house—if I tell you that the bishop's
diaconus or *secretarius* or *canonicus* (you can't be a man of God
unless you have a Latin title)—if I tell you that such a man with
a Latin title has the key to his door hanging on a nail in his bedroom, I do not mean to imply thereby that that man has locked
us out from God and hung the key on a nail in his bedroom; I
merely mean to say that we who have gathered here cannot enter

the church this evening to hold divine service—we who have slaved for six days, making shoes, weaving cloth, we who have brewed the ale, baked the bread, and dressed the flesh for six days for these worshipful priests in order that on the seventh day they might have the strength to hold divine service for us. No, I do not reproach the right reverend canons or blame the bishop, for they are but mere men, like us, and it was only God who could work for six days and rest on the seventh.

CITIZEN: Blasphemy! You blaspheme against God!

GERT: No need to worry. He can't hear me. The door is closed.

WOMAN IN THE CROWD: Holy Mother of God! An antichrist!

GERT (*pounding on the door*): Hear how hollow it sounds. The veil of the temple separated men from the Holy of Holies. But when Christ was crucified the veil was rent in twain from top to bottom. This must be true because it's in the Bible. But whether the priests sewed the veil together again, the Bible does not say. And what the Bible does not say is not necessarily a lie.

> *The crowd of townspeople surge toward Gert. The children cry out in fear.*

CITIZEN: A Lutherist! Woe unto you! A Lutherist! We have sinned! That is why the Lord has closed to us the door of His house. Can't you hear how the children cry at the very sight of you, as at the sight of an evil spirit!

GERT: You are trampling them beneath your feet, my friends!

WOMAN IN THE CROWD: Don't you dare go near him! He has the devil in him!

CITIZEN: Down with him! Down with him!

GERT: Touch me not! This is God's sanctuary! This place is sanctified!

CITIZEN: God does not shield Lucifer! Lucifer was cast out!

GERT: Perhaps God does not, but the Holy Church does! And I stand within its consecrated walls.

CITIZEN: Take him! Drag him outside the walls!

GERT: If ye have no fear of God, ye should at least have fear of thy Holy Father who will rebuke thee.

WOMAN IN THE CROWD: Drag him from the door! It is his evil spirit that has bewitched the church!

CITIZEN: True! True! God does not open his house to the devil!

> *They are about to set upon Gert when the Bishop's Secretary enters, preceded by a deacon, who calls for silence.*

SECRETARY (*reading from a proclamation*): "Inasmuch as the people of this diocese have not fulfilled their obligations and paid their tithes to the bishop's see, and inasmuch as the people of Strängnäs have continued to neglect these obligations, the cathedral chapter, in conformity with its rights and with the full approbation of the consistory, has deemed it necessary to close the doors of this church and to cease the holding of mass and the offering of oblations until the aforementioned grievances have been corrected. Let it be published and made known that whosoever does not fulfill his obligations will incur the extreme disfavor of the chapter. *Datum vigilia assumptionis Mariae.* Strängnäs Chapter." (*He leaves.*)

GERT: Now what do you have to say, my good people?

CITIZEN: No mass on the eve of Pentecost! It's scandalous!

GERT: Take care! Speak not ill of the priests. They are not to blame.

CITIZEN: Then who is?

GERT: The church. The invisible, all-powerful church. The institution. It is *the* Church that has closed *this* church.

> *Murmurs of displeasure from the crowd.*

> *Olof has come forward, and now he takes hold of a rope hanging down from the tower and rings the vesper bell.*

OLOF: If the services mean so much to you, I shall celebrate mass with you.

CITIZEN: We thank you, Master Olof. But we don't wish to get you in trouble. Do you realize what they might do to you?

OLOF: It is better to fear God than to fear men.

The people kneel.

OLOF: Dear friends, brothers and sisters in Jesus Christ, we are gathered here—

CITIZEN: Master Olof.

OLOF: Yes?

CITIZEN: We want to have a proper mass. Nothing newfangled.

GERT: Yes, Master Olof. It has to be in Latin. If it isn't in Latin how can we poor Swedes understand what you're saying?

CITIZEN: It has to be in the holy language. Otherwise anyone could say mass.

OLOF: Very true, my good friend. That is exactly how it should be. Every man a church unto himself and with God.

Protests from the crowd: "Lutherist!" "Go back to Germany!" "We don't need your sort here!"

CITIZEN: I see, Master Olof, I see. You are young and hot-headed. You've been infected by that German devil. Now I'm an old man and I know the world. I wish you well, Master Olof; and I say to you: turn back while you're still young. . . . And now, Master Olof, give us what we wish to have: the mass we're accustomed to.

OLOF: No! It's time to put an end to that farce. —In truth should ye worship, in the spirit should ye pray, and not in words ye do not understand.

CITIZEN: My young friend, do you not suppose that our Lord understands Latin?

GERT: Of course. Only Swedish is beyond His comprehension!

CITIZEN: Master Olof, are you going to let these people walk away from here without the words that their souls crave? Do you not see how they thirst for God? Offer up your sinful obstinacy for their sake, and let them not wander as sheep without their shepherd.

OLOF: My obstinacy? Sinful?

CITIZEN: You are a hard man.

OLOF: Am I? A hard man? Do you know what it has cost me to ring this bell?

CITIZEN: Your pride.

GERT: And your peace! That bell was the tocsin calling all men to arms. This is it! The war begins! The bells in Stockholm will soon answer, and then the blood of Huss, of Zizka, the blood of all those thousands of peasants who died in Germany and Bohemia will be upon the heads of the princes and the papists!

WOMAN IN THE CROWD: Oh, my God! He's a lunatic!

CITIZEN: Do you know this man, Master Olof?

OLOF: No.

GERT: Olof! Not know me? Deny me not, Olof! Are you afraid of these poor wretched souls who don't know what's best for them? Who have never heard the word "Freedom"?

OLOF: Who are you?

GERT: If I were to tell you, you would tremble! Yes, and why not? Ye must tremble lest ye never waken from your sleep. I am the fallen angel, who will rise again ten thousand times. I am the liberator who came before his time. I am called Satan because I loved you more than life itself. I have been called Luther; I have been called Huss; and now I am called Anabaptist!

> *The people in the crowd huddle together in fear, crossing themselves and muttering, "Anabaptist!"*

> *Gert removes his disguise. Without it, he looks much older.*

GERT: Do you know me now, Olof?

OLOF: Father Gert!

CITIZEN: He calls him "Father"!

> *The people draw back, repeating, "Anabaptist! Anabaptist!"*

WOMAN IN THE CROWD: Do you see who that is? He's the man they excommunicated, it's—

CITIZEN: Yes. Gert the Printer. The printer for Bishop Brask.

MAN IN THE CROWD: He printed Luther!

WOMAN IN THE CROWD: God have mercy on us and on our town! Alas for our priests when they make friends with the antichrist.

CITIZEN: He denies baptism!

WOMAN IN THE CROWD: He denies God.

> *The crowd breaks up and disperses.*

OLOF: Well, Father Gert, that was quite a speech. And very dangerous.

GERT: Dangerous, do you think, Olof? God bless you for that.

OLOF: I meant dangerous for you.

GERT: And for no one else?

OLOF: Let's hope not.

GERT: You knew Luther, didn't you?

OLOF: Yes. And now I want to do his work in my land.

GERT: That's all?

OLOF: What do you mean?

GERT: I mean it's not enough. Luther is dead. He made a beginning. We have to carry on where he left off.

OLOF: Whither wilt thou lead me, Father?

GERT: Far, Olof. Far.

OLOF: You make me fear you, Father.

GERT: Good, good. I shall make you sore afraid. I want to set you upon a very high mountain where you can look out over the world. This is the feast of Pentecost, Olof. It was then that the Holy Spirit descended and poured itself over the apostles – nay, over all flesh. You can receive the Holy Spirit, Olof, just as I received it, because I believed in it. The spirit of God descended unto me, I feel that. And that is why they locked me up as a madman. But now I am free; now I shall speak the word because – don't you see, Olof? – because now we stand on that high mountain. Look at those people crawling on their knees. Crawling toward those two men sitting on thrones. The bigger one holds two keys in his right hand and a thunderbolt in the other. That is the pope. When the pope raises the thunderbolt, a thousand souls are forever sent to perdition. And the ones who are not kiss his foot and sing *Gloria Deo*. And the man on the throne turns his head and smiles. Now look at the other one. He holds a sword and a scepter. Bow down before his scepter, or his sword will smite you. He frowns and glowers, and all the people tremble. He turns his head toward his friend on the other throne, and now they both smile. Two idols of Baal. But there's a rumbling in the air. Like the murmuring of a crowd. "Why that clamour?" roars the pope, and he shakes his thunderbolt. "Who is grumbling?" And the emperor shakes his sword. No one answers. But there is still a rumbling in the air and a rustling, and the sound forms a word and that word is "Think!" The pope is startled, and the emperor turns pale with rage and demands to know who spoke. "Who said, 'Think!' Bring him before me, and I shall have his head." And the pope roars, "Bring him before me, and I shall take his soul!" But there is no one to be brought forward. No one spoke. It was the wind in the trees. But the voice grows louder, and the wind becomes a storm sweeping across the Alps, roaring through Bavaria, churning the Baltic Sea, echoing against the shore. And then, multiplied a thousand times, the cry goes out over the world: "Freedom! Freedom!" And the pope throws his keys into the ocean, and the emperor puts his sword back into its sheath. What can they do against the word? – Olof, you want to strike down the pope, but you forget the emperor. The emperor who murders untold num-

bers of his subjects because they moan when they are trampled
underfoot. You want to strike down the pope in Rome, but, like
Luther, you want to give them a new pope: Holy Scripture. Olof,
listen to me! Don't put any bonds whatsoever on the human spirit.
Do not forget the great day of Pentecost and what it means: the
descent of the Holy Spirit. Don't forget what your goal must be:
a life of the spirit and the freedom of the spirit. Close your ears
to those deadly words: "All that is, is good." Because if you do,
the millennium will never come and man will never enter the kingdom of the free. That kingdom beckons us now.

> *Olof is silent.*

Does the thought make your head reel?

OLOF: You go too far, Gert.

GERT: Too far! The day will come when I shall be called a papist!
He shoots higher who shoots at the moon than he who aims at
the tree.

OLOF: Turn back, Gert. You will bring ruin to yourself and to
the kingdom. The land is still shaking from the wounds and fever
of the last war. And now you want to sow the seeds of civil war.
That's ungodly.

GERT: Once the surgeon's knife is in the flesh, he must cut that
the body may live.

OLOF: I'll report you as a traitor.

GERT: You! You have set yourself irreversibly against the church
today. There's no going back. . . . Moreover . . .

OLOF: Well, what is it? You look like Satan himself.

GERT: I'll let you in on a secret. Make of it what you will. The
king travels to Malmö today, and the day after tomorrow, or there-
abouts, Stockholm will be in revolt.

OLOF: How do you know?

GERT: Have you heard of Rink and Knipperdollink?

OLOF (*startled*): The Anabaptists!

GERT: Why so amazed? Two middle-class clods fighting the wrong battles. Up in arms against infant baptism because it can have no meaning, since an infant has no soul. And in their innocence devoting their energies to abolishing the oath of confirmation because it is nothing more than premeditated perjury extorted from an unthinking adolescent. Who the hell cares?

OLOF: There must be more to Rink and Knipperdollink than that.

GERT: What might that be?

OLOF: They are possessed.

GERT: Yes! Possessed of the spirit! The mighty wind that will sweep us into the future howls through their souls. Take care if you are caught in its path.

OLOF: It must be stopped. I shall go to the king.

GERT: Wait, Olof! We should be friends, you and I. . . . Your mother lives in Stockholm, doesn't she?

OLOF: You know she does.

GERT: But do you know that my daughter Christina is living with your mother?

OLOF: Christina?

GERT: Yes, for the time being. You see, if we win, my daughter will stand as surety for your mother. And if the Catholics win, well, then my daughter will be safe because of your mother's presence. And you do care about Christina?

OLOF: Gert! Gert! Where did you learn to be so clever and calculating?

GERT: In the madhouse.

OLOF: Get thee from me! You want to make my life miserable. You want to deprive me of my happiness.

GERT: Yes! if to be miserable is to be deprived of all earthly happiness, to suffer poverty, to be clapped in jail, to be mocked and reviled, all for the sake of the truth. If that's what you mean by a miserable existence, you don't deserve it. I thought you of all people would understand me. I counted on you, because you have a soul of fire. But I see now that the world tempts you. Go; swim with the current. And be happy.

OLOF: No one man can remake his time.

GERT: Luther did.

OLOF: One man alone cannot turn the current.

GERT: You fool! Lead the current. What is the current? It is we, the multitude, the people. The old ones are stagnant pools; you won't have to struggle against them. But don't let them dry up and turn to muck. Cut a channel for them, and they too will be swept up.

OLOF: I do understand you! You have spawned a thought in my soul, and if I do not strangle it at birth, it will be the death of me.

GERT: Believe me, you shall become a Daniel, who will show the truth to the kings. And they will seek thy life, but the Lord will be thy shield. —Now I can leave; now I am confident. Thine eyes are as lamps of fire, and the cloven tongues of fire flicker above thy head. Happy Pentecost, Master Olof! (*He starts to leave; then turns back.*) Here comes the Prince of Flies. Don't let him speck your immaculate soul.

OLOF: Lord Jesus, stand by me now.

> *Enter Hans Brask, Bishop of Linköping, and Magnus Sommar, Bishop of Strängnäs. Magnus approaches Olof; Brask stands to one side, looking the place over.*

MAGNUS: *Canonicus!* Who rang the vesper bell?

OLOF (*quietly but firmly*): I did.

MAGNUS: Were you not aware of the injunction?

OLOF: That it was prohibited I was well aware.

MAGNUS: And you deliberately defied it!

OLOF: Yes. When I saw the people milling around like sheep without their shepherd, I thought I should gather them.

MAGNUS: So you think to reproach us for the action we have taken. The truth is you are an impudent young man.

OLOF: The truth is always impudent.

MAGNUS: I do believe our young hero wants to play the apostle of truth. You will win no plaudits for that.

OLOF: No, I expect to be hissed.

MAGNUS: Well, don't peddle your ideas here. There's no market for them.

OLOF (*passionately*): Advice worthy of the Father of Lies! (*Humbly.*) I'm sorry. Forgive me.

MAGNUS: Do you know whom you are talking to?

OLOF (*heatedly*): To Magnus Sommar, bishop, *servus servi servorum*, the servant of all those who serve.

BISHOP BRASK (*coming forward*): Who is this man?

MAGNUS: One of the assistants at this church.

BRASK: What is his name?

MAGNUS: Olof Pedersson, also known as Olaus Petri.

BRASK: (*taking a long look at Olof*): So you are Master Olof!

Olof bows and looks at Brask.

BRASK: Young man, I like you. Will you serve as my secretary?

OLOF: I thank you, Your Grace. But I'm afraid I don't have the proper references.

BRASK: Bishop Magnus, what do you make of him?

MAGNUS: I believe he was highly praised by Martin Luther.

BRASK: So I have heard. A hot-headed youth—that's what we have here. We shall take him in hand and educate him.

OLOF: I'm afraid it's too late for that.

BRASK: A twig can be bent.

MAGNUS: This young branch already inclines strongly toward heresy. This very day he dared to defy our orders.

BRASK: Is that so?

MAGNUS: The celebration of mass was interdicted on entirely legal grounds. Yet he dared to hold mass. What's worse, a Lutheran mass; and by doing so, he stirred up the people. Your Grace should not take asps to his bosom.

BRASK: Take care, young man. As you well know, the penalty for preaching Lutheranism is excommunication.

OLOF: Yes. But I fear no other god than God.

BRASK: Weigh your words before you speak. I wish you well, and you repulse me.

OLOF: I have a cure for your sick faith. You want to buy it. And here I am impudently refusing to sell it to you.

BRASK: By Saint George, I swear you are utterly out of your mind!

OLOF: If I am, don't cure me as you would cure Gert the Printer. You put him in an asylum. It made him very clever, I'm afraid.

BRASK (*to Magnus*): You know this Gert fellow, don't you?

MAGNUS: No, your Grace.

BRASK: A madman. He worked for me—trained as a typesetter. When I gave him anti-Lutheran documents to print, he used my presses to print pro-Lutheran pamphlets. A fanatic, raving about the apocalypse and the millennium. (*To Olof.*) Have you seen him?

OLOF: He was just here. And little good can you expect from him.

BRASK: He's loose again, is he?

OLOF: He will soon be in Stockholm, where I am sure he will make his presence known. A warning, my Lord Bishop.

BRASK: Ah ha. Nothing to fear for a while.

OLOF: No? There are Anabaptists in Stockholm.

BRASK: What?

OLOF: The Anabaptists. They are in Stockholm.

BRASK: The Anabaptists!

King Gustav Vasa enters hastily.

GUSTAV: What the hell is going on?! The whole town is in an uproar. People storming up and down the streets demanding mass. What's behind all this?

BRASK: Mischief, Your Majesty, mischief.

GUSTAV: Bishop Magnus!

MAGNUS: Strängnäs has not paid its tithes, Your Majesty.

GUSTAV: And because of that you refuse to hold services!! 'Sdeath!

BRASK: Your Majesty would do well to bear in mind that—

GUSTAV: Bishop Magnus! I want an answer.

MAGNUS: Your Majesty would do well to bear in mind that matters of this kind, which come under the jurisdiction of the church, should—

GUSTAV: Yes, and I'm ordering you to stick to your business and do your job.

BRASK: Must I remind you, Sire, that the bishops in the kingdom of Sweden take their orders only from the highest authority: the pope and the canon law.

GUSTAV (*subdued*): I know. I know. But the pope can't always keep his eye on you.

BRASK: That is our affair.

GUSTAV (*flaring up, but controlling himself*): You are right, Brask. It shall be your affair.

BRASK: To change the subject, I hear that Stockholm is about to break out into rebellion.

GUSTAV: Where have you heard that?

MAGNUS: From our *canonicus* here.

GUSTAV: Your schoolmaster? Where is he? (*Turning in the*

direction indicated by Magnus.) You're the *canonicus?* What's your name?

OLOF: Olof Pedersson.

GUSTAV: Ah! Master Olof. So you're the heretic. Plotting against the Holy Church, hm? A dangerous undertaking.

BRASK: Today he found the occasion for unmasking himself. He openly violated the chapter's prohibition against holding mass. Consequently, we request Your Majesty's consent to what may be the appropriate and condign punishment.

GUSTAV: That's a matter for the chapter to settle. It's none of my business. (*To Olof.*) Now what's this about a rebellion in Stockholm?

OLOF: The Anabaptists are there.

GUSTAV: Is that all?

BRASK: Sire, you surely know what trouble these mad fanatics have caused in Germany. We would suggest that Your Majesty return to Stockholm with his troops.

GUSTAV: That is a matter that you must leave to my discretion.

BRASK: But civil war, Your Majesty!

GUSTAV: That is my affair. —Master Olof, I am appointing you secretary in chief of the city council in Stockholm. You will proceed immediately. Once there you will speak to the people. I am counting on you, Olof.

BRASK: Sire, for the sake of the fatherland I beg you to bear in mind how foolish it is to reason with fools.

GUSTAV: One doesn't bend the spirit with the sword. Bear that in mind, my lords.

BRASK: The church has never attempted—

GUSTAV: No, nor with keys either. (*To Olof.*) Go to my chancellor. He'll give you the necessary papers.

BRASK: One moment! I would advise our canon to think the matter over.

GUSTAV: He is our secretary. Our orders take precedence over yours.

BRASK: The church must first exact its claims on him. —Olaus Petri—

GUSTAV (*correcting him*): Secretary Olof Pedersson.

BRASK: Secretary Olof Pedersson: you are not free to leave Strängnäs until the chapter has pronounced sentence on you.

GUSTAV: The chapter does not pronounce sentence until it has tried the case.

BRASK: That is our affair!

GUSTAV: It is not your affair. Your diocese is Linköping. A canon in Strängnäs cannot be judged by a bishop of Linköping. Am I right, Bishop Magnus?

MAGNUS (*hemming and hawing*): I . . . in the light of what has occurred, I . . . would be inclined to think that . . .

BRASK: That further explanations should be unnecessary!

GUSTAV: Or that Bishop Brask should not involve himself. —Or that he should withdraw while I talk privately with Bishop Magnus. —Privately, I said.

Bishop Brask steps to one side.

Now what have you to say, Lord Magnus?

MAGNUS: I see no alternative . . . other than . . . since Bishop Brask . . .

GUSTAV: We are talking about Master Olof now. —I'm sure that your lordships can postpone the inquiry. Now if your lordships might take your leave of us—

Brask and Magnus leave.

GUSTAV (*turning to Olof*): Will you join with me?

OLOF: As Your Grace's secretary?

GUSTAV: No: as my right hand. On condition that for the time being the left hand doesn't know what the right hand is doing. Go to Stockholm.

OLOF: The cathedral chapter here will demand my return and excommunicate me.

GUSTAV: Before they go that far, I shall let you lay the blame on me. But until then you will be your own man, as far as possible.

OLOF: What does Your Grace want of me?

GUSTAV: I want you to talk to those fanatics in Stockholm.

OLOF: And then what?

GUSTAV: I don't dare think that far ahead. . . . Let the Anabaptists preach. Our people are apathetic and half-asleep. It can't hurt them to hear some new ideas, even if they are crazy ones. But I won't tolerate any violence! If violence breaks out, the sword will come into play. Fare thee well, Olof. (*He leaves.*)

OLOF (*alone*): Interesting! The emperor would prefer not to shake hands with the pope.

> *The students William and Peter, who have been waiting in one of the tree-lined walks, come forward.*

WILLIAM: Should we go on with the play, Master Olof?

OLOF: Playtime is over, children.

WILLIAM: You're not going to leave us, are you?

OLOF: Yes, I'm afraid so. And I probably won't be coming back.

WILLIAM: Why can't you stay through Pentecost? Then we could put on our play.

PETER: And I can be the angel Gabriel!

WILLIAM: Please don't go, Master Olof. You were the only one who was nice to us. You didn't make us fast all the time.

PETER: Please, Master Olof. Don't leave us!

OLOF: Oh, my children, ye know not what ye ask. The day shall come when you will thank God that I went away from you. — No, no, no! May that day never come! . . . Well, let's not waste any time saying goodbye. (*He embraces them, and they kiss his hand.*) Goodbye, Peter. Goodbye, William.

> *Lars Andersson has entered and observed the leave-taking.*

WILLIAM: Aren't you ever coming back, Master Olof?

LARS ANDERSSON (*coming forward*): Are you ready?

OLOF: No, I am never coming back.

PETER (*leaving*): Goodbye.

WILLIAM (*leaving*): Don't forget us!

> *Olof follows them with his eyes as they depart.*

LARS ANDERSSON: I have spoken with the king.

OLOF (*absentmindedly*): You have?

LARS ANDERSSON: Do you know what he said?

OLOF: No.

LARS ANDERSSON: He said, "Well, I've got myself a hunting dog that will raise the game. But I wonder if he'll come when I whistle."

OLOF: Look at them! Playing among the gravestones, playing and picking flowers, and singing Pentecostal hymns.

LARS ANDERSSON (*taking him by the arm*): You child!

OLOF (*startled*): What?

LARS ANDERSSON: I thought that today you had put your hand to the plow. No man, having done so, and looking back, is fit for the kingdom of God.

> *Olof waves at the students.*

LARS ANDERSSON: Still dreaming?

OLOF: A last lovely morning dream before we go to work. Forgive me. Now I'm awake.

> *They go toward the right. Reaching the wings, Olof turns to take one last look at the students. But at this moment the Dominican friars Martin and Nils, wearing their long black mantles, appear just where the students exited.*
>
> *Olof gasps in astonishment, and his hand flies to his forehead.*
>
> *Lars leads him off.*

CURTAIN

ACT II

Scene I

Stockholm. A tavern in the wall of the Great Church. At back a counter with tankards, mugs, steins. To the right of the counter is a table, and behind it an iron door that leads to the interior of the church. The monks Martin and Nils, clad like ordinary townspeople, are seated at this table, drinking beer. Farmers, sailors, and German soldiers are seated and standing around the other tables. The door to the street is at the right. Sitting on a barrel is a musician, fiddle in hand. The soldiers are throwing dice. All those in the room are in various stages of drunkenness and talking noisily.

Gathered around one of the tables are a Farmer from the province of Småland (at this time under the Danish crown), a Dane, a German, and Hans Windrank, a sea captain.

THE GERMAN (*addressing The Dane*): You mean to sit there and defend that bloody king of yours, that tyrant King Christian!

THE DANE: God preserve us, he's a man like the rest of us!

THE GERMAN: He's a monster! A bloody butcher! A cowardly, sneaking, lying Dane! How many Swedes didn't he kill when he marched into Stockholm and had himself crowned king of Sweden! One hundred Swedes in one day! The massacre of Stockholm.

THE DANE: Holy Jesus! Look who's talking about blood! What about those murders – not a mile from here – in 1389 – when you Germans dragged the Swedes out of Parliament, locked them in a shed, and burned them!! On Corpus Christi Day!!

WINDRANK: Gentlemen, gentlemen! We're supposed to be

enjoying ourselves. Now let me tell you about America. Now there's —

THE GERMAN (*to The Dane*): Why blame me? I'm not German. I'm from Lübeck.

THE DANE: For God's sake, all I'm saying is that the Germans are just —

WINDRANK: What's the point of arguing! (*Shouts at The Innkeeper.*): Schnapps here! Four! —Now let's settle down and have a good time. America—now there's a place! The last time I was there, let me tell you—

> *The Innkeeper serves the liquor.*

THE GERMAN (*tasting it*): *Wunderbar!* Just think, gentlemen, what progress we have made! Today the grain is growing in the field and—

WINDRANK: And tomorrow it will be made into whiskey. I wonder, just who was the man who made that discovery.

THE GERMAN: Begging your pardon—it's a German *invention.* I say invention. One *discovers* America.

WINDRANK: Yes. And the Germans never *discover* anything!

THE GERMAN: *Verdammt!*

WINDRANK: What's the matter? You're not German. You're from Lübeck.

THE DANE (*to The German*): All right. Here's one for you. Who invented the story that the Germans made Gustav Vasa king of Sweden?

> *General laughter.*

THE GERMAN: Ah, ha! We did. It was us. We Lübeckians made Gustav king of Sweden when the country was on the verge of collapse.

WINDRANK (*raising his cup*): To the king! Skoal!

THE DANE: To Lübeck! Skoal!

THE GERMAN (*flattered*): That's very kind. I don't know how to express —

WINDRANK: Hell, you're not the king!

THE GERMAN: Begging your pardon, it was my Danish friend's toast —

THE DANE: Hell, you're not a Lübecker! What are you doing here? You're a Stockholmer!

WINDRANK (*turning to The Farmer from Småland*): You're not saying much. Why aren't you drinking?

THE FARMER: I don't mind drinking your schnapps, but as for your toast, this is what I think of it!

> *He crushes the tin cup and throws it on the floor. Windrank reaches for his knife.*

WINDRANK: You refuse to drink to our King!?

THE FARMER: I've drunk from his cup so long I ain't got no desire to drink his health. Like hell I'll drink to him!

WINDRANK: 'Sblood!

THE GERMAN (*suddenly interested in The Farmer*): Shut up! Let's hear what he's got to say.

THE DANE (*also involved*): Yes, for God's sake, let him talk.

THE FARMER: Lord help me when I get home. (*He seems to be on the verge of tears.*)

WINDRANK (*moved*): What the hell's the matter, old boy? You look like you lost your last friend. Money? Is that it? Look! (*He takes out his purse.*) There. Help yourself. Half my pay's there. — Come on, what's the matter?

THE FARMER: I don't want to talk about it. More schnapps! (*Signals to The Innkeeper.*) Schnapps! — Money? I got money. Look! (*He puts a small purse on the table.*)

> *The Innkeeper brings the liquor.*

Trouble is, it's not mine. What the hell! I'm going to drink it all up – every damn cent of it! And if you're my friends, you're going to help me.

WINDRANK: That's not your money? What's going on?

THE GERMAN: Oh, somebody's done you in, huh? I can tell. Something awful?

THE FARMER: I'm ruined. Lost everything. I come up from Småland to sell two hundred head of cattle. Borrowed money to get them. When I get here to Stockholm, the king's bailiff steps in and says I have to sell at the price the king decides. No higher. It's the king who sets the prices, not us farmers. It's the king who's ruined me.

THE GERMAN: I don't believe it!

THE FARMER: There's a lot more you won't believe. He's going to take the monks and the priests away from us. That's what I heard. You know why? To make the nobles richer. Take from the church, give to the lords.

THE DANE: To the lords and landowners! God!

THE FARMER: It's true, every word. That bloody king of yours, that King Christian, he should be here right now to lop off a few more Swedish heads. God bless him!

WINDRANK: Well, I'll be swiggered! King Gustav setting that course! For the nobles! I thought he was sitting on them.

THE FARMER: Sitting on them! Ha! He's letting them hatch and run wild. They'd be cutting the oak trees on my land – if I had any land left. Oh, I had a parcel of land – once. Then along comes a high-and-mighty lord and he says my great-grandmother had it on loan from his great-grandfather. And he grabbed it – my land!

THE GERMAN: Is that what the king is up to! I had absolutely no idea.

THE FARMER: Ha! The lords even let their kids run around in our woods with their guns, killing deer just for the hell of it! But if one of us was dying of starvation and knocked off a deer, he wouldn't die of starvation, let me tell you! He'd be hung from

a tree. And not an oak tree! God forbid! That would be a disgrace
to the oak. The oak is the royal tree. Because its branches form
a crown, you see. But the pine tree isn't meant to have a crown.
So it isn't royal. Like the song says:

> "The peasants rose and burned the crops;
> The land was red with blood and fire.
> Then came the lords and raised them higher,
> Strung them up in the pine tree tops."

See! Pine tree tops; no crowns.

THE GERMAN: But the pine tree stands straight and tall.

THE FARMER: Right, right. Come on, slug it down! Here's to
you! I mean it.

They drink.

Oh, that's good. Kill you or cure you. . . . It's the wife and
kids, you know. If I didn't have them—. Oh, what the
hell! . . . Oh, there are things I could tell you. Such things. But
I ain't opening my mouth.

WINDRANK: What sort of things?

THE GERMAN: Something funny, I'll bet.

THE FARMER: Yeah, something funny. Like: if you counted
them all up, there'd be a lot more pines than oaks.

THE GERMAN: Is that right?

WINDRANK: Now wait. I don't like this. You say only bad
things about the king. I don't know what he's up to, and it's none
of my business. But I know one thing for sure: he's building up
the merchant fleet. Who outfitted those ships for the Spanish
trade? King Gustav. Who made me a captain? King Gustav. So
I damn well ain't got nothing to complain about.

THE GERMAN: Yes, but why? Out of spite! To hurt the
Lübeck shippers. But it's Lübeck money that's kept him going.
And this is how he repays them. Pure spite, I tell you!

THE FARMER: He'll get his! You can castrate a bull, but he's still got horns. — Thanks, fellows, for your company. I've got to be going.

THE GERMAN: Oh, come on. Just one more. We've got a lot of talking to do.

THE FARMER: No, thanks. You've been good. But I don't dare. I've got a wife and kids at home waiting for me, and I've got to go and tell them that we've lost — everything. I can't face it. . . . All right, Deutschman, I'll take you up on that. Let's have another.

THE GERMAN: Now you're talking!

> *They drink.*
>
> *The Farmer empties his cup, then jumps up.*

THE FARMER: Oh, God! Hell and damnation! What the devil's in it? Bitter. (*He stumbles out of the tavern, obviously sick.*)

THE GERMAN (*to The Dane*): I wouldn't want to be in his shoes when he sobers up.

> *The Dane nods.*
>
> *The din in the tavern has gotten worse. The fiddler plays louder and faster. And then the sound of the church organ is heard over the din.*

WINDRANK: I still say it's strange that the king allows a beer tavern within the church wall.

THE GERMAN: Don't tell me you're particular, Captain. The king doesn't know about this.

WINDRANK: Maybe. Still, it doesn't sound right — church music and this kind of singing. I've always been a god-fearing man, you see. Brought up that way.

THE GERMAN (*ironically*): Lucky you! No doubt your mother — your dear mother —

WINDRANK (*sentimentally*): My mother!

THE GERMAN: Tucked you into bed every night and told you

to say, "Now I lay me down to sleep; I pray the Lord . . . "

WINDRANK: She did, she did.

THE GERMAN: What a good, kind woman.

WINDRANK (*becoming maudlin*): Oh, if you only knew!

THE GERMAN: God has heard her prayers. You're crying. . . . You really are a good man.

THE DANE: God almighty, yes.

THE GERMAN: Oh, if your mother could only see you now! With those tears in your eyes!

WINDRANK: I'm just a poor sinner, I know that. But one thing I know: I've got a heart. God damn me if I don't. If some wretch told me he needed a bite to eat, I'd give him the shirt off my back.

THE GERMAN: Good for you! Let's have another round.

WINDRANK: No, no. No, I don't think so.

> *A few loud blows are heard on the iron door leading to the church. Commotion in the tavern.*

WINDRANK (*frightened*): Oh, my God!

THE GERMAN: No cause for alarm. It's not Peter, and it's not the gate to heaven.

WINDRANK: I'll never take another drink. I swear to God!

THE GERMAN (*to The Dane*): Nothing like liquor. A blessed drink. It can transform a rascal like this into a Bible thumper. Worse. It's made him a teetotaler. Nothing but liquor can do that!

THE DANE: Right, right! There's nothing like it!

THE GERMAN: It swells the heart and shrinks the head. That's how it makes good people out of us. Because to be good means to have a lot of heart and little brains.

THE DANE: Right. But that ain't all. It makes us religious because it stop us from thinking. And reason blocks the way to the soul.

THE GERMAN: Oh, it's a holy thing, liquor, a holy thing! Strange that no one—

THE DANE: Enough said.

> *More pounding on the iron door.*
>
> *Windrank has dropped off, but the pounding wakes him with a start.*

WINDRANK: Help! Help! I'm dying!

THE GERMAN: Pity! Such a sweet soul, too.

> *The iron door is thrown open, and as it swings, it knocks over the table at which the monks Nils and Martin are sitting. Mugs and steins crash to the floor.*
>
> *A woman wearing a black and red skirt—the required dress of a prostitute—and with a nun's veil over her face is virtually thrust into the room. Momentarily Gert can be glimpsed behind the door, which is quickly slammed shut.*

THE PROSTITUTE (*looking about, stunned and afraid*): Please help me! They want to kill me!

A GERMAN SOLDIER: A whore—in a nun's veil! Ha! (*He laughs, and others join in.*)

MARTIN (*crossing himself*): A whore! Who brought her in here? This is a respectable place. —Innkeeper, take her out. You want to ruin your reputation and stain the sanctity of the church?

THE PROSTITUTE: Please! Won't someone help me?

> *The Innkeeper has grabbed her arm and is pulling her toward the street door.*

THE PROSTITUTE: Please! Don't turn me over to that mob out there! All I wanted was to slip into the house of the Lord. All I wanted was a bit of His mercy. And the monks drove me back. They set the people on me. They would have killed me, but Father Gert saved me. Brought me here.

MARTIN: Do you hear that? She has profaned the sanctity of the church. Look at her! Trying to conceal the skirt of shame with the veil of holiness!

THE GERMAN: Only the veil wasn't long enough!

MARTIN: Off with the mask! Let's see you for what you are—an abomination! (*He goes to her and tears the veil from her face. He gasps in surprise.*)

THE PROSTITUTE: You! Martin! —Murderer!

THE GERMAN: What do you know—old acquaintances!

MARTIN: A dirty lie! I've never seen her before. I'm Friar Martin, a Dominican, and Brother Nils here is my witness!

NILS (*drunk and slobbering*): 'S true. I can vouch for that. Brother Martin's never seen this woman.

THE PROSTITUTE: Nils, how can you? You yourself showed me Martin's letter of absolution. I was cast out of the cloister, but they gave Martin absolution.

NILS: 'S true! Can't deny it.

MARTIN (*in a rage, grabs Nils and shakes him*): You lie! (*Turning to the crowd.*) You can see he's drunk!

THE GERMAN: My good friends, I can vouch that this holy man is drunk—and therefore is lying.

> *Noises of displeasure and indignation from the crowd. "A drunken priest." "A Dominican, and drunk!"*

THE GERMAN: Ah, well! Liquor absolves the liar. Isn't that so, Father Martin?

THE INNKEEPER: Quiet! Quiet! I can't have any disturbances here. I'd lose my customers. I might get brought before the church chapter. Now will you please remove this wretched person from the premises? She's the cause of all this trouble.

MARTIN: Get her out of here, or I'll see to it that you're excommunicated. Don't you realize that we are within the walls of the holy church? The chapter has set aside this part of it for travelers—for their bodily refreshment.

THE GERMAN: Good people, don't you see?! This is a holy room. Look about you! Isn't this God's dwelling place?

> *The crowd forcibly drags The Prostitute toward the street door.*

THE PROSTITUTE: Jesus, help me! Please, help me, Jesus!

> *Master Olof stands in the doorway. He pushes his way through the people, takes The Prostitute by the hand and draws her away from the mob.*

OLOF: Who is this woman? Answer me!

MARTIN: This is no woman.

OLOF: What do you mean?

MARTIN: Not a man, either—although she is disguised.

OLOF: You said "she"; so she is a woman.

MARTIN: A whore!

OLOF (*shocked, lets go of her hand*): A whore?

THE GERMAN: Don't let go of her, Master Olof. She'll run away.

OLOF: Why are you laying hands on her? What has she done?

THE GERMAN: She went into the church.

OLOF: I see. (*Looking around.*)

MARTIN: What are you looking for?

OLOF (*taking note of him*): A priest?

MARTIN: I am a Blackfriar.

OLOF: Yes, I thought so. So you're the one who roused the mob against her.

MARTIN: It was I who protected the church from this slime,

who sought to keep the church free from vice. This woman has been excommunicated. She commits usury of the flesh. She sells her body, which should be the temple of God.

She falls on her knees before Olof.

OLOF (*taking her by the hand*): A Blackfriar, are you? I am taking this woman by the hand and setting her up against you. She has sold her body, you say. How many souls have *you* bought? . . . I too am a priest. No, merely a human being, and not so presumptuous as to lock the door of God's house. Being a sinful creature, I reach my hand to a fellow creature, who cannot be without sin. Come forward, he that is without sin among you. Let him first cast a stone at her. . . . Come forward, Brother Martin, you angel of light. You have dressed yourself in the black robes of austerity, and you have shaved your head so that no one can see that you have grown grey with sin. What? You have no stone to throw? Alas, what have you done with them, all those stones you were to give to the people when they ask for bread? Have you already given them away? . . . Come forward, you respectable citizen.

Olof addresses Captain Windrank, who in his drunken stupor has slipped off his chair and is lying asleep on the floor.

You who sleep like a beast, why don't you wake up and hurl your knife at her? Do you see how red he is? Red from shame at finding himself in this doubtful company, or red from debauchery?

The people in the tavern murmur resentfully.

Why do you grumble? Are you embarrassed by my words or ashamed of yourselves? Why do ye not cast stones? Ah, of course, ye have none. Well, open the door. Call up the people, let them run her down. If you fear that fifty men could not tear her to pieces, be assured that five hundred women would. . . . Still silent? . . . Woman, stand up. They do not condemn you. Go, and sin no more. But don't show yourself to the priests. They will throw you to the women.

During this speech Martin has repeatedly tried to interrupt Olof but has been prevented from doing so by The German. Now he has his way and produces a paper.

MARTIN: Listen to me! This man is a heretic. I don't have to tell you that. His words make it clear enough. A heretic! And he has been excommunicated!! It's in this paper. See for yourselves! (*He takes a candle from one of the tables and throws it in the middle of the floor.*) "As this light is extinguished, which we here cast down, so shall all joy and contentment be extinguished in him, along with all good he might have from God!"

The people cross themselves and shrink back from Olof. He stands alone with The Prostitute in the middle of the floor. The people mutter, "Anathema!"

MARTIN (*to The Prostitute*): You see! What good is Master Olof's absolution now?

Olof has been stung and silenced by Martin's words.

OLOF: Woman! Do you fear to put your trust in me? Do you dare to put your faith in my words? Don't you hear the lightning bolts of excommunication striking over our heads? Why don't you join those twenty righteous men who stand within the shadow of the holy church? . . . Answer me! Do you believe God has cast me out, as these have done?

THE PROSTITUTE: No!

OLOF (*taking the broadsheet containing the order of excommunication*): Very well. The great bishop in that little town of Linköping has sold my soul to Satan for life—no more, because his power reaches no farther than that. And this he has done to me because I invited the people to seek God—at the wrong time. Here is the contract. Just as the church through this has bound me to hell, so I free myself from it— (*He tears the sheet to pieces.*) —and from the excommunication! May God help me! Amen.

The people howl, "Anathema!"

MASTER OLOF [ACT II]

MARTIN: Grab him! Strike him down! He is excommunicate.

OLOF (*places himself in front of The Prostitute*): Listen to the devils howling for their victim! – Touch me not!

MARTIN: Come on! Down with him!

> *One of the soldiers raises his weapon to strike at Olof. At that moment the iron door is flung open, and a group of Anabaptists, led by Knipperdollink, storm in, shouting and carrying broken crucifixes, fragments of statues of saints, and shredded ecclesiastical vestments.*

KNIPPERDOLLINK (*starts speaking as soon as the door is opened*): What do we have here! Look at this! One more house of holiness. What does this signify? A beer tavern in the temple itself. It means, look you, that the abomination has grown so great that the sanctuary itself is defiled. But I shall cleanse it with fire. The church into the flames! The saints onto the bonfire!

> *The people in the tavern have thronged toward the street door.*
>
> *Olof steps forward.*

OLOF: Be sure you know what you are doing!

KNIPPERDOLLINK: Do you fear that the beer barrels will burst from the heat, you Belial? Are you the pope's tavernkeeper that you think nothing of building a chapel of vice in the walls of the church?

OLOF: I am secretary of the town council. In the name of the king and by virtue of the authority invested in me, I order you to keep the peace!

KNIPPERDOLLINK: Ah ha! You are the man the king sent to defeat our sacred cause. Forward, you men of god! Seize him! Seize him first. Time enough later to rid the Lord's house of this idolatry.

MARTIN: Lay hold of him! He is a heretic! He is excommunicate!

KNIPPERDOLLINK: Heretic? Not a Catholic?

OLOF: Hardly, since I've been excommunicated.

KNIPPERDOLLINK: Then you are one of ours!

Olof is silent.

KNIPPERDOLLINK: Answer! Are you for us or against us?

MARTIN: He is Olof Pedersson, the king's man.

KNIPPERDOLLINK: Olof Pedersson, are you?

OLOF: Yes.

KNIPPERDOLLINK: But you are a heretic?

OLOF: I am proud to say I am.

KNIPPERDOLLINK: A heretic – in the king's service?

OLOF: Yes.

> *The Anabaptists shout and surround Olof.*
>
> *The iron door opens, and Gert the Printer enters quickly.*

GERT: Stop! What are you doing?

KNIPPERDOLLINK: Gert! – You can tell us. Who is this man?

GERT: One of ours. Let him go, my friends. – There, there stand the devil's emissaries!

> *He points at Martin and Nils. The Anabaptists assault them. Martin and Nils run out through the street door, pursued by the Anabaptists.*
>
> *Gert has followed as far as the door. He turns and faces Olof.*
>
> *The tavern is quiet. The Prostitute has crept into a corner. Captain Windrank is still asleep under the table. Olof, deep in thought, stands in the middle of the room. Gert throws himself down on one of the benches, exhausted.*

GERT: It's hard work, Olof.

OLOF: What have you done?

GERT: Done? We've done with the church. Cleaned it out. That's a beginning.

OLOF: That will cost you dearly.

GERT: We still have the upper hand. The whole town is in an uproar. Right now Rink is at work in St. George's chapel. — Tell me, did the king pick you to fight us?

OLOF: Yes.

GERT: Very wise.

OLOF: Tomorrow I am to preach. In the new pulpit.

GERT: New pulpit?

OLOF: Yes. I designed it. After the ones in Germany.

GERT: Indeed! This royal mission—how are you handling that? Here you stand with your arms across your chest, doing nothing.

OLOF: Come to church tomorrow. Bring your Anabaptist friends.

GERT: To hear a Catholic sermon? Or what?

OLOF: I was excommunicated today.

GERT (*leaps up to embrace Olof*): God bless you, Olof! This is truly a rebaptism. Now you are reborn.

OLOF: I still cannot understand you. Why do you carry on like wild animals? You defile all that is sacred.

GERT (*picking up a piece of one of the broken wood statues*): Is this sacred? This? A St. Nicholas, I believe. Jesus came in vain to dwell among us if we still worship sticks of wood. Do you call that a god: a stick I can break? Like this!

OLOF: But he is sacred—to the people.

GERT: So was the golden calf. So was Zeus. And Thor and Odin. And yet they were struck down. (*He notices The Prostitute.*) What woman is that? Oh, I see. The one I pushed in here for you to save. . . . Olof: tell me something. Has the king bought you?

OLOF: Go away, Gert. I abhor you.

GERT (*seeing Windrank*): Who is that pig sleeping on the floor?

OLOF: Don't you see? When I face you, I shrivel up. Please leave me alone. I want to do my work, not yours.

GERT: Now listen—

OLOF: You want to weave the fabric of your life into mine.

GERT: Now listen to me—

OLOF: No. You have spun an invisible web around me. You have proclaimed me an Anabaptist. How will I explain that to the king?

GERT: Which king?

OLOF: King Gustav.

GERT: Oh, that king. . . . Goodbye, Olof. . . . Preaching tomorrow, are you? . . . (*Pointing to The Prostitute.*) Why does she hang around here? . . . Goodbye. (*He leaves.*)

OLOF: God's errand boy, or Satan's?

THE PROSTITUTE (*approaches Olof and kneels before him*): Let me thank you.

OLOF: Give your thanks to God alone, who saved your soul. And do not go from here believing your sins have been atoned for. You must find strength to know yourself as damned and cursed for all your life. God has forgiven you. Human beings never will.

> *Olof takes her by the hand and starts to lead her toward the street door. The iron door opens, and Friar Martin steps into the room, followed by Olof's Mother and Christina, Gert's daughter.*

MARTIN: We must have come the wrong way.

> *Olof's Mother catches sight of Olof holding the hand of The Prostitute.*

MOTHER (*beside herself*): Olof! Olof!

CHRISTINA: Who is that? That woman, she looks so sad.

MARTIN: What a horrible place. Let us get out of here!

Olof turns and runs to the iron door, which Martin slams shut.

OLOF: Mother! Mother!

He rushes out through the other door.

The stage grows dark.

INTERLUDE

Once again the door to the church opens, slowly this time. Bengt, the Sexton, who serves as organ blower and general caretaker of the Great Church, steps cautiously into the room. He is accompanied by his wife, Catherine.

SEXTON: Catherine, sweet! Hold the lantern while I put the padlock on the door.

CATHERINE: Bengt, dear, let's have a look round at this mess first. I had no idea the tavern was so close. Why, this is terrible. Look at these huge barrels of beer.

SEXTON: And there's aquavit and liquor. What a smell! It's giving me a headache. Let's get out of here.

CATHERINE: God's mercy, what ungodly things must have gone on here.

SEXTON: Katey, my sweet.

CATHERINE: Yes, love?

SEXTON: I don't think I'm feeling very good. It's so cold and clammy down here.

CATHERINE: Maybe we'd better go home.

SEXTON: I think I'd better sit down and rest for a moment on this bench.

CATHERINE: You shouldn't be sitting in the damp and cold. Let's go back into the church.

SEXTON: I don't know. I think it was colder in there.

CATHERINE: Don't have a fever, do you?

SEXTON: I think maybe I do. I'm burning.

CATHERINE: Would you like something to drink?

SEXTON: There's an idea. Might help.

CATHERINE: I'll see if I can find some water.

SEXTON: Water? You wouldn't find water in a hole like this.

CATHERINE: Well, you can't drink beer when you've got a fever.

SEXTON: To tell the truth, the fever's gone. I've got a terrible chill, that's what.

CATHERINE: I'll find some small beer for you.

SEXTON: I don't think it will do any good. Won't have any effect unless it's strong. There's some. That butt: Rostock, number 4, marked A.W.

CATHERINE (*searching*): I don't see it. . . . Here's an Amsterdam, number 3.

SEXTON: Try the fourth shelf up and toward the right.

Catherine looks.

SEXTON: The spigot's there to the left, right next to the funnel.

CATHERINE: Don't see it.

SEXTON: I ought to know.

CATHERINE: Found it! Here it is.

> *As the Sexton gets up to help her, he stumbles over Captain Windrank.*

WINDRANK (*waking up slowly, and mumbling*): Oh, oh. Jesus Christ. . . . Saints Peter and Paul . . . and Ferdinand and Isabella . . . and St. George and the dragon and whatever else . . . in came . . . Judgment of God . . . Hocus-pocus . . . the Big Dipper wrongside up . . . spills out . . . don't cry over it. . . . And the cow jumped over the moon. . . . Now I lay me down to sleep. . . . Four angels to my bed, Gabriel stands at the head. . . . Avast! Who's stepping on my stomach?

SEXTON (*frightened*): Would you, sir, deign to tell me what or who you are?

WINDRANK: A dog, usually; tonight, a pig.

SEXTON: A dog? What sort, may I ask?

WINDRANK: A sea dog. I sail with the wind. But that is no reason why you, good sir, should take the wind out of me by stepping on my bellows.

SEXTON: Good sir, I make my living by stepping on bellows — for the organ here in the Great Church.

WINDRANK: Ah ha, the organ blower. I'm honored.

SEXTON: Sexton, really. I also run a little clothing shop, within the church wall.

WINDRANK: So you are organ blower, church sexton, and clothes pedlar —

SEXTON: Three in one. "Conjoined without confusion and without change."

WINDRANK: A most respectable trinity!

SEXTON: One shouldn't joke about such things.

WINDRANK (*yelling*): Oh, oh! I'm drowning! Help!

SEXTON: What in the name of the Lord is going on?

WINDRANK: Look at this flood! Foh!

SEXTON: Katey, my sweet! Where are you, angel? (*Rushing about.*) Oh, Jesus, you've scared the wits out of my wife. She's run out of here and taken the spigot with her, and all the beer's running out of the cask. Get up, good sir, get up! Let's leave this ungodly doghole.

WINDRANK: Leave? My good friend, I have just come into my element. I'm for staying.

SEXTON: Whatever you say, but the clock is striking twelve. The witching hour!

WINDRANK (*getting to his feet hurriedly*): You've changed my mind!

The Sexton starts to lead Windrank out.

WINDRANK: Sexton, I'm being assailed by strong doubts about the trinity.

SEXTON: What's that you say? Dear me!

WINDRANK: I mean *your* trinity.

SEXTON: What do you mean, Captain?

WINDRANK: There are four of you, or you can hang me from the yardarm.

SEXTON: Four? Which four?

WINDRANK: What about the beer tapster? Ha, ha! Have to include him, hm?

SEXTON: Sh! Sh! He's included only at night.

They both fall over the broken statue of St. Nicholas.

WINDRANK: Oh! Oh! Spooks! Holy Mother of God!

SEXTON (*getting to his feet and picking up the statue*): It's enough to make your hair stand on end. St. Nicholas, smashed to bits and swimming in beer. Things have come to a pretty pass when holy things are dragged into the dirt like this. The world can't last long. "If they do these things in a green tree, what shall be done in a dry?"

WINDRANK (*has picked himself up*): Wet, don't you mean?

SEXTON: Captain, you blaspheme. St. Nicholas is my patron saint. I was born on his day.

WINDRANK: That must be why both of you like beer so much.

SEXTON: It's all the fashion now to be a heretic.

WINDRANK: Yes, it must be in the air. Usually I'm a very God-fearing man. But don't you cry. I'll glue the pieces of your St. Nicholas together.

SEXTON (*yelling into the church through the iron door*): Katey! Catherine!

WINDRANK: Sh! Sh! Hell, man, you'll raise the devil's dam!

SEXTON: That's not nice! I have to live with her!

> *They leave.*

TABLEAU CURTAIN

Scene 2

> *The sacristy of the Great Church. A large door is visible, and a smaller one leading to the pulpit. Chasubles and copes are hanging on the walls. Prayer stools and some small chests. The sun is shining in through a window.*
>
> *Bells are ringing. From behind the left wall can be heard the monotonous sound of a voice intoning prayers.*
>
> *The Sexton and his wife, Catherine, enter through the large door, stop, and say a silent prayer.*

SEXTON: That's that. Well, get a move on, sweet, and do a little dusting.

CATHERINE: Well, there's no need to be particular. It's only Master Olof who's preaching today. And I don't understand why the chapter allows it.

SEXTON: He has the support of the king, that's why.

CATHERINE: Yes, yes, I know.

SEXTON: The ambo isn't good enough for him. He's built himself a special speaking place, up in the air. A pulpit, he calls it. A basket, that's what it is. Crazy, newfangled notions. Luther! Luther!

CATHERINE: I suppose it will be the same shambles today as yesterday. I thought they would tear down the whole church.

SEXTON (*as he takes a cup of water up to the pulpit*): I suspect he'll be needing to wet his whistle today, poor fool.

CATHERINE (*while the Sexton is in the pulpit*): It's all the same to me.

SEXTON (*from the pulpit*): Catherine! Master Olof's coming!

CATHERINE: He can't be! How awful! They haven't rung the sermon bell yet. Well, I suppose they wouldn't bother ringing it for someone like him.

> *Olof enters, looking solemn and serious. He goes to the prayer stool and kneels.*
>
> *The Sexton has come down from the pulpit. He takes a robe and holds it for Olof.*

OLOF (*standing up*): God's peace.

> *Catherine curtsies and leaves.*
>
> *The Sexton offers to put the robe on Olof.*

OLOF: Hang it up again.

SEXTON: Master Olof, you have got to wear your robe.

OLOF: No.

SEXTON: But it's always done. The napkin?

OLOF: Not necessary.

SEXTON: Well, I must say!

OLOF: If you don't mind, please leave me, my friend.

SEXTON: You want me to go? I've always—

OLOF: Yes, if you don't mind.

SEXTON: Oh, I see. Yes. Well, I've put the missal to the right as you come up, and I've stuck a spill in to mark the place, and

I've put the water next to it. And don't forget to turn the hour-glass, otherwise things just might go on too long, you know—

OLOF: Have no fear. Many out there will tell me when to stop.

SEXTON: Oh, yes, Lord help us. Beg your pardon. But we do have our customs, don't you know.

OLOF: What's that mournful mumbling I hear?

SEXTON: A pious brother reading prayers for some lost soul. (*He leaves.*)

OLOF: "Thou therefore gird up thy loins, and arise, and speak unto them all that I command thee." . . . God help me. (*He kneels at a prie-dieu and finds a piece of paper on it. Reads.*) "Do not go into the pulpit today. They seek your life." —Words of the tempter! (*He tears the paper to bits.*)

Olof's Mother comes in.

MOTHER: You've gone astray, my son.

OLOF: Who's to say?

MOTHER: *I* am. Your mother. And I am still here. I reach out to you. Turn back!

OLOF: Where would you lead me?

MOTHER: To the path of virtue and to the fear of God.

OLOF: If the decrees of the pope's chancery stand for virtue and the fear of God, I'm afraid you've come too late.

MOTHER: It's not just what you teach; it's the way you live.

OLOF: You say that because of the woman you saw me with last night. I'm too proud to answer you. What good would it do, anyway?

MOTHER: So this is how I'm repaid for all I had to sacrifice that you might see the world and receive a good education.

OLOF: Mother, I swear your sacrifices shall not be wasted. It is to you that I owe my thanks for this day, when at long last I can come forward and openly speak the truth as I see it.

MOTHER: You talk of the truth! You who have made yourself the prophet of lies!

OLOF: Harsh words, Mother.

MOTHER: Did I and all my people before me live a lie? Believe in and die for a lie?

OLOF: It *was* not a lie; it has *become* a lie. When you were young, Mother, you were right. When I grow old, perhaps I'll be in the wrong. One doesn't grow with the times.

MOTHER: I don't understand you.

OLOF: I know. That is the single greatest sorrow of my life: that everything I say and do, however pure my intentions, strikes you as wrongdoing, as godlessness.

MOTHER: Olof, I know that you've made your decision and I know that you are confused. I can't do anything about that, since you know so much more than I do. And I trust God that he will bring you back into the fold. But, Olof, I beg you, don't risk your life today; don't hurl yourself into hell. Don't throw your life away!

OLOF: What do you mean? They won't kill me while I'm in the pulpit.

MOTHER: Haven't you heard that Bishop Brask is negotiating with the pope to bring to Sweden the law that condemns heretics to the stake?

OLOF: The Inquisition?

MOTHER: Yes! The Inquisition!

OLOF: That's enough, Mother! I must speak to the people today; I must go into the pulpit.

MOTHER: I won't let you go!

OLOF: Nothing can stop me.

MOTHER: I have prayed to God to change your heart. I will tell you something, but you must never mention it to anyone. Old as I am—my legs could hardly carry me—I sought out a servant of the Lord and pleaded with him, who stood closer to God, to say

mass for your soul. He denied me because you were excommunicated. . . . Oh, I did a terrible thing. God forgive me for
it. I bribed him, yes, fouled his soul with gold, the devil's gold,
all to save your soul.

OLOF: No, Mother, no! I don't believe it.

>*Olof's Mother takes him by the hand and leads him*
>*toward the wall at the left.*

MOTHER: Listen! . . . Listen. . . . He is praying for you
now in the chapel.

OLOF: So that was the mumbling I heard. Who is it?

MOTHER: A Blackfriar. You know him: Martin.

OLOF: You've got Satan himself saying prayers for me. Forgive
me, Mother, I know you mean well, but—

MOTHER (*crying and kneeling*): Olof! Olof!

OLOF: Don't! Don't! A mother's prayers can tempt angels to fall.
They have finished the hymn. I have to go into the pulpit.
They're waiting.

MOTHER: You are driving me to my grave, Olof.

OLOF (*violently*): The Lord will raise you! (*Kisses her hand.*)
Don't say anything more. I don't know what I'm saying.

MOTHER: Listen! Listen to that muttering.

OLOF: I'm going. I'm going. That God who held His hand over
Daniel in the lions' den shall protect me. (*Olof goes up into the
pulpit.*)

>*During the following scene, Olof's voice can be heard, a*
>*strong orator's voice, delivering the sermon, but the*
>*words cannot be made out. A few moments into the*
>*sermon, murmurs of discontent can be heard, which*
>*grow into a roar, punctuated by shouts of disapproval.*
>
>*Christina, Gert's daughter, enters.*

CHRISTINA: Did you see him?

MOTHER: You here, child? I told you to stay home.

CHRISTINA: Why am I not allowed to enter the house of the Lord? You're hiding something from me.

MOTHER: Go home, Christina.

CHRISTINA: I can't hear Olof preach? Why not? If it is the word of God—. It is, isn't it?

Olof's Mother is silent.

CHRISTINA: Why don't you answer, Mother? What is going on? Doesn't he have permission to preach? The people out there looked as if they were hiding something. They were muttering when I walked in.

MOTHER: Don't ask, child. Go back home and thank God for your ignorance.

CHRISTINA: You treat me like a child. You don't dare tell me—

MOTHER: Your soul is like the living water. Don't let it be muddied. You have no part in this quarrel.

CHRISTINA: Quarrel! I thought as much.

MOTHER: Yes, the battle is raging. Keep clear of it. You know what our lot is when men wage war.

CHRISTINA: At least let me know what it's all about. I can't stand being left in ignorance. I see darkness all around me, and shadows that move. Give me light that I may know where I am. Perhaps I know who these ghosts are.

MOTHER: You will tremble when you recognize them.

CHRISTINA: I would rather tremble than be tormented by this horrible calm.

MOTHER: Don't call down the lightning. It will destroy you.

CHRISTINA: If you mean to frighten me, you have succeeded. But I still want to know the truth. If you don't tell me, I'll find someone who will.

MOTHER: You said you had decided to become a nun and enter a convent. Is that your firm decision?

CHRISTINA: My father wishes it.

MOTHER: That means *you* have doubts.

Christina is silent.

MOTHER: Something is holding you back?

CHRISTINA: You know there is.

MOTHER: Yes, I do; and you must break that bond.

CHRISTINA: That will soon be impossible.

MOTHER: I can help you, my child. You can be saved. I shall offer unto the Lord the greatest sacrifice I can make if that will save one soul from damnation: my son.

CHRISTINA: Olof!

MOTHER: He is lost. It's true. That his own mother should have to say it!

CHRISTINA: Lost?

MOTHER: He is a prophet of lies. The devil has seized his soul.

CHRISTINA (*passionately*): It's not true!

MOTHER: I wish to God it weren't.

CHRISTINA: Why did you wait till now to tell me? Why? — Of course, because it's a lie; that's why! (*She goes to the door and opens it slightly.*) Look at him there in the pulpit! Is that the evil spirit speaking through his mouth? Is that the fire of hell burning in his eyes? Can a lie be uttered by lips that tremble with conviction? Can the darkness send light? Don't you see the glow around his head? No, you are wrong. I know it! I don't know what ideas he preaches. I don't know what ideas he denies. Whatever they are, he is right. He is right, and God is with him!

MOTHER: How little you know the world and the cunning of the devil. Take care. (*She pulls Christina away from the door.*) You mustn't listen to him! Your spirit is weak. He is an apostle of Antichrist!

CHRISTINA: Who is Antichrist?

MOTHER: Those who believe in Luther.

CHRISTINA: You have never told me who Luther is. But if Olof is his apostle, then Luther must be a great man.

MOTHER: Luther is possessed by the devil.

CHRISTINA: No one told me this before. Why not? I don't believe it now.

MOTHER: I am telling you now. Forgive me; I wanted to keep you untouched by the evil in this world, so I kept you in ignorance.

CHRISTINA: I don't believe you! Let go of me! I must see him, I must hear him. He doesn't talk like the others.

MOTHER: Oh, Jesus, my Savior! You too are possessed by unclean spirits.

CHRISTINA (*at the door*): Listen! "Ye shall not bind the souls of men." That's what he is saying to them. . . . "Ye are free, for God has made you free!" They tremble at his words. Some are standing. Some are protesting. . . . "If ye do not wish to be free, then woe unto you! That is a sin against the Holy Ghost!"

SEXTON (*as he enters*): I don't think it's advisable for you ladies to remain here. The people are up in arms. Oh, dear, I'm afraid this won't end well for Master Olof.

MOTHER: Oh, Holy Mother of God, what are you saying?

CHRISTINA: Don't be afraid. The spirit of God is with him!

SEXTON: I don't know about that, but I never heard a sermon like that one. Even an old sinner like me couldn't help crying as I sat up there in the organ loft. I don't understand it—how a heretic and an Antichrist can talk like that! Well, I must say, that Luther!

Cries and yells are heard from within the church.

SEXTON: What did I tell you! There's going to be a terrible row. Why did King Gustav have to be out of town just now?

MOTHER: We had better go. If God is with him, they cannot harm him. And if it is the devil—well, Lord God, let Thy will be done. But pray forgive him.

> *More yelling is heard from within the church. Christina and Olof's Mother leave.*
>
> *The stage is empty for a moment. Olof's voice can be heard, louder than before. Catcalls and the sound of stones hitting the pulpit door.*
>
> *Christina returns, closes the door behind her, and throws herself down on one of the hassocks.*
>
> *Sound of stones striking the pulpit door and of tumult within the church. It grows quiet, and Olof comes in from the pulpit, looking wan and defeated, blood on his forehead. Not seeing Christina, he flings himself into a chair.*

OLOF: All for nothing! They don't care. I loosen his bonds, and the captive strikes me. I tell him he is free, and he doesn't believe me. Is that little word so big that the mind of man can't take it in? If only there were one person who believed. But to be all alone—a fool, whom no one understands.

CHRISTINA: I believe in you, Olof.

OLOF: Christina!

CHRISTINA: *You* are right.

OLOF: How do you know that I am?

CHRISTINA: I don't know how. I only believe it. I was listening.

OLOF: And you don't curse me?

CHRISTINA: Aren't you preaching the word of God?

OLOF: Yes.

CHRISTINA: Why haven't we heard these things before? Why do they speak a language we don't understand?

OLOF: Young woman, someone has been putting words in your mouth. Who?

CHRISTINA: I don't know. I never thought about it.

OLOF: Your father?

CHRISTINA: He wants me to enter a convent.

OLOF: Has it come to that? What do you want?

CHRISTINA (*noticing Olof's injury*): You've been hurt, Olof. Oh, my God! Let me put a bandage on it.

OLOF (*sitting down*): Have I undermined your faith?

CHRISTINA (*takes Olof's napkin—left behind when he went into the pulpit—tears it into strips and binds his forehead during the following*): My faith? I don't understand. . . . Tell me, who is Luther?

OLOF: I mustn't tell you.

CHRISTINA: That's what you all say. It's what my father says, it's what your mother says, it's what you say. Does no one dare to tell me the truth? Is the truth so dangerous?

OLOF: It is! Look! (*He points to his forehead.*)

CHRISTINA: So you want to see me shut up in a nun's cell, living in ignorance—not living at all, really.

Olof says nothing.

CHRISTINA: You want to see me weeping away my life, my young years, saying my prayers endlessly until my soul sinks into sleep. Well, I don't want it. I've been awakened. People are fighting. They're suffering, they're in despair. I've seen it, but I'm not to be allowed a part, not even allowed to look, not even to know what it's all about. You treat me like a stupefied animal. Don't you suppose I have a soul, a soul that cannot be nourished on bread or the stale prayers that you put in my mouth. "Ye cannot bind the souls of men"—that is what you said. Oh, if you only knew how those words struck me. The light dawned for me, and those words struck me. The light dawned for me, and those wild yells out there sounded to me like the singing of birds at daybreak.

OLOF: Christina, you're a woman. You were not born to fight.

CHRISTINA: All right. Then for God's sake let me at least suffer. Anything is better than to sleep my life away. Don't you see? God awakened me after all. You wqould never have dared to tell me who the Antichrist is, never let me know who Luther is. When your mother frightened me by saying you were another Luther, I called down a blessing on him. Whether he's a heretic or a believer, I don't know. I don't care. Because neither Luther nor the pope nor the Antichrist can give me peace of soul if I do not have faith in the everlasting God.

OLOF: Oh, Christina! Will you help me? Be at my side in the battle? You could be all things to me. For me, there is no one but you.

CHRISTINA: Yes, Olof! Yes, with all my heart! I know what I want. I don't have to run to Father and ask him. I feel free. Because I am free!

OLOF: Do you know what you're doing? – what sort of life you're asking for?

CHRISTINA: I do now. Don't worry. You won't have to destroy any illusions. They're gone. . . . Although I admit I have dreamed of a knight in armor who would come to offer me a kingdom and who would speak of love and flowers. . . . Olof, I want to be your wife. Here is my hand. But there is one thing you should know. You were never that shining knight of my dreams. Thank God he never came. He would have vanished as all dreams do.

OLOF: Yes, you shall be mine, Christina, and you shall be happy. I promise you. You were always in my mind when despair seized me and the devil tempted me. Now you shall be at my side. You were always the fair maid of my dreams, held captive in a tower by the lord of the castle. Now you are mine.

CHRISTINA: Beware of dreams, Olof.

Knocking at the door.

OLOF: Who is it?

GERT (*from outside*): Gert.

OLOF: What will he say now? I promised him!

CHRISTINA: Afraid? Let me open the door.

Olof opens the door.

GERT (*startled*): Christina! —Olof? —You have broken your promise!

OLOF: No!

GERT: Liar! You have stolen my child, my life's consolation.

CHRISTINA: Olof isn't lying.

GERT: You have been to church, Christina?

CHRISTINA: I have heard what you didn't want me to hear.

GERT: Lord, You have begrudged me my one joy!

OLOF: Open the floodgates, you said. Let the torrent rage, you said. Well, it claims whatever stands in its way.

GERT: You have stolen my child from me.

OLOF: Then give her to me, Father Gert!

GERT: Never!

OLOF: Isn't she free to make up her own mind?

GERT: She is my child!

OLOF: So much for the freedom you preach! No, she is mine. God has given her to me, and you cannot take her back.

GERT: You are, Olof—and God be praised for it—a priest!

OLOF *and* CHRISTINA: A priest!

GERT: And therefore prohibited from marrying.

OLOF: And if I marry anyway?

GERT: You wouldn't dare.

OLOF: Yes, I would.

GERT: Would you want a husband who is excommunicate, Christina?

CHRISTINA: I don't even know what that means.

OLOF: You see, Gert, you see!

GERT: Oh, Lord, you have chastened me sore.

OLOF: Truth is not partial.

GERT: Your love is greater than mine. Mine was a selfish love. God bless you both. Now I stand alone. (*Embraces them.*) There! Go home, Christina, and set their minds at ease. I want to talk to Olof.

Christina leaves.

GERT (*to Olof*): Now you are mine.

OLOF: What do you mean?

GERT: My kinsman. — Did you get my note?

OLOF: So it was you that warned me not to go into the pulpit.

GERT: Quite the contrary, Olof. It's just that I expressed myself in a roundabout way.

OLOF: I don't understand.

GERT: Of course not. You're still too young. That's why you have need of providence. To a man like you one says "don't do it" when one wants it done.

OLOF: Why weren't you in church with your friends?

GERT: Only the sick need doctors, Olof. We were at work elsewhere. You've done a good job today, and I see that you got paid for it. Today I made you a free man, Olof.

OLOF: You?

GERT: The king ordered you to calm the rebellious spirits. And look at what you have done!

OLOF: I begin to understand you, Gert.

GERT: I'm delighted! Yes, indeed, you set a fire under the sluggards.

OLOF: I did indeed.

GERT: Now what do you suppose the king will say to that?

OLOF: I'll take responsibility.

GERT: Good!

OLOF: The king will approve of what I have done. He wants a reformation, only he's afraid of carrying it out himself.

GERT: You've got it wrong, boy.

OLOF: I know what you want: to set me against the king.

GERT: Tell me, how many masters do you think you can serve?

Olof says nothing.

GERT: The king is back in town.

OLOF: What?

GERT: He just returned.

OLOF: And the Anabaptists?

GERT: Imprisoned, of course.

OLOF: And you stand here doing nothing.

GERT: I'm getting on in years. I once carried on as you do now, but it only exhausted me. Rink and Knipperdollink have formed my advance guard. They had to fall, that was obvious. Now I begin my work.

Drums are heard in the street outside.

OLOF: What's that?

GERT: The royal drums marching the captives to prison. Take a look.

OLOF (*stands on a bench and looks out through the window*): Women and children! Dragged off by soldiers!

GERT: They threw stones at the king's guard. That was naughty.

OLOF: Next they'll be putting the mad and the sick in prison.

GERT: There are two kinds of madmen: one kind gets prison, pills, and cold baths. The other kind gets his head lopped off. A radical cure – but then the disease *is* dangerous, wouldn't you say?

OLOF: I'm going to see the king. He won't allow these atrocities.

GERT: Watch out for your head, Olof.

OLOF: Watch out yourself, Father Gert.

GERT: I'm in no danger. I've been certified mad.

OLOF: I can't bear to see this. I'm going to the king even if it costs me my life. (*Goes toward the door.*)

GERT: It's not a matter that the king can settle. You should appeal to the law.

OLOF: The king is the law.

GERT: Yes, unfortunately. (*He looks out the window.*) Stupid horses. If they knew their strength, you couldn't harness them. When a horse does wise up, it runs away. They call that a crazy horse. . . . Let's pray to God for the sanity of these poor wretches.

CURTAIN

ACT III

Scene 1

A large room in the castle in Stockholm. At back, a gallery, which will later be closed off by a curtain.

An old Servant is pacing his round in the gallery.

Olof enters.

OLOF: Is the king receiving today?

SERVANT: Yes.

OLOF: Can you tell me why I've been kept waiting for four days?

SERVANT: I'm sure I wouldn't know.

OLOF: It seems very strange that I haven't been admitted.

SERVANT: What is your business?

OLOF: No concern of yours.

SERVANT: No, no, of course not. I merely thought that I might provide some information.

OLOF: Are you customarily in charge of the king's audiences?

SERVANT: No, no, nothing like that. But anyone who gets to hear as much as I do picks up things here and there.

Pause.

OLOF: How long will it be?

The Servant pretends not to hear.

OLOF: I say, do you know if the king will be here soon?

SERVANT (*with his back to Olof, slighting him*): Beg pardon, what –?

OLOF: Do you know whom you're talking to?

SERVANT: Have no idea, sorry.

OLOF: I am the king's secretary in the council.

SERVANT: Bless me, Master Olof is it! I knew your father, Peter the blacksmith. You see, I'm from Örebro, too.

OLOF: That's hardly an excuse for poor manners.

SERVANT: True, my boy. When one rises in the world, the poor relations are forgot. Sad but true, my dear boy.

OLOF: It's possible my father honored you with his acquaintance, but I'm sure that when he died, he didn't make you my father. So if you don't mind—

SERVANT: My, my, we are touchy! Pity your poor mother. (*He moves off to the left.*)

> *A moment's silence. Olof is alone. Then Lars Siggeson, National Marshal and Lord High Constable, enters from the right.*
>
> *Without really looking at Olof, the Marshal casually tosses his coat to him.*

MARSHAL: Will the king be here soon?

> *Olof drops the coat on the floor.*

OLOF: I wouldn't know.

MARSHAL: Bring me a chair.

OLOF: That's not one of my duties.

MARSHAL: I am not provided with a list of the doorman's duties!

OLOF: I am not a doorman!

MARSHAL: I don't care what you are. I don't have a list of servants with me, either. It's your duty to be polite.

> *Olof says nothing.*

MARSHAL: Don't stand there! What the devil's got into you?

OLOF: I beg your pardon. As secretary of the council, I am not obliged to wait on people.

MARSHAL: What! —Ah, it's Master Olof! So it amuses you to stand by the door and play the servant in order to reveal yourself as God Almighty. And I thought you had some pride! (*During this, he has picked up his coat and placed it on a bench.*)

OLOF: Lord Marshal—

MARSHAL: Never mind! You're a vain upstart. No need to stand lurking there. Come, sit here, Mr. Secretary. (*Shows him a place, and then goes into a side room.*)

> *Olof sits down.*
>
> *A young Nobleman enters and greets Olof from the gallery.*

NOBLEMAN: Good morning, Mr. Secretary! Good morning! Anyone arrive yet? How are things here in Stockholm? I've come directly from Malmö.

OLOF: Deplorable!

NOBLEMAN: So I have heard. As usual, the mob blusters when the king has his back turned. And the priests—what a stupid lot they are! Oh, forgive me! But you are a freethinker, are you not, Mr. Secretary?

OLOF: I'm afraid I don't quite follow.

NOBLEMAN: Don't be embarrassed on my account. I was educated in Paris. You see? Francis the First, oh *Saint-Sauveur!* That man will go far. Do you know what he said to me at a *bal masque*—only recently in carnival time?

> *Olof lets the question hang.*

NOBLEMAN: *"Monsieur,"* he said, *"la religion est morte, est morte."* That's what he said. That doesn't prevent him from attending mass, however.

OLOF: Really?

NOBLEMAN: And do you know what he said when I asked him why he went to mass? "*Poésie*," he said, "*poésie*." Isn't he divine?

OLOF: And what did you say?

NOBLEMAN: "Your Majesty," I said – in French, of course – "happy the land that is ruled by a king who sees so far beyond the limited horizons of his time that he can comprehend the tenor of things to come without compelling the sleeping masses to embrace those higher ideals for which they will not be ready until centuries have passed." Well said, don't you think?

OLOF: Absolutely. Though it lost something in the translation. Some things have to be said in French.

NOBLEMAN (*momentarily disconcerted*): Perfectly right, of course, indeed you are. Dear fellow, you could *faire fortune*, you're so far ahead of the times.

OLOF: Not so far, I'm afraid. Unfortunately, my education was somewhat scanted. I went to Germany for it, as you know, and the Germans have not got beyond religion.

NOBLEMAN: How true, how absolutely true! Can you tell me why they are making such a fuss over that reformation in Germany? Oh, Luther is an enlightened man, I know that; I am sure of it. But why can't he keep it to himself? – the reformation, I mean. Why throw brilliant ideas out to the masses? Pearls before swine. Anyone who looks out over the wide world, anyone who is part of the great intellectual movements, can see the cause of that imbalance, that loss of equilibrium, which is apparent in all the cultured lands. I speak not of Sweden, which has no culture. Do you know what that center of gravity is? That center any disturbance of which turns the world upside down? That center of gravity is – the nobility. The aristocracy, the intelligentsia! Feudalism has had its day – *hoc est* the way of the world! Civilization is collapsing, culture is dying. I see you don't believe it. But a mere glance at history proves me right. Had there been no aristocracy there would have been no crusades! Without the nobility – none of this, none of that. Why is Germany torn to pieces? Because the peasants have risen in revolt against the nobility. They're cutting off their own head. Why does France – *la France*

—stand firm and solid? Because France *is* the aristocracy, and the aristocracy is France. They are one and the same, an identity. And—to put another question—why is Sweden today shaken to its very foundations? Because the nobility has been crushed. Now Christian the Second, there was a genius! He knew how to conquer a land. He didn't saw off a leg or an arm; he cut off the head. Ah, well! Sweden shall be saved. King Gustav knows how. The nobility shall be restored and the church crushed.—What do you say to that?

OLOF (*getting to his feet*): Nothing.

A moment's silence.

OLOF: You're a freethinker?

NOBLEMAN: But of course!

OLOF: And therefore you don't believe that Balaam's ass could talk?

NOBLEMAN: My God, no!

OLOF: I do.

NOBLEMAN: Extraordinary!

LARS ANDERSSON (*coming in*): God's peace, Olof.

OLOF (*embracing him*): Welcome, Lars.

NOBLEMAN (*as he leaves*): *Racaille!*

LARS ANDERSSON: Does your new job agree with you? How do you like it here in Stockholm?

OLOF: It's too stuffy.

LARS ANDERSSON: I'm sure.

OLOF: And the ceilings are too low.

LARS ANDERSSON: He must stoop who has a low door.

OLOF: In just ten minutes here I've become so much the courtier that I've learned to hold my tongue when an ass brays.

LARS ANDERSSON: No harm in that.

OLOF: What's the king up to?

LARS ANDERSSON: He keeps his own counsel.

In the meantime several people have come into the room and are waiting to see the king.

OLOF: How does he look?

LARS ANDERSSON: Like a question mark followed by several exclamation points.

Bishop Brask enters. Everyone makes way for him.

Lars Siggeson, the National Marshal, already on the scene, approaches him and greets him.

Thereupon Olof greets him. Brask is amazed.

BRASK (*to The Marshal*): Are these the clerks' quarters?

MARSHAL: They shouldn't be, but our king is infintely obliging.

BRASK: Patronizing, is more like it.

MARSHAL: Quite.

BRASK: Rather large attendance today, I see.

MARSHAL: Yes. Mostly social calls, congratulating His Majesty on his safe return.

BRASK: I shall find it a pleasure, my Lord Constable, to inform His Majesty that I am in complete sympathy with his felicitous solution to a difficult problem.

MARSHAL: My Lord Bishop is most gracious to put himself to so much trouble. It's a long journey from Linköping, especially for a man of your years.

BRASK: Yes, it is. More so, since my health isn't too reliable.

MARSHAL: Indeed. I'm sorry to hear that my Lord's health isn't what it should be. It's always depressing not to be in full vigor, and especially so when one occupies a high position with all its responsibilities.

BRASK: I must say you look in good shape.

MARSHAL: Yes, thank God.

The conversation dies for a moment.

BRASK (*sitting down*): Do you feel a draft, my Lord Marshal?

MARSHAL: Yes, it's possible I do. Perhaps we should have them close the door?

BRASK: No, thank you. I don't think that is necessary.

Again the conversation dies.

MARSHAL: The king seems to be taking his time.

BRASK: Yes.

MARSHAL: Perhaps there is no point in waiting for him.

BRASK: Perhaps not.

MARSHAL: If you wish, I could call your servants.

BRASK: Having waited this long, I suppose I can wait a while longer.

Silence. Then the Servant announces the arrival of King Gustav.

SERVANT: His Majesty!

GUSTAV: Welcome, my lords. (*He sits down at a table.*) If my lords will be good enough to step out into the antechamber, I shall receive you one at a time.

Everyone except Bishop Brask starts to withdraw.

GUSTAV: Our National Marshal may stay.

BRASK: But Your Majesty—!

GUSTAV (*raising his voice*): Lars Siggeson!

Lars Siggeson, the National Marshal, turns and approaches Gustav. Bishop Brask leaves.

Silence.

GUSTAV: Well, speak up! What should I do?

MARSHAL: Your Majesty: the situation is clear. The state is tottering because it has lost its main support. Its existence is in peril because it has acquired an enemy stronger than itself. Strengthen the main support, the nobility, and crush the enemy, the church.

GUSTAV: I dare not.

MARSHAL: Sire, you have no choice.

GUSTAV: No choice! No choice!

MARSHAL: Begging your leave, Sire, no. Bishop Brask is negotiating right now with the pope to bring the Inquisition here. Lübeck is becoming more insistent in its exorbitant demands for the repayment of our debts, and is even threatening war. The national treasury is empty; there are insurrections in every part of the country —

GUSTAV: Enough, enough! . . . What matters is that I have the people behind me.

MARSHAL: Have you? Forgive me, Your Majesty, but take the Dalesmen, for example. A spoiled tribe, who dispute the Lübeckers the honor of having provided Sweden with a king, who stand ready to revolt at the first opportunity, and who issue demands such as — (*He reads from a slip of paper.*) "No foreign styles in clothes, such as slashed and pouched apparel and brocaded fabric, which have recently been introduced at court, shall be countenanced."

GUSTAV: Damnation!

MARSHAL: "Anyone who eats meat on Fridays or Saturdays is to be burned at the stake or otherwise deprived of his life." Or this: "No new faith or creed or Lutheran doctrine is to be imposed on us." —I tell you, a faithless and insolent people!

GUSTAV: Still, they were real men once, when I stood alone and had need of them.

MARSHAL: Real men? When their houses were on fire, they carried water. Who wouldn't? Real men? How many times haven't they broken their word? For words mean nothing to them — except of course words of praise. And those they have heard so often that they now actually believe that their crude insolence is good old Swedish bluntness.

GUSTAV: You belong to the nobility.

MARSHAL: I do. And I am convinced that the yeoman has played out his part: the exercise of brute muscle power to drive the enemy out of Sweden. . . . Your Majesty: eliminate the church, which keeps the people in chains; use the wealth of the church to pay off the nation's debts; and return to the prostrate nobility the gold that the church cheated them of.

GUSTAV: Call in Brask!

MARSHAL: But Your Majesty —

GUSTAV: Bishop Brask, I said!

The Marshal leaves.

Bishop Brask enters.

GUSTAV: Now, Bishop Brask, let me hear what you have to say.

BRASK: May I offer our warmest wishes for your —

GUSTAV: Thank you, my Lord Bishop. To business.

BRASK: Regrettably, there have been rumors of complaints from various parts of the kingdom concerning Your Majesty's unpaid loans from the church. I refer to the silver tribute levied by Your Majesty.

GUSTAV: And you have come to demand payment. Does the church actually use all those chalices for communion?

BRASK: Yes, Your Majesty.

GUSTAV: Let them drink out of tin mugs.

BRASK: Your Majesty!

GUSTAV: Any other business?

BRASK: The most serious of all: heresy.

GUSTAV: That doesn't concern me. I am not the pope.

BRASK: I am bound to inform Your Majesty that the church will insist upon its rights even at the risk of running into conflict. . . .

GUSTAV: With whom?

BRASK: With the state.

GUSTAV: Your church can go to the devil! Is that clear enough?

BRASK: It was clear enough before.

GUSTAV: And you only wanted to hear it from my own lips?

BRASK: Yes.

GUSTAV: Take care! You travel with two hundred men in your retinue and dine off silver while the people eat the bark off trees.

BRASK: Your Majesty takes too narrow a view of the matter.

GUSTAV: And you are a broad-minded, enlightened man? What about Luther? How do you account for that phenomenon? What about the movements now sweeping through Europe?

BRASK: Reaching forward but stepping backward. Luther's role is simply to provide the purgative fire for what is centuries old, tried and true, in order that, through strife, it may prove itself victorious.

GUSTAV: I'm not interested in your sophistries.

BRASK: But Your Majesty harbors criminals and encroaches on the rights of the church. Your Master Olof has grievously offended the church.

GUSTAV: Excommunicate him.

BRASK: That has been done. Yet he is still in Your Majesty's service.

GUSTAV: What more do you want to do to him? . . . Well?

Pause.

BRASK: Furthermore, there seems to be no stopping him. I have learned that he has secretly married in direct violation of canonical law.

GUSTAV: Well, well! He does move fast.

BRASK: Your Majesty can turn his back on that, of course. Suppose, however, he rouses the people?

GUSTAV: Then I shall take the matter into my hands. — Is there anything else?

BRASK (*waits before speaking*): I beg you, Sire, for heaven's sake, do not drive the country into wrack and ruin again. It is not ready for a new religion. We are frail reeds that can bend. But the church? No! The faith? No, never!

GUSTAV (*extending his hand*): Perhaps you are right. Let us be avowed enemies, Hans, old Hans, rather than false friends.

BRASK: Fair enough. But do not do anything you might regret. Every stone you take from the wall of the church the people will cast at you.

GUSTAV: Do not drive me to extremes, Bishop. We do not want the horrible spectacles that Germany has witnessed. For the last time: will you make concessions if the welfare of the country is at stake?

BRASK: The church . . . never . . .

GUSTAV: The church first, yes. Very well. God be with you.

Brask leaves.

The Marshal enters.

GUSTAV: Bishop Brask confirmed what you said. That was precisely the idea. Now we need masons, not for building but for demolishing. The walls may stand; the cross may remain on the roof and the bells in the tower. But I shall leave the cellars in ruins. Begin with the foundations, always.

MARSHAL: The people think that we are depriving them of their faith. They will have to be taught otherwise.

GUSTAV: We shall have Master Olof preach to them.

MARSHAL: A very dangerous fellow.

GUSTAV: And the very man we need now.

MARSHAL: He has been acting like an Anabaptist instead of fighting against them.

GUSTAV: I know. That will come later. Send him in.

MARSHAL: Chancellor Lars would be better.

GUSTAV: Have them both come in.

MARSHAL: Or Olof's brother, Lars Pedersson.

GUSTAV: Won't do just now. He's too tender-hearted. His time will come, too.

> *The Marshal brings in Olof and Chancellor Lars Andersson.*

GUSTAV (*addressing Lars Andersson*): I need your help, Lars.

LARS ANDERSSON: As regards the church?

GUSTAV: Yes. It must be demolished.

LARS ANDERSSON: I'm not your man. Perhaps Your Majesty should ask Master Olof.

GUSTAV: You mean you won't help?

LARS ANDERSSON: I mean I cannot. But I can provide you with a weapon.

> *He hands to Gustav the Swedish translation of the Bible. Gustav opens it and turns a few pages.*

GUSTAV: It's done. A Swedish translation of the Holy Scriptures. A job well done, Lars! A good weapon. Will you make use of it, Olof?

OLOF: Yes, with God's help.

Gustav signals to Lars Andersson to leave.

GUSTAV: Have you calmed down yet, Olof?

Olof doesn't reply.

I gave you four days to think things over. How did you fare with the assignment I gave you?

OLOF (*brusquely*): I have spoken to the people –

GUSTAV: Yes. Which left you as hot-headed as ever. You intend to defend those crazy fools, the ones they call Anabaptists?

OLOF (*boldly*): Yes!

GUSTAV: Calm yourself. . . . I hear you got married in all haste.

OLOF: Yes.

GUSTAV: And you have been excommunicated?

OLOF: Yes.

GUSTAV: And you're still as brash as ever. Now suppose that as a troublemaker in the realm you accompanied the others to the gallows – what would you say to that?

OLOF: I would regret that I had been unable to complete my work – and thank God for what little I was able to accomplish.

GUSTAV: Good, very good. Would you dare to go to Uppsala, that old owl's nest, and tell those doting professors that the pope is not God and that he has nothing to do with Sweden?

OLOF: Is that all?

GUSTAV: Will you tell them that God's word is to be found only in the Bible?

OLOF: Is that all you want of me?

GUSTAV: One thing more: you are not to mention Luther's name.

OLOF (*thinks about it for a moment*): No. I can't agree to that.

GUSTAV: Would you prefer to die with the others?

OLOF: No. But I think my king has need of me.

GUSTAV: It isn't very magnanimous of you to take advantage of my situation. — Very well, say what you want to say. However, you will have to forgive me if I make some revisions later on.

OLOF: One doesn't haggle over the truth.

GUSTAV: Damnation! (*Abruptly changing his tone.*) Do as you wish.

OLOF (*on his knees*): I am allowed to say exactly what I want said?

GUSTAV: Yes.

OLOF: Then my life won't be wasted—not if I cast a spark of doubt into these complacent souls. There shall be a reformation, after all.

GUSTAV (*taking time to reply*): Yes.

> *Pause.*

OLOF (*worried*): What will become of the Anabaptists?

GUSTAV: Why ask? To the gallows, that's what.

OLOF: Will Your Majesty allow me a question?

GUSTAV: Tell me, what do these crazy fools want?

OLOF: The trouble is that they don't really know themselves. If I might—

GUSTAV: Yes? Speak out.

> *Gert the Printer enters in haste, acting insane.*

GUSTAV: How dare you burst in here! Who are you?

GERT: Sire, I most humbly petition Your Majesty to attest to the correctness of this certificate.

GUSTAV: Wait until you are called.

GERT: Oh, *I* can wait, Sire. But the guards won't wait for me. I fled, you see, from the prison. It wasn't the place for me.

GUSTAV: Were you with the Anabaptists?

GERT: Yes, I got mixed up with them. But I have a certificate that I belong in the asylum. Division number three – for incurables, that is. Cell number seven.

GUSTAV (*to Olof*): Call the guards.

GERT: That isn't necessary, Sire. All I'm asking for is justice, and the guards aren't in charge of that.

GUSTAV (*staring at him*): Didn't you take part in the sacrileges committed against the churches here?

GERT: That would follow. Would a sane man do such crazy things? We had in mind to make only a few changes – stylistic ones. The ceilings were too low, in our opinion.

GUSTAV: What did you really accomplish?

GERT: Oh, so much, so much, and still only half of it done. So much and so quickly that our thoughts can't keep up. They are always a little behind. Oh, yes, refurbish the walls in the church, that's what we wanted. And the windows removed to get rid of the musty smell. Some other things, too, but that should do for now.

GUSTAV (*to Olof*): A fearful illness. Can't be anything else.

OLOF: Who knows?

GUSTAV: I'm tired. You have two weeks to get ready. Give me your hand and your promise that you will help me.

OLOF: I shall do my part.

GUSTAV: Give orders for the removal of Rink and Knipperdollink to Malmö.

OLOF: Then what?

GUSTAV: They can escape – to Germany. And this idiot you can send back to the asylum. Fare thee well.

Gustav leaves.

Gert shakes his fist at Gustav's back.

GERT: Shall we go?

OLOF: Where?

GERT: Home.

Olof is silent.

GERT: You wouldn't put your father-in-law in the madhouse, would you, Olof?

OLOF: Wouldn't I? My duty!

GERT: Are there no higher duties than obeying orders?

OLOF: Don't start that again.

GERT: What would Christina say if you left her father among the mad folk?

OLOF: Don't tempt me.

GERT: You see how hard it is to serve the king.

Olof is silent.

GERT: Dear boy, I won't cause you any distress. Here is absolution for your conscience. (*He shows Olof a piece of paper.*)

OLOF: What is it?

GERT: A bill of health. A release from the asylum. You see, you have to be mad among the sane, and sane among the mad.

OLOF: How did you get this?

GERT: You sound as if I don't deserve it.

OLOF: I wonder.

GERT: Of course. You're still afraid.

The Servant enters.

SERVANT: I'll have to ask you to leave. The room has to be swept.

GERT: And aired out?

SERVANT: You can be sure of it.

GERT: Don't forget to open the windows.

SERVANT: Never fear. It needs it. We're not used to this kind of company.

GERT: Oh, by the way, old boy, I have greetings from your old man.

SERVANT: Oh?

GERT: You do know your father?

SERVANT: What's that to you?

GERT: You know what he said?

SERVANT: No.

GERT: He said, "He that blows into the dust fills his eyes with it."

SERVANT: I don't see the point.

GERT: We all have excuses. (*He leaves.*)

SERVANT: Riffraff!

TABLEAU CURTAIN

Scene 2

Olof's study. Windows at the back with the sun shining through them. Trees outside. Christina is standing at one of the windows, watering flowers and talking to songbirds in a cage. Olof is at his desk, writing. From time to time he looks up from his work and glances impatiently at Christina. This is repeated several times until Christina knocks down a flower pot. Olof stamps the floor in irritation.

CHRISTINA: Oh, my poor, dear flower. Look, Olof, four buds broke off.

OLOF: Yes, yes, I'm not blind.

CHRISTINA: You're not even looking. Come here and see.

OLOF: Dearest, I haven't time.

CHRISTINA: You haven't even looked at the goldfinches I bought for you this morning. Don't you think they sing beautifully?

OLOF: Like a bird.

CHRISTINA: Like a bird?

OLOF: Frankly, it's hard to work with that screeching.

CHRISTINA: They don't screech, Olof. You're just partial to screeching at night. The owl doesn't bother you. What does that owl mean that you have on your signet ring?

OLOF: The owl is an ancient symbol of wisdom.

CHRISTINA: That's silly. A wise man wouldn't like the dark.

OLOF: A wise man hates the dark, he hates the night. But he turns night into day with his keen vision.

CHRISTINA: You always have the right answer, Olof. I wonder why?

OLOF: Because, my sweet, I know you enjoy letting me be right.

CHRISTINA: Right again! —What are you working on?

OLOF: I'm translating.

CHRISTINA: Read some of it to me.

OLOF: Oh, I don't think you would understand this.

CHRISTINA: Isn't it Swedish?

OLOF: Yes, but it's very abstract.

CHRISTINA: Abstract? What does that mean?

OLOF: I can't explain it. Let me put it this way: if you don't understand what I read, then you'll know what abstract means.

CHRISTINA (*taking up her knitting*): You read, and I'll knit.

OLOF: Listen carefully now, and don't blame me if I bore you.

CHRISTINA: I'll understand. I'm determined to.

OLOF (*reading*): "Matter, conceived as an abstraction from form, is completely without predicates, undefined and undifferentiated. Because not from pure non-being but only from the non-being of reality, that is, from being as potentiality, can anything originate. Potential being is no more non-being than reality. Every existence is therefore a realized possibility. Matter is thus for Aristotle a more positive substratum than it is for Plato, who explained it as pure non-being. From this it is possible to understand how Aristotle could conceive of matter in contrast to form as a positive negativity."

CHRISTINA (*throwing aside her knitting*): Oh, stop! I don't understand a word! Why? Why? I'm ashamed of myself, Olof. I must make a pretty poor wife, who can't understand what her husband is saying. I'd best stick to my knitting. I'll clean your study and dust your books. At least I'll learn to understand the looks in your eyes. Oh, Olof, I'm not worthy of you. Why did you take me as your wife? You overrated me, because you were momentarily infatuated with me. You'll come to regret it, and we'll both be unhappy.

OLOF: Christina, calm yourself. Now sit down here, darling, beside me. (*He picks up the knitting.*) Would you believe me if I told you that it is absolutely impossible for me to do work like this? Absolutely impossible. I could never manage it. So you must be more skillful than I am, and I must be less than you.

CHRISTINA: Why can't you do it?

OLOF: For the same reason that you didn't understand me just now: I haven't learned. Will it make you happy if I tell you that you can learn to understand this book—which is not mine: be sure you understand that—while I, on the other hand, can never learn how to do your work?

CHRISTINA: Why not?

OLOF: Because I'm not made that way. And because I don't want to.

CHRISTINA: But if you did want to?

OLOF: That, darling, is my weak point. I could never make myself want to. Believe me, you are stronger than I am. You are the master of your will; I'm the slave of mine.

CHRISTINA: Do you really think I could learn to understand that book of yours?

OLOF: I'm convinced of it. But you mustn't.

CHRISTINA: I must always be kept in ignorance, is that what you want?

OLOF: No, no, it's not that. But suppose you understood everything I understand. You wouldn't look up to me.

CHRISTINA: As a god?

OLOF: Whatever. Believe me, you would lose what makes you greater than me: the strength to curb your will. Then you would be less than me, and I couldn't look up to you. You see what I mean? We're happy because we overrate each other. Let's hold on to our delusions.

CHRISTINA: Now I don't understand you at all. Still, I have to believe you, Olof. I'm sure you're right.

OLOF: I need to be alone, Christina. Do you mind? Please.

CHRISTINA: Am I disturbing you?

OLOF: Christina, I have serious business to attend to. Today is decisive. The king has abdicated because Parliament wouldn't accept his proposals. Today I'll either reach my goal or start from scratch again.

CHRISTINA: I want to be happy today. It's Midsummer Eve, Olof.

OLOF: Why should you be especially happy today?

CHRISTINA: Why shouldn't I be? I was a captive. I've become your wife.

OLOF: I hope you will forgive me if I find it difficult to share all your joy. I've paid for my bliss: it cost me a mother.

CHRISTINA: I know what it cost you. I feel it deeply, too. When she learns of our marriage, your mother will forgive you, but she will curse me. Who will have the harder time of it? I don't mind—it's for your sake. I understand that. I know that enormous struggles lie ahead, that daring ideas are fermenting in your brain. Know that I can never take part in the struggle, never help with advice, never defend you against abuse and smears. Have to see it happening and still live in my small world, doing all the little things that I don't believe you appreciate but that you'd miss if I didn't do them. Since we can't cry together, Olof, maybe we could laugh together. That would make things easier for me. Come down from the heights where I can't reach you. Come home once in a while from those battles you fight in the mountains. If I can't climb up to you, can't you come down to me for a moment? Forgive me for talking like a child, Olof. You are sent by God; I know that. I have felt the blessing of your words. But you are also a man; you are my husband, or at least you should be. You won't lower yourself too much if you would drop the solemn talk and just for once let me see the sun on your face rather than the clouds. Are you so great that you can't look at a flower or listen to the birds sing? I put the flowers on your desk, Olof, to give your eyes something restful to look at; you had the girl take them away because they gave you a headache. I wanted to relieve the lonely silence of your work with the song of birds; you called it screeching. I asked you to come to dinner a while ago; you didn't have time. I want to talk with you now; you haven't got the time. Although you despise this little world of mine, you tell me to live in it. If you don't want to lift me up to your world, at least have the kindness not to trample on mine. I'll take away everything that disturbs your precious thoughts. You'll be rid of me and all my rubbish. (*She throws the flowers out the window, takes the birdcage, and starts to leave.*)

OLOF: Christina, dearest, I'm sorry. Forgive me. You just don't understand.

CHRISTINA: That's all you ever say: "You don't understand." It comes to me now—that moment in the sacristy with you. I grew up so fast that I became old in an instant. A different person.

OLOF: Christina, come. I'll look at your birds; I'll talk to your flowers.

CHRISTINA (*carrying the birdcage away*): No. No more baby talk. We'll be serious. Don't be afraid of my noise and laughter. It was all for you, but since it doesn't suit you or your great calling—(*She bursts into tears.*)

OLOF (*taking her in his arms and kissing her*): Christina, Christina, dearest. You're quite right. I'm sorry.

CHRISTINA: Olof, that gift you gave me, the gift of freedom—it was too much. I don't know what to do with it. I have to have someone I can obey.

OLOF: I think we'll find someone. But let's not talk about that now. Off to dinner! I'm really quite hungry.

CHRISTINA (*happily*): I don't believe it! You hungry? (*She happens to look out the window and is startled by what she sees.*) Why don't you go in, Olof, and I'll come right away. I want to straighten up here a little.

OLOF (*as he leaves*): Don't make me wait as long as you had to wait for me!

> *Christina clasps her hands in prayer and stands waiting for someone to enter through the street door.*
>
> *Pause.*
>
> *Olof's Mother enters and walks past Christina without deigning to look at her.*

MOTHER: Is Master Olof home?

> *Christina has approached her in a friendly way, but struck by the woman's snub and by her tone of voice, she adopts the same tone.*

CHRISTINA: No, he isn't. If you care to wait, he'll be here soon.

MOTHER: Thank you. (*She takes a seat.*)

Pause.

MOTHER: Give me a glass of water.

Christina serves her.

MOTHER: Now leave me.

CHRISTINA: As the wife in the house, I'm obliged to keep you company.

MOTHER: And since when does a priest's housekeeper call herself his wife?

CHRISTINA: I am Master Olof's wife in the sight of God. Don't you know that we are married?

MOTHER: You are a harlot! That I know.

CHRISTINA: I don't know what that means.

MOTHER: That woman Olof spoke to in the tavern that night—she was a harlot.

CHRISTINA: She looked so miserable. It's true, I'm not happy.

MOTHER: I can well believe it. Get out of my sight! Your presence here is an insult to me.

CHRISTINA (*on her knees*): For the sake of your son, don't treat me as if I were some shameless creature.

MOTHER: As his mother, I order you out of his house, whose threshold you have desecrated.

CHRISTINA: As his wife and as mistress of the house, I'll open the door to anyone I please. I would have shut it on you, if I had known what you had to say.

MOTHER: Mighty fine talk! I order you to leave this house!

CHRISTINA: What gives you the right to force your way in here and drive me out of my own house? You bore a child, yes, brought him up: that was your purpose in life; and you can thank God that you fulfilled it so well. Not everyone is so fortunate. Now you stand on the brink of the grave. Don't stand in his way any longer. Let him stand on his own two feet before you come to the end of your journey. Or did you bring up your son so badly that like a child he still has to hold your hand? If it's gratitude you want, you won't get it that way. Do you think that one's purpose in life is to sacrifice oneself to one's parents out of gratitude? A voice is calling him to forge ahead. Your voice calls him back. "Come here, you thankless child!" Is he to stray from his true path in life, sacrifice his strength and talent, which belong to the world, to humanity itself, merely to satisfy the petty wishes of one selfish mother? Do you think that bearing and rearing a child earns you its everlasting gratitude? Didn't that child provide you with an aim and a purpose? Shouldn't you be grateful to God for having given meaning to your life? Or did you do it all in order to be repaid bit by bit till your dying day? Don't you realize that that one word "gratitude" destroys all you have done? And what gives you rights over me? You seem to think that by marrying I mortgaged myself and my free will to whomever nature selected as the mother and father of my husband, who unfortunately wouldn't be here but for the two of them. You are not my mother. I never swore to be true to you when I took Olof as my husband. And I have enough respect for my husband not to let anyone insult him without hearing from me—not even his mother! That's why you're hearing from me!

MOTHER: Now I see the fruits of the doctrines my son is spreading.

CHRISTINA: If you insist on insulting your son, you'll have to do it to his face! (*She goes to the door and calls.*) Olof!

MOTHER: Already the sly one, aren't you?

CHRISTINA: Already? Wasn't I always? I just didn't know I was sly until I needed to be.

OLOF (*entering*): Mother! Welcome.

MOTHER: Thank you. And goodbye!

OLOF: Goodbye? Why? I want to talk to you.

MOTHER: That won't be necessary. She has said everything. You won't have to show me the door.

OLOF: What in the name of God are you talking about? Christina, what's going on?

MOTHER (*starts to go*): Goodbye, Olof. I will never forgive you for this. Never!

OLOF (*standing in her way*): Wait! At least explain to me.

MOTHER: You ought to be ashamed. You send her out to tell me that you owe me nothing, that I'm no longer of any use to you. That's hard. (*She leaves.*)

OLOF: What did you say to her, Christina?

CHRISTINA: I don't remember. A whole lot of things. I don't know where the words came from. I said things I didn't even dare think about before. Things I must have dreamed about all the years my father kept me under his thumb.

OLOF: Christina, you're so different. I hardly recognize you.

CHRISTINA: I'm not surprised. I'm beginning to wonder myself who I am.

OLOF: You must have been very unkind to Mother.

CHRISTINA: Yes, I suppose I was. Don't you think I've become hard? Olof?

OLOF: Did you tell her to leave?

CHRISTINA: I'm sorry, Olof. I didn't behave properly. —I—

OLOF: For my sake at least, you might have shown her more consideration. Why didn't you call me right away?

CHRISTINA: I wanted to see if I could take care of myself. —Olof, are you going to take her side against me when she asks you to?

OLOF: I'd have to think about that.

CHRISTINA: I can answer for you. You don't mind giving in to your mother voluntarily because you're strong. It amuses you. It's different with me. I'd be mortified, because I'm weak. I'll never give in to her.

OLOF: Not even if I beg you?

CHRISTINA: You can't ask that of me. Not unless you want me to hate her. . . . Tell me, Olof, what is a harlot?

OLOF: You do ask the strangest questions.

CHRISTINA: Don't you think I deserve an answer?

OLOF: Will you forgive me if I don't answer?

CHRISTINA: Always the same. No answers. Am I never to be told anything? Am I supposed to remain a child? Then put me in the nursery; dandle me on your knees!

OLOF: It means an unfortunate woman, a fallen woman.

CHRISTINA: No, there's more to it than that.

OLOF: Has anyone dared to call you that?

CHRISTINA (*hesitates*): No.

OLOF: You're not being straight with me, Christina.

CHRISTINA: No. . . . Since yesterday I've become wicked.

OLOF: Something happened then that you're keeping from me.

CHRISTINA: Yes. I thought I could deal with it, but I can't. I can't.

OLOF: Tell me, please.

CHRISTINA: Don't say I'm weak. . . . A crowd of people pursued me right to the door, calling me this name. "Harlot! Harlot!" And I didn't know what they could mean. "Harlot." One doesn't laugh at an "unfortunate" woman.

OLOF: Yes, my dear, that's exactly what they do.

CHRISTINA: I didn't understand what they were saying, but their gestures made everything clear enough. And since then I've been full of hate.

OLOF: And in spite of all that, you've been so kind to me. Forgive me for being so hard on you. —"Whore"—that's what brutes call their victims. You'll be hearing more about what it means. But I warn you: never defend one of these "unfortunate" women. You'll be dragged into the dirt.

Enter a Messenger with a letter.

OLOF: At last! (*He reads the letter hastily.*) Read it to me, Christina. I want to hear the good news from your lips.

CHRISTINA (*reading*): "Victory is yours, young man. I, who fought against you, want to be the first to tell you this. I do not write to you in humiliation. You wielded the weapons of the spirit when you spoke for the new faith. Whether you are right or not, I do not know, but I believe you are entitled to the counsel of an old man. Go no further, now that your enemies have fled the field. Do not grapple with shadows. They will cripple your arm, and you will wither and die. Neither rely on the princes of the realm. This is the advice of a once-powerful man, who now steps aside and commits to the hands of the Lord the fate of His ruined church." Signed "Johannes Brask." —Olof, you have won!

OLOF (*ecstatic*): Oh, God, I thank thee for this moment! (*Pause.*) No—I'm afraid, Christina! It's wrong. It's too much. I'm too young to have reached my goal. Nothing more to accomplish— what a terrible thought. Not to fight anymore, not to struggle— that's death.

CHRISTINA: Rest awhile, and be thankful it's over.

OLOF: Can it ever be over? Can such a beginning have an end? No, no! I want to begin all over again. It wasn't victory I wanted but the battle itself.

CHRISTINA: Don't tempt God, Olof. I feel it's far from over, far.

The Nobleman enters.

NOBLEMAN: Good day, Mr. Secretary. Wonderful news!

Christina excuses herself and leaves.

OLOF: Good day to you, sir! I've already heard some of it.

NOBLEMAN: My thanks to you—and my congratulations—for that remarkable defense you made in the debate at Uppsala University against that—that—professor of theology—what's his name? —Galle. A stupid man, really. You cooked his goose, I must say. Overdid it perhaps. Too much heat. A dash of malice in the sauce would have been more subtle.

OLOF: You have some news from the king?

NOBLEMAN: Oh, I do indeed; indeed I do! Here are the enactments of the estates, in sum. (*He takes out a paper and consults it.*) First. Mutual agreement to resist and punish all rebels.

OLOF: Go on.

NOBLEMAN: Second: the right of the king to take possession of the castles and strongholds of the bishops, to determine their revenues, and—

OLOF (*interrupting*): Third.

NOBLEMAN: Yes. Now comes the best part, the kernel of the whole enterprise. Third: the right of the nobility to reclaim those estates that they possessed in fee simple and that fell to the churches and monasteries as a result of the perquisitions of King Charles VIII in 1454, provided—

OLOF: Yes, yes! Fourth.

NOBLEMAN: —provided that the claimant upon the sworn oaths of twelve men can confirm his birthright before the judicial assembly. (*He folds up the paper.*)

OLOF: Is that all?

NOBLEMAN: Isn't it superb?

OLOF: There's nothing more?

NOBLEMAN: Oh, some minor points. Nothing of significance.

OLOF: Could I hear them?

NOBLEMAN (*unfolding the paper and looking at it*): There's a fifth item about the right of preachers to promulgate the Gospel. But they had that before, didn't they?

OLOF: And nothing else?

NOBLEMAN: Well, there's the decree itself. "The incomes of bishops, dioceses, and canons shall be recorded, and the king shall have the right to determine—"

OLOF: That's irrelevant.

NOBLEMAN: —"how much of this income they may retain and how much shall be given him for the needs of the crown." . . . "That priestly offices"—yes, this ought to interest you—"that priestly offices, lower as well as higher, shall henceforth be filled only with the crown's approval, so that—"

OLOF: The point about the faith, about God's word, please read that to me.

NOBLEMAN: The word? . . . The faith? . . . There's nothing about that. Ah, yes, here it is. "The Bible shall from this day forward be studied in all schools."

OLOF: That's all?

NOBLEMAN: That's all. —No, I almost forgot. I have special orders—very sensible, I must say—from the king to you, that as long as the people are unsettled by these changes, you are not in any way to disturb the old traditions—not to do away with the mass, or holy water, or other rites. Nor are you to attempt any radical changes whatsoever. For the king, you see, is not going to close his eyes to your actions as he did before when he was powerless to do anything else.

OLOF: I do see. And the new faith that he told me I could preach—what about that?

NOBLEMAN: It is to ripen slowly. It will come, it will come.

OLOF: Anything else?

NOBLEMAN (*rising to his feet*): No. Be calm and patient, young man, and you'll go far. —Oh, the best news! It almost slipped my mind. Rector Pedersson, may I offer you my compliments! Here is your letter of appointment. Rector of the Great Church of Stockholm, with three thousand dalers a year—and at your age! My word, now you can settle down and enjoy life—even if you never rise any higher. . . . Isn't it wonderful to have attained your goal at such an early age! My congratulations! (*He leaves.*)

OLOF (*throwing the letter of appointment on the floor*): An appointment! I fought and suffered for this? A royal appointment! I served Belial instead of God! Woe to you, false king, who sold out your Lord and your God! Woe to me, who sold my life and my life's work to Mammon! God in heaven, forgive me! (*He collapses on a bench, crying.*)

> *Christina and Gert enter, Christina coming forward, Gert remaining in the background.*

> *Christina picks up the letter of appointment, reads it, and then goes to Olof with a happy expression on her face.*

CHRISTINA: Olof! I'm so happy for you. Congratulations!

> *She starts to embrace and kiss him. He stands up and thrusts her away.*

OLOF: Get away from me! You, too!

GERT (*coming forward*): Well, Olof. How stands it with you and your faith?

OLOF: With me and the faithless, you mean!

GERT: Come, look at it this way. We've taken care of the pope. Shall we have a go at the king now?

OLOF: Yes. We began at the wrong end.

GERT: Ah! At last!

OLOF: You were right, Gert. Now I'm your man. Let there be war. But fair and square.

GERT: You've been living in a dreamworld, like a child, until today.

OLOF: I know. Now comes the flood. Now let it come! Woe to them and to us!

CHRISTINA: Olof, you can't! For heaven's sake, stop!

OLOF: Go, Christina, go away. You'll drown here. Or you'll draw me under with you.

GERT: He's right, my girl. What can you do out in the storm?

> *She leaves.*
>
> *The ringing of bells, shouts of joy, music and drums are heard.*
>
> *Olof goes to the window and looks out.*

OLOF: What's all the shouting for?

GERT: The king is treating the people to a Maypole and music outside North Gate.

OLOF: And they don't realize that in place of the rod he has given them the sword.

GERT: If only they did realize! If only they did!

OLOF: Poor souls! They dance to his pipes, and to the beat of his drums they march to their deaths. Are all to die that one may live?

GERT: No. One shall die that all may live!

> *Olof recoils, stunned.*

CURTAIN

ACT IV

A room in the house of Olof's Mother. To the right, a four-poster bed, Olof's Mother, ill, asleep in it. Christina is dozing in a chair. Lars Pedersson, Olof's younger brother, fills the night lamp with oil and turns the hourglass.

LARS (*talking to himself*): Midnight. . . . A decision has to be made. (*He goes over to his Mother's bed and listens.*)

> *Christina moans in her sleep. Lars goes to her and wakes her up.*

LARS: Christina!

> *She wakes with a start.*

LARS: Go to bed, Christina. I'll keep watch.

CHRISTINA: No, I want to be here. I have to talk to her before she dies. . . . Olof will be here soon, I know.

LARS: You're sitting here for Olof's sake, aren't you?

CHRISTINA: Yes. You won't tell him I fell asleep, will you?

LARS: Dear Christina! . . . You're not very happy.

CHRISTINA: Did anyone say we are supposed to be happy?

LARS: Does Olof know you're here?

CHRISTINA: No, he would never allow it. He sees me as a saint, a statue on a shelf. The smaller and weaker I become in his eyes, the more he enjoys laying his strength at my feet.

MOTHER (*stirring*): Lars!

> *Christina holds Lars back and goes to the bed.*

97

MOTHER: Who is that? Who is here?

CHRISTINA: Your nurse.

MOTHER: Christina!

CHRISTINA: Can I get you anything?

MOTHER: I want nothing from you.

CHRISTINA: Please let me help.

MOTHER: You can help by leaving. Don't embitter my last moments. Leave this house!

LARS (*coming to the bed*): What do you want, Mother?

MOTHER: Take this woman away from here. Bring my father confessor before I die.

LARS: Don't you think your own son should hear your last confession? Isn't he worthy of your trust?

MOTHER: He's done nothing to make himself worthy of it. —Has Martin come yet?

LARS: Martin!—that disreputable monk!

MOTHER: God, Thy punishment is too great for me. My own children put themselves between Thee and me. Am I to die without the consolations of my faith? You have been the death of me, isn't that enough? Now do you want to send my soul to perdition—your mother's soul? (*She sinks back in a faint.*)

LARS: You heard that, Christina. What should we do? Which is it to be? Either she dies swindled by that wretched Friar Martin—and maybe thanks us for it—or else in her last prayer she will curse us. No. No. Let them give the last rites. Who do you think, Christina?

CHRISTINA: I don't dare think anything.

LARS (*goes out to fetch the monks in. Returns almost immediately*): It's dreadful! They are drunk and asleep. They've been sitting out there throwing dice and drinking. And they're supposed to purge my mother's soul before she dies!

CHRISTINA: You've got to tell her the truth.

LARS: She wouldn't believe it. To her it would be one more lie to be held against us.

MOTHER: Lars! It is the last thing I shall ask of you. Don't deny me.

LARS (*going out*): God forgive me!

CHRISTINA: Olof would never have done it.

> *Lars accompanies the friars Martin and Nils into the room, then leaves, taking Christina with him.*
>
> *Martin goes to the bed.*

MARTIN: She's sleeping.

> *Nils has carried in with him a chest, which he places on the floor, and draws from it holy water, censers, ampullas, palm branches, and candles.*

NILS: So we can't go to work yet.

MARTIN: If we've waited this long, we can wait a little longer. As long as that devil of a priest doesn't show up.

NILS: Master Olof, you mean. . . . Say, you don't think he saw anything out there, do you?

MARTIN: So what if he did! As long as the old lady forks out the money, I'm not worried.

NILS: You really are a son-of-a-bitch, aren't you.

MARTIN: Maybe. But I'm getting tired of all this. I need some peace and quiet. Do you know what life is?

NILS: No.

MARTIN: It's pleasure. The flesh is God. Says so somewhere, doesn't it?

NILS: "The Word was made flesh"—that's what you're thinking of.

MARTIN: Is that what it says? Oh, well.

NILS: You could really have amounted to something—with a mind like yours.

MARTIN: You are right. I could have become somebody. That's what they were afraid of. I had too much spirit. So they beat it out of me in the monastery. I had a soul then. Now I'm just body. And the body wants to make up for the harm done.

NILS: They must have whipped the conscience out of you at the same time.

MARTIN: Pretty much. . . . What about that recipe for mulled Rochelle you were telling me about, before we fell asleep out there?

NILS: Did I say Rochelle? I meant claret. Hell, it doesn't make any difference. Here's what you do. You take half a gallon wine, half a pound cardamom, well husked—

MARTIN: Shut up, damn it! She's stirring. Get the book out!

During the following, Nils recites softly:

NILS:

Aufer immensam, Deus aufer iram;
Et cruentatum cohibe flagellum:
Nec scelus nostrum proferes ad aequam
*Pendere lancem.**

MOTHER: Is that you, Martin?

MARTIN: It's Brother Nils supplicating the Holy Virgin.

While he recites, Nils lights the censer.

MOTHER: What a great comfort it is to hear the Lord's word in the holy tongue.

MARTIN: No offering is so pleasing to the Lord as are the prayers of pious souls.

* "Put aside, Lord, put aside Your boundless wrath, and stay Your bloodied scourge. Drag forth not our sins to be weighed on the scales." From a hymn by Georg Thymus.

MOTHER: Like incense my heart is kindled by holy devotion.

MARTIN (*sprinkles her with the aspergillum*): From the filth of thy sins God washes thee clean.

MOTHER: Amen. . . . Martin, I am going hence. The ungodliness of King Gustav forbids me to give earthly gifts to the Holy Church that they may strengthen its power to save souls. So I ask you, Martin, as a man of God, to receive my possessions and to pray for my children. Pray to the Almighty that they shall turn their hearts away from the lie and that one day we shall meet in heaven.

MARTIN (*accepting a money bag from her*): Madam, your gift is pleasing to the Lord, and for your sake God will hear my prayers.

MOTHER: Now I want to sleep awhile. To gather my strength for the last sacrament.

MARTIN: No one will disturb your last moments. I shall see to it. Not even those who once were your children.

MOTHER: It is a hard thing, Father Martin, but it is God's will. (*She sleeps.*)

> *Martin and Nils move away from the bed. Martin opens the money bag and kisses the gold coins.*

MARTIN: Ah, what a treasure! How many hours of voluptuous delights lie hidden in these cold, hard coins. Ah!

NILS: Should we leave now?

MARTIN: I could do that, certainly, having performed the service. But it's a shame to let the old girl die unblessed.

NILS: Unblessed?

MARTIN: Yes.

NILS: You don't believe that?

MARTIN: It's hard to know what to believe right now. Some enter the kingdom of heaven this way, some that way. Everyone claims to have found *the* way.

NILS: What if you were to die now, Martin?

MARTIN: Not possible.

NILS: I said "if."

MARTIN: Oh, I'd go to heaven like everybody else. Only I'd have a little score to settle with Master Olof first. You see, Brother Nils, there is one pleasure sweeter than all the rest. Revenge.

NILS: What's he done to you?

MARTIN: He has seen through me. Ripped off my mask. Read my thoughts. Damn!

NILS: And for that you hate him?

MARTIN: Could there be a better reason?

Knocking at the street door.

MARTIN: Somebody's at the door! Read, damn it!

Nils rattles off the Latin verses.

Sound of a key being inserted into the lock of the door, which is then opened from the outside. Olof enters, looking distracted and perturbed.

MOTHER (*wakes up and calls*): Father Martin!

OLOF (*going to her bed*): It's Olof, Mother! I'm here. Why didn't you let me know you were ill?

MOTHER: Goodbye, Olof. I'll forgive you, Olof, the hurt you've given me if you will leave me alone while I prepare myself for heaven. —Father Martin! Give me extreme unction that I may die in peace.

OLOF: So this is why you did not send for me! (*He catches sight of the money purse that Martin had neglected to conceal and snatches it from him.*) You're trading in souls! And this is the price! Get out of this house! Leave this deathbed! This is my place, not yours.

MARTIN: You can't keep us from carrying out our duties.

OLOF: I'm telling you to get out!

MARTIN: Our office here is by authority not of the pope but of the king, as long as we have not been suspended.

OLOF: I shall cleanse the house of the Lord, even if the pope and the king will not have it so.

MOTHER: Olof! Would you have me cast into the fire? Would you have me die with a curse on my lips?

OLOF: Be calm, Mother. You shall not die trusting in a lie. Seek God yourself, in your prayers. He is nearer than you think.

MARTIN: Only a disciple of the devil would not want to spare his own mother the throes and torments of purgatory.

MOTHER: Jesus, come! Succor my soul!

OLOF (*to the monks*): Get out of here before I throw you out! And take this superstitious nonsense with you! (*He kicks the sacramentals.*)

MARTIN: Hand over the money your mother gave to the church. Then I'll go.

MOTHER: Is that why you came, Olof? For my gold? Give it to him, Martin. Olof, you can have it all, all. Just leave me in peace. You shall have more. Everything!

OLOF: In the name of God, take the money and go! I beg you!

Martin snaps up the purse and starts to leave with Nils.

MARTIN: Madam, where the devil walks, our power ceases. (*To Olof.*)—As a heretic, you are damned for all eternity. As a law-breaker, you will receive your punishment here in this life. Beware the king.

They leave.

Olof kneels by his Mother's bed.

OLOF: Listen to me, Mother! Hear me before you die!

She is half-unconscious.

OLOF: Mother, please. Mother, if you can still hear me, talk to me. Forgive me. I cannot do otherwise. I know you have suffered all your life for my sake. You have prayed to God that I should do His bidding. And the Lord has heard your prayers. Do you want me to confound all that you have done? Do you want me to break what you have built, what has cost you so much effort and so many tears, by doing your bidding now? Forgive me!

MOTHER: Olof, my spirit no longer belongs to this world. I am speaking to you from the hereafter. Turn back, Olof, loosen the unclean bond that your body has made. Receive again the faith I gave you; and I shall forgive you.

OLOF (*with tears of despair*): Mother! Mother!

MOTHER: Swear to me that you will!

OLOF (*is silent, then*): No!

MOTHER: You are under the curse of God. I can see Him. I see God in His wrath! Help me, Holy Mother of God!

OLOF: Isn't God love? That isn't the God you see.

MOTHER: No, He is the God of vengeance! It is you who have offended Him. It is you who cast me into the fire of his fury. —Cursed be the hour I gave you birth! (*She dies.*)

OLOF: Mother! Mother! (*He takes her hand.*) She's dead. Without forgiving me. . . . Oh, Mother, if your spirit dwelleth in this place, look down upon your son. I shall do thy will; what is sacred to you shall be sacred to me. (*He lights the tall wax candles left by the friars and places them around the bed.*) You shall have the consecrated tapers to light you on your way—(*He places a palm branch in her hand.*)—and with the palm of peace you shall forget your last struggle with earthly matters. Mother, if you see me now, I know you will forgive me!

> The sun has begun to rise and it lights up the window curtains with a reddish glow.

OLOF (*springing to his feet*): Morning sun, you put my candles to shame. There is more loving-kindness in you than in me. (*He goes to the window and opens it.*)

Lars enters quietly. He is astonished to see Olof.

LARS: Olof!

OLOF (*embracing him*): Dear brother! It's all over.

LARS (*goes to the bed, kneels, and rises*): She is dead. (*He says a silent prayer.*) You were alone here.

OLOF: You were the one who let in the monks.

LARS: You drove them out!

OLOF: Yes. It's what you should have done.

LARS: She didn't forgive you, did she?

OLOF: She died cursing me.

Silence.

LARS (*pointing to the candles*): Who arranged the ceremony?

Pause.

OLOF (*nettled and embarrassed*): A moment of weakness.

LARS: You are human, after all. I'm glad to see it.

OLOF: Are you sneering at me because I was weak?

LARS: No, I'm admiring you for it.

OLOF: And I hate myself for it. God in heaven, am I not right?

LARS: No, you're not.

CHRISTINA (*has just entered*): You are so right it hurts.

OLOF: Christina! What are you doing here?

CHRISTINA: I couldn't stand it at home—so quiet and lonely.

OLOF: I asked you not to come here.

CHRISTINA: I thought I might be of some help, but I see I'm not. Next time I'll stay home.

OLOF: You've been up all night.

CHRISTINA: It was no hardship. I'll go if you want me to.

OLOF: Go in the other room and rest. I want to talk to Lars.

> *Lost in her thoughts, Christina puts out the candles.*

OLOF: What are you doing, Christina?

CHRISTINA: It's broad daylight.

> *Lars looks at Olof.*

OLOF: My mother is dead, Christina.

> *Tender but restrained, Christina goes to Olof to be kissed on the forehead.*

CHRISTINA: You have my sympathy, Olof. (*She leaves.*)

> *Pause. Lars and Olof follow Christina with their eyes, and then look at each other.*

LARS: As your brother, Olof, and as your friend, I beg you not to carry on as you have.

OLOF: You never change, do you, Lars? Harping always on the same string. But the ax is now laid unto the root of the tree, and one doesn't stop chopping until the tree falls. The king has abandoned our cause; now it lies in my hands.

LARS: The king is no fool.

OLOF: He's a greedy muckworm, that's what he is—a traitor who licks the boots of the nobility. First he treated me like a dog; now he kicks me away.

LARS: He has more insight than you. If you went out and spoke to three million people and said to them, "Your faith is a false one; trust me!" do you really believe that on an impulse they would rid themselves of those deep convictions and beliefs that have sustained them year in and year out, in sorrow and in joy? Never! The human soul would be a sorry mess if it were that easy to throw overboard all that's tried and true.

OLOF: It isn't like that at all! The whole nation is torn by doubt. There is scarcely one priest who knows what to believe in—that is, if he has any beliefs at all. Everything points to a change. And the blame rests with you, you who are weak of heart, who dare not take it on your consciences to cast out doubt when the only faith is a frail and wavering one.

LARS: Take care, Olof! You want to play God.

OLOF: Someone has to. Haven't you heard? God no longer comes down to us His miracles to perform.

LARS: But you only tear down, Olof. Soon there will be nothing but emptiness. What are you going to put in place of the old? Not that, you say. And not that. Then what? You never answer.

OLOF: What presumption! Do you think faith is something one gives? Has Luther given us anything new? No. He has simply torn down the screens that shut out the light. The new idea that I represent is distrust of the old—not because it is old but because it is rotten.

Lars gestures toward their Mother.

OLOF: I know what you mean. But the truth is she was too old, and I thank God that she died. Now I am free, now for the first time in my life! It was God's will!

LARS: You are out of your mind—or else you are inhuman.

OLOF: You mustn't reproach me. I value her memory as much as you do. But if she had not died now, I don't know how much longer I could have gone on compromising my principles. . . . In the spring the dead leaves cover the ground and smother the young plants that want to grow. What do they do? They shove the dry leaves to one side, or they push right straight through them. Because they *have* to grow.

LARS: You're not entirely wrong, Olof; I admit that. . . . The laws you broke were broken during a time of trouble and strife in the church. But what was forgivable then must now be punished. Don't compel the king to show himself worse than he is. Don't force him to punish your infractions when he knows how much he owes you. You cannot do whatever you like.

OLOF: Doing whatever he likes is how he rules. He must learn to tolerate it in others. . . . You're in service with the king. You'll be working against me, won't you?

LARS: Yes.

OLOF: So we are enemies. Good, I need them, since the old ones are gone.

LARS: Olof, the blood tells.

OLOF: Not to me. Except at its source: the heart.

LARS: You wept for Mother.

OLOF: Frailty. Perhaps devotion and gratitude. But not blood. What is blood, anyway?

LARS: You look dog-tired, Olof.

OLOF: I'm exhausted. I've been up all night.

LARS: You came so late.

OLOF: I wasn't at home.

LARS: Your work shuns the light of day.

OLOF: The light of day shuns my work.

LARS: Beware, Olof, the false apostles of freedom.

OLOF (*fighting against sleep and exhaustion*): A contradiction in terms. No more talking, if you don't mind. I'm done in. I've spoken so much at our meetings. —I forgot: you wouldn't know about our secret meetings. . . . *Concordia res parvae crescunt.* . . . Sallust. . . . "Concord makes small enterprises succeed; discord destroys the great ones." . . . We're going to pursue the reformation to its end. . . . Gert is a far-sighted man. I'm nothing next to him, I'm nothing. . . . Goodnight, Lars. (*He falls asleep in a chair.*)

LARS (*looking at him with sympathy*): My dear brother. God protect you.

Loud knocking on the outside door.

LARS: Who can that be? (*He looks out the window.*)

GERT (*from outside*): Open up, for God's sake!

LARS (*going out*): It can't be that important, Father Gert.

GERT (*still outside*): For the love of heaven, let me in!

> *Christina comes into the room, carrying a blanket.*

CHRISTINA: Olof, why do they keep knocking? – He's asleep. (*She covers Olof with the blanket.*) I wish I were Morpheus; then you would come to my arms when you are weary of the battle.

> *The rumbling of a heavy cart in the street outside can be heard. It comes to a stop.*

OLOF (*wakes up suddenly*): Five o'clock already?

CHRISTINA: It's only three, Olof.

OLOF: I thought I heard the baker's cart.

CHRISTINA: I don't think it is. It wouldn't sound so heavy. (*She looks out the window.*) Look, Olof. What is that?

OLOF (*at the window*): The hangman's wagon! – No, it isn't. What–?

CHRISTINA: It's a cart for the dead!

LARS (*entering, followed by Gert*): The plague!

OLOF *and* CHRISTINA: The plague!

GERT: Yes, it's broken out! Christina, my child, you must leave this house. The angel of death has placed his mark on the door.

OLOF: Who sent that cart to this house?

GERT: Whoever put that black cross on the door. The bodies of the dead have to be carted away immediately.

OLOF: Friar Martin – he's your angel of death. The whole thing is a fabrication.

GERT: No. Look out the window. The cart is filled with corpses.

Pounding on the door.

GERT: Do you hear? They're waiting.

OLOF: Without proper burial! Never!

LARS: What price ceremonies, Olof?

GERT: Come, Christina, you must leave with me. This is a pesthouse. I'll take you out of town to some safer place.

CHRISTINA: My place is with Olof. If you had loved me a little less, Father, you would have done less harm.

GERT: Olof, she will listen to you. Tell her to come with me.

OLOF: I took her out of your hands once. You wanted her all to yourself. She will never go back.

GERT: Christina, at least leave this house.

CHRISTINA: Not a step until Olof orders me out.

OLOF: I don't order you to do anything, Christina. Remember that.

Two Draymen enter.

FIRST DRAYMAN: Was told to pick up a body here. Got to hurry.

OLOF: Get out of here!

FIRST DRAYMAN: King's orders.

LARS: Olof, don't be rash. It's the law.

GERT: It won't do to delay. The people are going crazy. They're up in arms against you, Olof. Yours was the first house to be marked with the cross. "The vengeance of the Lord—upon the heretic!" That's their hue and cry.

OLOF (*on his knees beside the bed*): Forgive me, Mother. (*Stands up.*) Do what you must.

The Draymen go to the bed and begin lifting it with ropes.

GERT (*aside to Olof*): "The vengeance of the Lord—upon the King!" That's *our* hue and cry.

CURTAIN

ACT V

Scene 1

The churchyard of the Convent of Saint Clara in Stockholm. At the back, a half-razed convent building, from which workmen are carrying old timber and debris. To the left, a burial chapel, candlelight shining through its windows. When the door to the chapel is opened later on, a strongly lighted statue of Christ can be seen within, above a sarcophagus.

In the yard some graves lie open. The moon is rising above the ruins. Captain Windrank is sitting on watch at the chapel door. From within the chapel singing can be heard.

Friar Nils enters and goes up to Windrank.

NILS: Good evening, Captain Windrank.

WINDRANK: Please. Don't talk to me.

NILS: Now what's the matter?

WINDRANK: Are you deaf?

NILS: Ah ha! So that dishonorable discharge from your ship has done you in, eh? Made you renounce the world.

WINDRANK: Fifty-two, fifty-three, fifty-four, fifty-five, fifty-six, fifty-seven —

NILS: Have you gone out of your mind?

WINDRANK: Fifty-eight, fifty-nine, sixty. For God's sake, will you get out!

NILS: Not until you've had a little nightcap with me.

WINDRANK: Sixty-four, sixty-five. I might have known. Go

away, tempter. I'm never touching the stuff again. . . . Not until the day after tomorrow.

NILS: It's medicine—against the plague. The air in a place like this is very dangerous to your health.

WINDRANK: Seventy. —It really works against the plague?

NILS: Like nothing else.

WINDRANK (*taking a drink*): Just a drop.

NILS: Just a drop. —Have you got dizzy spells? Why are you counting to a hundred? Does it work?

WINDRANK: Shhh! Shhhh! A new era!

NILS: What? A new era?

WINDRANK: Yes. Begins day after tomorrow.

NILS: That's why you're counting?

WINDRANK: No. I'm counting so I'll keep my mouth shut. (*Slapping himself.*) Shut up, damn it! —Get out of here before I ruin everything. Seventy-one, seventy-two, seventy-three.

NILS: Who's in there?

WINDRANK (*firmly*): Seventy-four, seventy-five—

NILS: A burial? Whose?

WINDRANK: Seventy-six, seventy-seven. —Why don't you go to hell!

NILS: One little shot more, eh? Makes the counting easier.

WINDRANK: One little one. What the hell! (*He drinks.*)

Singing is heard.

NILS: It's the nuns of Saint Clara, coming to celebrate her memory for the last time.

WINDRANK: What a hoax! In these enlightened times!

NILS: The king gave them permission. The plague broke out in the parish of Saint Clara. So they blame it on the sacrilegious tearing down of her convent.

WINDRANK: So now they expect to use songs to drive the plague away? That devil of a plague can't have an ear for music. On the other hand, I'd be surprised if he didn't flee from this caterwauling.

NILS: Tell me, who's profaning this last sanctuary? The bones of Saint Clara are to be buried here before they tear it down.

WINDRANK: There's going to be a brawl, for sure.

> *The singing has grown louder, and now a procession of Dominican monks, in black, and Franciscan nuns or Poor Clares, in gray, enter, Friar Martin leading the way. They stop but continue to sing. The laborers are all the while noisily at work in the back.*

THE MONKS *and* NUNS:

> *Cur super vermes luteos furorem*
> *sumis, o magni fabricator orbis!*
> *Quid sumus quam fex putris, umbra, pulvis*
> *glebaque terrae!**

MARTIN (*to the Abbess*): You see, sister, how they have laid waste the dwelling place of the Lord.

ABBESS: The Lord who has delivered us into the hands of the Egyptians will redeem us out of Egypt when he sees fit.

MARTIN (*to the workmen*): You there! We are here to do reverence to a saint, and you are disrupting and interfering with our ceremonies.

---

* "Why do you rage against the worms in the mud, You the creator of the wide world? What are we other than putrefying slime, shadows, dust, lumps of turf?" From the hymn by George Thymus quoted in Act IV.

FOREMAN: We are under orders to work round the clock till this place is leveled to the ground.

ABBESS: I see that impiety has infected even the lowest level of people.

MARTIN (*to the Foreman*): May I remind you that the king has authorized our presence here. We have his permission to bless the memory of Saint Clara.

FOREMAN: Don't let me stop you.

MARTIN: On his authority I demand that you stop what you're doing. I shall take it up with your workers. You have forced them into this nefarious undertaking. I shall appeal directly to them. We shall see if they have any respect for what is holy and sacred.

FOREMAN: I wouldn't, if I were you. I give the orders around here. Let me tell you something. They're happy to be getting rid of this wasp's nest. They're the ones who had to pay for it. Besides, they're thankful to be getting some work and pay during this famine. (*He walks upstage.*)

MARTIN: Sister, let us put aside the wickedness and tumult of this world, and let us enter the sanctuary to pray for them.

ABBESS: Lord God, Thy holy cities are a wilderness; Zion is a wilderness; Jerusalem a desolation.

WINDRANK (*barring Martin and the Abbess from the chapel*): One hundred! No one goes in!

> *From within the chapel voices raised in unison can be heard: "We swear!"*

MARTIN: Who is in there? Who has profaned the chapel?

WINDRANK: What chapel? It's the king's storehouse.

> *The door to the chapel is flung open. Enter the conspirators: Olof, Lars Andersson, Gert, The German, The Dane, The Farmer from Småland, and others.*

OLOF (*seeing the nuns and monks; heatedly*): What sort of tomfoolery is this?

MARTIN: Make room for the dedicated servants of the holy Saint Clara!

OLOF: Do you think that your idols can dispel the plague — which the one true God has sent to punish you? Do you suppose that the Lord is so pleased by those bits of bones that you are carrying in that reliquary that He will forgive your grievous sins? Away with the abomination! (*He snatches the chest from the Abbess and throws it into one of the open graves.*) Dust thou art and unto dust shalt thou return — even if you are Sancta Clara da Spoleto and ate only three slices of bread a day and slept with the pigs at night.

> *The nuns shriek.*

MARTIN: If you fear not your Lord in heaven, perhaps you will fear your lord on earth. He, at least, has so much respect for the divine that he fears the wrath of the saints. (*He hands Olof an offical-looking document.*)

OLOF: You know what the Lord did to the king of Assyria when he endorsed idolatry. He slew him *and* his people. For when the king is wrong, the righteous suffer with the unrighteous. In the name of the one Almighty God I hereby abolish this adoration of Baal, even though all the kings of earth countenance it. The pope wanted to sell my soul to Satan, but, as you may remember, I tore that contract to pieces. Why should I now fear a king who will sell his people to the Baalim? (*Olof tears the order to pieces.*)

MARTIN (*to the nuns and monks*): You are my witnesses that he defames the king!

OLOF (*to the conspirators*): You are my witnesses before God that I have turned His people away from an impious king.

MARTIN: Hear me, you true believers, it is because of this heretic that the Lord has struck us with the plague. And the punishment of the Lord descended first on his mother!

OLOF: Hear me, you papist infidels! The Lord punished me because I served Sennacherib against Judah. Now I shall atone for my sins. I shall lead Judah against the kings of Assyria and Egypt!

The rising moon has turned red and a reddish glow fills the stage. The people are frightened. Olof steps up on a grave mound.

OLOF: You see, Heaven itself weeps blood for your sins, for your idolatries! Punishment shall happen. It shall fall upon us because of those who rule and have the power. It is they who have offended! Do you not see how the very graves gape, awaiting the victims?

Gert grabs Olof's arm, whispers to him, and brings him down.

The people mill about, frightened.

ABBESS: Give us back our reliquary and allow us to quit this desolate place.

MARTIN: Sister, better that the saint's bones should rest in this holy ground than that they should be desecrated by the hands of heretics.

OLOF: Cowards! It is the plague you fear! Where now is your faith in the power of sacred bones?

Again Gert whispers to Olof.

By this time most of the crowd has dispersed. Only a few people remain on stage.

OLOF (*to Martin*): Are you quite satisfied now, you hypocrite? Why don't you tell your earthly master that a silver casket is buried here? He'll rip it out of the earth with his fingernails. Go tell your lord and master that the silver moon has turned to gold. Then for once in his life he'll raise his eyes from earth to heaven. Tell him that you have succeeded, by means of this blasphemous trumpery, in arousing the indignation of a true man of principle. Tell him—

Martin and the rest of the procession have left the stage by this time.

GERT: That's enough, Olof. (*To the conspirators, except for Olof and Lars Andersson.*) Leave us.

> *The conspirators whisper and mutter among themselves and leave.*

GERT (*to Olof and Lars*): It's too late to turn back. You know that.

OLOF: What's on your mind, Gert? Speak out.

GERT (*takes out a manuscript*): To you two servants of God, a whole nation—(*He taps the manuscript.*)—comes forward to make a confession. Do you acknowledge your oath?

OLOF *and* LARS: We have sworn.

GERT: This book is the fruit of my silent labors. Each page—each line—each word is a cry from a people who in their blindness believed it was God's will that they were oppressed. To them it was a sacred duty not to believe in their deliverance.

> *Olof reads here and there in the manuscript.*

GERT: From those pages you will hear cries of distress rise up from the most remote villages of the Norrland to the seaports on the Sound. Cries that come to this: out of the debris of the church the nobility builds castles for itself and prisons for the people. You shall read how the king traffics in justice and barters with the law, letting even murderers escape punishment if only they will work for him in the salt furnaces. You shall learn how he profits from sin, making prostitutes pay taxes to his coffers. Yea, the very fish in the rivers, the salt ocean itself pays tribute to him. But that's over now. The eyes of the people have been opened. The times are seething, the pot is coming to a boil. The oppressors shall be overwhelmed; the people shall be made free!

OLOF: Who has written this?

GERT: A whole people! Call them folksongs. This is what they sing when they plod along with yokes on their necks. I have gone from street to street, from town to town. I have asked, "Are you happy?" And here are the answers. I have held inquests, and here the findings are set down. Olof, do you think that the millions are meant to be ruled by one person? Do you believe that God bestowed this land, this wealth, these human beings, on one person to do with as he wishes? Or do you not rather believe that that one person should do the will of all? . . . You do not answer. Of course. You tremble at the thought that it can be, that one can put an end to it. . . . Now let me make confession to you. Tomorrow the oppressor is to die, and you shall all be free.

OLOF *and* LARS: What?!

GERT: Have you understood nothing of what I said at our meetings?

OLOF: You have tricked us into this!

GERT: Not at all. You are free to do as you wish. Two voices less make no difference. Everything is prepared.

LARS: Have you thought of the consequences?

GERT: Idiot! It was for the sake of the consequences that I have done this.

OLOF: Can you be right? What do you say, Lars?

LARS: I was not born to lead the way.

OLOF: Everyone is born to lead, but not everyone wants to lay down his life.

GERT: Only the man who has the courage to be laughed at and scoffed at marches in the vanguard. Hatred is nothing; it is ridicule that kills.

OLOF: If the plan should fail—?

GERT: A risk worth taking. You don't seem to know that Thomas Münzer has set up in Mühlhausen a spiritual kingdom where the means of life are owned in common. You don't seem to realize that the whole of Europe is in revolt. Here in Sweden, when Dacke led the rebellion of the people of Småland against King Gustav, who was he if not a defender of the downtrodden? Why did the Dalesmen north of here rise up if not to defend their freedom against a king who had broken faith and violated his promise? And he goes unpunished. But when the people defend themselves, they are called faithless traitors and rebels!

OLOF: So this is the point to which you have been leading me all this time?

GERT: No, it was the current that carried you here. You didn't dare act out your wishes. Tomorrow in the Great Church the mine explodes: the signal for the people to rise up and choose a ruler after their own hearts.

OLOF (*flipping the pages of the manuscript*): If everyone wants it, then nothing can stop it. Gert, let me take this book to the king, and let him hear the people speak. Then he must do them justice.

GERT: What an innocent you are! He might be frightened for a moment—even give back a silver stoup to some church. But a moment later he would point to heaven and say, "It is not my will that causes me to sit here and be unjust to you; it is God's will."

OLOF: Very well. Let God's will be done!

GERT: How?

OLOF: All right. Let him die that all may live. —Murderer, ungrateful wretch, traitor—that's what they will call me. So be it. I have sacrificed everything else—my honor, my conscience, my faith. There is only one thing left for me to give to these poor souls who cry for deliverance. —Come, let us go, before I have regrets.

GERT: Wouldn't matter. It's too late for regrets. That Friar Martin is one of the king's spies—or didn't you know? Sentence is probably even now being pronounced on the man who instigated the rebellion.

OLOF: No matter. I shall have no regrets. Why should I? I am executing the decree of God! Onward, in the name of the Lord!

> *They leave.*
>
> *The Prostitute has come in and knelt at one of the graves. She strews it with flowers.*

PROSTITUTE: Have I not been struck often enough? Am I now not worthy of Thy forgiveness?

CHRISTINA (*entering in great haste*): Please, good woman, have you seen Master Olof?

PROSTITUTE: Are you a friend of his, or an enemy?

CHRISTINA: That's insulting!

PROSTITUTE: Sorry. I haven't seen him since the last time I said my prayers.

CHRISTINA: You look done in. . . . I recognize you now. You were the woman Olof talked to that night in the Great Church.

PROSTITUTE: You shouldn't be seen talking to me. Don't you know what I am?

CHRISTINA: Yes, I do.

PROSTITUTE: You mean they told you? Who?

CHRISTINA: Olof told me.

PROSTITUTE: God! And you don't disdain me?

CHRISTINA: An unfortunate, unhappy woman, Olof said. Trampled on. Why should I disdain unhappiness?

PROSTITUTE: You would, unless you are unhappy yourself.

CHRISTINA: Yes. We have something in common.

PROSTITUTE: So I've got company. You fell in love with some scampt who wasn't worth it.

CHRISTINA: Wasn't worth it?

PROSTITUTE: Sorry. If he makes us love, he's worth it. Who was it?

CHRISTINA: Do you know Master Olof?

PROSTITUTE: Not Master Olof! It can't be true. Don't take away my faith in him. It is all I have left—since God took my child from me.

CHRISTINA: At least you have had a child. You have known some happiness.

PROSTITUTE: Happiness? I thank God for never letting my child know how unworthy of him I was.

CHRISTINA: Your sin cannot be that terrible.

PROSTITUTE: It is. I buried it here not long ago.

CHRISTINA: Your baby? I don't believe it. Every day I pray to God that he will give me a child, one child, for me to love.

PROSTITUTE: You poor girl! God keep you.

CHRISTINA: I don't understand. What are you trying to say, my good woman?

PROSTITUTE: Don't call me that. You know what I am.

CHRISTINA: We all hope to be something better. One prays in church for those who hope.

PROSTITUTE: Not for the likes of us.

CHRISTINA: "Likes of us?"

PROSTITUTE: You pray for the other sort. You damn our kind.

CHRISTINA: "Other sort?"—What do you mean?

PROSTITUTE: Do you know Master Olof's wife?

CHRISTINA: I am Master Olof's wife.

PROSTITUTE: You! Of course. Forgive me. I shouldn't have said those things. You and him—you wouldn't know sin if you saw it. —Leave me. You're an innocent child. You don't know how evil the world is. You mustn't talk to me anymore. God bless you. Goodbye. (*She prepares to leave.*)

CHRISTINA: No, don't leave me. Whoever you are, stay, please, for God's sake! They've broken into my house. My husband has disappeared. Take me with you—to your place—anywhere. You're a good woman. I know you're not a criminal.

PROSTITUTE: (*interrupting*): Stop that! Whatever they say or do to you, the mob can't hurt you half as much as keeping company with me would. You'll thank me if I go now.

CHRISTINA: What have you done?

PROSTITUTE: Done, I'm damned, that's all. The curse that God pronounced on woman at the Fall has come true in me. Don't ask any more questions. If I answered, you'd damn me some more, and I'd have to defend myself, and that would be even more damnable. — Here comes someone who might be a gentleman and take care of you, that is, if you give him your honor and your reputation and your eternal peace of mind in return for his trouble. That's all he wants for offering his protection to young girls late at night. — I'm sorry. I'm bitter, but it has nothing to do with you.

WINDRANK (*enters, drunk*): Damn it! Can't a man be alone even among the corpses? Listen, ladies, please don't ask me anything. I can't be responsible — for my responses. Until day after tomorrow, when I'll tell all. Because it'll be too late. . . . Ladies, you're not from a nunnery, are you? And without a place to lay your heads? Ha, ha! Your ladyships — ships of the night? — Well, well, I don't presume to have the right to be ungentlemanly. Even though the sun has set. There's an old law: no one can be nabbed after sunset. But the law is a scoundrel. In spite of which he's gentleman enough not to force himself upon women. — Shut up, shut up. My tongue keeps on rattling like a spinning wheel. It's that damned liquor. . . . I mean, why me? Why drag me into it? Huh? . . . They're paying me, that's why? I'll be well off. Don't get me wrong; I'm not doing it for the money. . . . Anyway, it's done. . . . But I don't want it, no part of it. I want to sleep in peace. No ghosts haunting me. . . . Maybe I could go and tell them. No, they'd nab me. — Someone else could go and tell 'em. One of you nuns, maybe. Would you?

Christina confers with The Prostitute.

CHRISTINA: If this is something weighing on your conscience, yes, tell us.

WINDRANK: Tell you? That's what I'm trying not to do! It's

awful. I can't take any more. I'll do it! — But why me? Why me? I don't want it, no part of it!

CHRISTINA: If you're thinking of committing —

WINDRANK: Murder! Who said so? — You know, huh? Thank God. Go, go and tell them. Right away. Otherwise I'll have no peace, never, for all eternity.

CHRISTINA (*astonished at first; controls herself*): Why — why murder him?

WINDRANK: Lots of reasons. Look how he's tearing down your monasteries!

CHRISTINA: The king?

WINDRANK: He's the one. Father of his country. Liberator of Sweden. Of course he's a pest and a plague. But you don't kill someone for that.

CHRISTINA: When?

WINDRANK: Tomorrow, that's it. In the Great Church. Right in the church itself.

At a sign from Christina, The Prostitute leaves.

CHRISTINA: Why did they choose you to do such a thing?

WINDRANK: Well, I've got some connections with the servants in the church. Besides, I'm poor. Got no work. Need the money. — Anyhow, doesn't make any difference who fires the gun. All depends on somebody clever to aim it. Besides, we've got other plans up our sleeve. Although I'm the one who starts it. I open fire. — Aren't you going to tell 'em?

CHRISTINA: It's already taken care of.

WINDRANK: Thanks be to God. — Goodbye money, riches, wealth.

CHRISTINA: Who is in this with you?

WINDRANK: Oh, no! You won't get that out of me.

Friar Nils, soldiers, and others pass across the stage.

CHRISTINA: They're already looking for you.

WINDRANK: I wash my hands of it!

NILS (*approaches Windrank without seeing Christina*): Have you seen Olaus Petri?

WINDRANK: Why?

NILS: He's being sought after.

WINDRANK: No, I haven't seen him. Anybody else they're looking for?

NILS: Oh, yes, quite a few.

WINDRANK: No, I haven't seen a soul.

NILS: We'll get to you soon enough. (*Leaves.*)

CHRISTINA: Were they looking for the conspirators?

WINDRANK: Yes. What a business! I've got to get away. Goodbye.

CHRISTINA: Before you go, tell me —

WINDRANK: No time to lose!

CHRISTINA: Was Master Olof one of them?

WINDRANK: Of course.

> *Christina falls senseless on one of the graves.*
>
> *Windrank suddenly sobers up and is deeply touched.*

WINDRANK: Oh, my God! It must be his wife. (*He goes to her.*) I think I've killed her! Oh, Hans, Hans! Now you can go and hang yourself. What business had you with your betters. — Hey, over here. Help this woman!

> *Olof is led in, surrounded by soldiers carrying torches. He breaks free of them, rushes to Christina, and falls on his knees by her side.*

OLOF: Christina!

CHRISTINA: Olof! You're alive! Thank God. Take me home with you.

OLOF (*crushed*): It's too late.

TABLEAU CURTAIN

Scene 2

A portion of the Great Church in Stockholm, near the west portal. The door to the sacristy is at the left. Pillories are to the right of the portal. A stool of repentance is next to the pillory.

Olof and Gert, in prison clothes, are in the stocks. The church organ is playing; bells are ringing. The service has ended, and the congregation is leaving.

The Sexton Bengt and his wife, Catherine, are standing to one side, downstage.

SEXTON: Chancellor Lars was pardoned, but not Master Olof.

CATHERINE: The Chancellor was always a peaceable man. Never did make much of a fuss. I simply don't understand how he could let himself become part of such awful goings-on.

SEXTON: Always a bit peculiar, I thought. Never said much. And now he's pardoned by the king. But it cost him every penny he owned. Still, I can't help feeling sorry for Master Olof. I always did like him, even though he was difficult a lot of the time.

CATHERINE: Why would they make such a young boy rector of the church, anyway?

SEXTON: Yes, he was pretty young. Bad mistake on his part. But give him time, he'll correct it.

CATHERINE: No he won't. He's going to his death today.

SEXTON: My God! I almost forgot. It's so hard to believe.

CATHERINE: Has he repented yet, do you know?

SEXTON: I doubt it. I'm sure he's as stiff-necked as ever.

CATHERINE: He'll turn to putty when he sees his students. He won't be confirming them this year.

SEXTON: I don't mind saying it: the king is pretty ruthless when he sets his mind to it. I can't get over it: making the rector suffer his punishment on the very day that his students are to be confirmed. Almost as disgusting as that time he made Dean George drink a toast to the public executioner. Or the time he made the prelates take off their mitres and ride through town with birch-bark baskets on their heads.

CATHERINE: The worst of it is that he's forcing Olof's own brother to make Olof ready for death.

SEXTON: Look! Here they come. All the students. How sad they look. Can't say I blame 'em. I think I'm going to cry.

> *Carrying bunches of flowers, the confirmands, boys and girls, pass by Olof. They look sad and depressed, their eyes downcast. The older people follow behind them. Some point their fingers at Olof, others reprimand them for doing so.*
>
> *The student William comes last. He stands shyly in front of Olof, kneels and places his flowers at Olof's feet. Olof has his cowl over his face and does not notice. Some of the people murmur disapprovingly, others express their approval. Friar Martin approaches Olof to remove the flowers, but some of the people thrust him back.*
>
> *Soldiers make way for Olof's brother, Lars Pedersson, who is dressed in full pontificals. The crowd slowly disperses, leaving Lars, Olof, and Gert alone.*
>
> *The organ stops playing, but the pealing of the bells continues.*

LARS (*to Olof*): Olof. The citizens of Stockholm presented a formal petition for your pardon to King Gustav. He has rejected it. . . . Have you made yourself ready for death?

OLOF: I can't think that far ahead.

LARS: I am here by order of the king. I have come to prepare you.

OLOF: You have your work cut out for you. I am far from ready. The blood still seethes in my veins.

LARS: Have you repented?

OLOF: No!

LARS: Would you enter the life eternal with an intransigent heart?

OLOF: Forget the formulary or I won't listen to you. I don't think I can die right now. There's too much left in me.

LARS: I agree. And that's why I can tell you that I am here to prepare you—for a new life in this world.

OLOF: You mean I am to live?

LARS: Yes. On condition you confess that your past life was in error and provided you retract your remarks about the king.

OLOF: How can I? That truly would be death to me.

LARS: I have given you the conditions. The decision is yours.

OLOF: Principles aren't negotiable.

LARS: Even a delusion can become a principle. Think it over, Olof. (*Lars goes out.*)

GERT: This was not the time to reap the harvest. Much snow will have to fall if the autumn seed is to rise and prosper. Civilizations will rise and fall before even the first seed sprouts. The conspirators have been caught. That's what they say, and offer thanks to God. But they are mistaken. The conspirators are all around us: in the king's rooms, in the churches, in the city squares. Only they don't dare as we have dared. Not yet. But they will, one day. . . . Farewell, Olof. You ought to live on; you're young, Olof. I'm perfectly happy to die now. Another martyr, a new name for a battle cry for a new pack of conspirators. Lies never fire the human spirit—never believe that. Never lose your faith in those emotions that shook you to the core when you saw violence, physical or spiritual, inflicted on a human being. Even if the whole world says you're wrong, believe what your heart tells you, if you have the courage to do so. The day you deny your own soul you are truly dead. And eternal damnation shall seem a tender mercy for those who have sinned against the Holy Ghost.

OLOF: You talk as if my release were a certainty.

GERT: The citizens of Stockholm have offered five hundred ducats for your ransom. Since it only cost two thousand ducats to have Birgitta declared a saint, I should think five hundred would be enough to have you declared innocent. The king doesn't dare take your life.

> *The Marshal, Lars Siggeson, enters with the executioner and several soldiers.*

MARSHAL: Take Gert the Printer! Away with him!

GERT (*as he is led out*): Farewell, Olof. Take care of my daughter. And, Olof, never forget the great day of Pentecost!

MARSHAL: Master Olof. You are a young man, and, being young, you were easily led astray. The king pardons you because of your youth. But as surety he demands that you publicly apologize for exceeding your authority and for acting contrary to the orders of the king.

OLOF: So the king still has need of me.

MARSHAL: There are many who have need of you. You must not, however, count on clemency until you have satisfied these conditions. I hold here the king's pardon. Your chains can be removed in an instant, if you wish it. On the other hand, this paper can be torn to shreds in an instant.

OLOF: Anyone who is satisfied with five hundred ducats is not going to trouble himself about a recantation.

MARSHAL: You are in error. The executioner is waiting for you also. . . . I beg you to listen to a few words from an old man. I was once young like you, and I too was driven by strong passions and high ideals. That's part of being young, and those passions are meant to be overcome. I was very much like you. Went about telling the truth to all and sundry, and all I got was ingratitude – at best, a laugh. I, too, wanted to build a little heaven here on earth – (*With emphasis.*) naturally on foundations other than yours. But I soon learned to listen to the voice of reason and I banished idle dreams. . . . I certainly don't believe that you are the kind that seeks to win fame by making trouble; I won't say that. You have good intentions, but your good intentions do a great deal of harm. You have hot blood in your veins. It rushes to your head and blinds you. You lash out at the world, heedless of consequences. You preach freedom, yet you drive thousands into the slavery of their passions. Turn back. Atone for your transgressions; rebuild what you have torn down. For this the people will bless you.

OLOF (*shaken and troubled*): It's true, what you say. I can tell it is. Where did you learn all this?

MARSHAL: Experience taught me. That's what you lack.

OLOF: Have I lived and fought for a lie? Must I profess that my youth and the best years of my manhood have been wasted – pointless – thrown away? No, let me rather die with my illusions.

MARSHAL: You are here because you have held on to them too long. . . . Now calm yourself. Your life is still ahead of you. The past has been an education – a hard one, admittedly, but all the sounder for that. Up to now you have followed your whims. You have indulged in folly. You have neglected the demands of reality. . . . Outside this door stand the people of Stockholm. They have claims on you. This pardon that I hold in my hand represents their investment in you. The clergy of the new church have a lien on you: they want you to live in order that you may complete the work you so brilliantly began. The citizens have their claim: they want you as secretary of the town council. The congregation wants its pastor; the students, their teacher. These are your legal claimants. But there is still someone else out there, perhaps the one to whom you owe the most, although she makes no claim on you: your young wife. You took her from her father, and now you're driving her out into the storm. You rooted out

her childhood faith, and sowed dread in her heart. Because of
your foolish actions an enraged mob has hunted her out of her
home. Yet she does not ask in repayment that you should love
her, only that she may live out her life sharing your sufferings
with you. . . . . You call us selfish, but you can see that we too
concern ourselves with our fellow men. . . . Now let me open
this door for you, the door that will lead you back into the world.
Bend your spirit while it is still young and supple, and thank God
for giving you the years that lie ahead in which to serve mankind.

OLOF (*sobbing*): I am lost!

> *The Marshal signals the executioner who releases Olof
> from the pillory and removes his prison attire. The
> Marshal then opens the door to the sacristy, and dele-
> gates representing the city council, the clergy, and the
> citizens of Stockholm enter.*

MARSHAL: Olaus Petri, lately Dean of the Great Church of
Stockholm, do you hereby plead guilty and ask the king's grace
and pardon for your infractions against the royal mandates? Do
you recant those statements made in excess of the authority
granted you by the king? Do you abjure those of your actions
taken contrary to the king's orders? And do you swear fealty to
the king of Sweden, avowing and affirming that you will serve
him faithfully?

> *Olof remains silent.*
>
> *Lars and Christina go to him. Gesturing, the delegates
> implore him to accept the terms of the king's pardon.*

OLOF (*coldly, decisively*): Yes.

MARSHAL: In the name of the king, I now declare you a free
man.

> *Olof and Christina embrace. The delegates gather
> around Olof, shake his hand, and wish him well.*

OLOF (*tonelessly*): Before I leave this place, let me have a moment alone with my God. I have need of it. It was here that not so long ago I struck my first blow. It was here —

LARS: It was here that you won your greatest victory. Today.

> *Everyone leaves, except Olof. He falls on his knees.*
>
> *The student William comes into the church, quietly, hesitatingly. He is astonished to see that Olof is alone and out of the pillory.*

WILLIAM: Master Olof. I've come to say goodbye to you, before you enter the life to come.

OLOF (*standing up*): William, my dear boy. You were always steadfast. Never gave up on me. . . . I feel like crying with you when I think of the happy moments of my youth.

WILLIAM: Before you die I want to thank you, Master Olof, for all that you have done for us. These flowers — I gave them to you — but you didn't see them. They're trampled on, I see. I wanted them to be a souvenir of that time we played under the linden trees in the garden at the monastery in Strängnäs. You said when you left that we would thank God if you never came back. I thought you might be happy to know that we never did thank God for that. We never forgot you. You stopped the cruel punishments. You opened those heavy monastery doors and let us out. You made us feel free. We saw how blue the sky was and how happy life could be. Why you should be made to die — we don't understand that. For us, you could only do right. They say you are dying because you helped some people who were oppressed. If that is so, then your death cannot be painful, even if it hurts us deeply, very deeply. You told us about how they burned Huss at the stake, because he dared to tell the truth to the high and mighty. You described how he stepped onto the pyre and with joy commended his soul to God, and how he prophesied that a swan would one day come to sing songs hailing a new age of freedom. That's how I've seen you going to meet your death, your head high, your eyes raised to heaven, while the people shout, "Like this, dies a witness to the truth!"

As if struck, Olof slumps down on the stool of repentance.

GERT (*his voice resounding from far within the church*): Renegade!

Olof collapses on the pillory, utterly crushed.

CURTAIN

Introduction
to
The Father

In 1871, not long before Strindberg conceived *Master Olof*, Georg Brandes, lecturing at the University of Copenhagen on the main currents in nineteenth-century literature, declared that Scandinavia was a stagnant pool unaffected by these currents. The reason for this state of affairs was that serious Scandinavian literature concerned itself almost exclusively with religious ideals and not with contemporary issues. If Scandinavian writers were to join the mainstream of development, said Brandes, they would have to follow the French example and "submit problems to debate."

Taking his cue from Brandes, Ibsen did just that. So did Strindberg, and together they made Scandinavia the fountain-head of modern drama. *A Doll's House,* published at the end of 1879, inaugurated a whole series of plays dealing with the problem of women's rights. Strindberg thought Ibsen's presentation of the feminist question was biased against normal couples who found pleasure in sex and was consequently of interest only to a small segment of the population, which Shaw would later call the "neurotic classes." In essays, short stories, and plays, Strindberg chafed, ridiculed, and assailed the Norwegian dramatist and his "bluestocking" followers. One of these plays, which after several rewritings was published under the title *Comrades*, ws a parody of *A Doll's House*. The husband is the doll in Strindberg's play, tyrannized by a woman who is a marauder, invading the male labor market. In place of Ibsen's famous tarantella scene, in which Nora dances as if she were sacrificing her life for her husband's honor, Strindberg has the husband almost persuaded to dress up in drag as a Spanish dancer for a costume ball. It is he who makes the sacrifice to save the marriage by switching numbers on his and his wife's paintings so that she can win a prize and thus feel equal or superior to her comrade-husband. The *raisonneur,* in one version of the play, twits Ibsen for his uncompromising and gloomy view of life in a speech that ticks off all the famous slogans and catchwords in Ibsen's plays.

135

Oh, give us back the joy we knew, you who preach
the joy of life. Give us the cheering spirit of compromise and send the troll kings home. They came down
from misty moors with mountainous demands and
bills for ideal expenses and made life dark and
unpleasant. Give us the sun again, just a little bit of
sunshine, enough for us to see that the old planet still
possesses a bit of the old heavens.

If Strindberg could have sustained the mood of this speech,
Comrades might have been a light-hearted romp through the
fields of feminism. Unfortunately Strindberg could not involve
himself in the women's rights question without becoming
increasingly acrimonious. He did not mind that his views were
attacked and ridiculed as long as he was allowed to reply, but he
was rightly infuriated when the feminists tried to silence him by
bringing him to court (not for writing against the feminists,
which was not a criminal offense, but for blasphemy against the
state church, which was).

Furthermore, his marriage to a career woman, an actress,
brought the feminist controversy into his own home, and he
began to magnify the importance of the women's rights movement. What at first had seemed to him a social question of secondary importance now became an issue that would fundamen-
tally affect the civilization of Europe. It was, in Strindberg's
view, no longer a matter of career spouses dueling with each
other or of a few neurotic women of ambiguous sexuality; it was
a conflict that pitted all women against all men in a struggle to
decide who would rule at home, in the courts, and in the councils
of state. He found his fearful intimations spelled out in an article
by the Marxist sociologist Paul Lafargue, "Le Matriarcat. Etude
sur les origines de la famille," printed in the 15 March 1886 issue
of *La Nouvelle Revue.* Lafargue believed that the pioneering
studies of such cultural historians as Bachofen, L. H. Morgan,
and Friedrich Engels offered unmistakable evidence that present
male-dominated society had been preceded in prehistorical times
by a society in which women were dominant by virtue of the fact
that it was only through the mother that indubitable parental
links could be established. The patriarchal family was, he said,
a comparatively new form, whose "development was marked by

as many crimes as we can probably expect in the event society should seek to return to the matriarchal form."

This ominous forecast, which Strindberg quoted in the preface to the second volume of his collection of stories *Getting Married,* came as a revelation. Lafargue explained why the women's rights question had assumed such alarming proportions and why the feminist hordes had descended on Strindberg when he tried to talk sensibly on the subject. He thought it was the beginning of a world revolution in which women would triumph over men through a series of crimes, a revolution without crimes being a logical impossibility.

What a subject for a drama! Not a trifling lampoon like *Comrades,* but a searching drama about the coming of a new order in society, a new order of morality. Lafargue had explained that the trial of Orestes at the end of Aeschylus's trilogy the *Oresteia,* in which the male principle replaces the female principle and fathers become more important in the social structure than mothers, encapsulated the revolution in communal life that had occurred before writing had been invented. Strindberg now conceived of a drama, the first in a proposed trilogy, that would reveal the vast wheel of history turning backward, with women fighting to gain ascendancy over men.

But what crimes could they commit if they were the weaker sex and the vassals of men? The crime of destroying man's faith in himself, of sowing the seeds of doubt in the one area that was essential to the patriarchy: fatherhood. Once this much was fixed in Strindberg's mind, his knowledge of abnormal psychology, a subject in which he was particularly well-read, provided the mechanism that would set the wheel turning.

The result was *The Father,* a play in which the protagonist, a man of science and of arms, representing the accomplishments and power of patriarchal society, finds himself in a house of women, women of all sorts and ages, forming a matriarchal society. One reason for the captain's defeat is that he is committed to a moral code developed by patriarchal society, whereas his wife can consider herself not subject to it. Hence she appears in the play as immoral, driven only by her instincts.

Once moral considerations have been put aside, the conflict becomes basically one of wills. The outer action seems erratic, spasmodic, illogical. But as Robert Brustein has remarked, *The*

Father possesses "a kind of internal logic, which makes all its external contradictions seem rather minor; and it maintains this dreamlike logic right up to its shattering climax. For it assumes total warfare between men and women, in which unconscious thoughts are as blameworthy as explicit actions."

The bitter conflict forces the unconscious thoughts to come to the surface, and in doing so it reveals that man has sown the seeds of his own destruction. Patriarchal society created the Christian religion and along with it evolved an ideal image of woman. Man became a slave to the image of the madonna, worshiping her purity while seeking sexual satisfaction from her. Torn by his irreconcilable longings for both the mother and the prostitute, the saint and the sinner, the captain destroys himself, using his wife as instrument. Not only does *The Father* suggest that a Nietzschean transvaluation of values is about to occur in European civilization; it adumbrates in the climactic scene at the end of Act II certain ideas that were to form the cornerstone of the new psychology of the unconscious.

The present translation of *The Father* is based on the latest scholarly edition, prepared by Gunnar Ollén and printed in *August Strindbergs Samlade Verk,* vol. 27 (Uppsala, 1984), as well as on Strindberg's own French translation, *Père* (Helsingborg, 1888). I have also consulted the Danish translation by Peter Nansen, *Faderen* (Copenhagen, 1888).

The Father

(Fadren)

A Tragedy in Three Acts

CHARACTERS

CAPTAIN, in the cavalry (Adolf)
LAURA, his wife
BERTHA, their daughter, about 14 years old
DR. EASTLAND
PASTOR, Protestant, Laura's brother (Jonas)
MARGARET, a maid, the Captain's old nurse
HAPPY, a corporal in the cavalry
ORDERLY, the Captain's

The action takes place in Sweden in a December in the 1880s.

ACT I

The parlor of the Captain's house. A door in the rear wall, to the right, leads to the entrance hall. In the middle of the room, a large round table, with newspapers, magazines, and scientific journals on it. To the right, a leather sofa with a table in front of it. To the far right, a wallpapered jib door, of the sort common in nineteenth-century Swedish homes. To the left, a secretary; a pendulum clock above it. Also to the left, the door to the inner rooms. Weapons of various sorts, hunting rifles and game-bags, hanging on the walls. Near the rear door, a clothes tree with military coats hanging on it. A lamp is burning on the center table.

[1]

The Captain and the Pastor are sitting on the leather sofa. The Captain is in undress uniform except for his boots and spurs. The Pastor is dressed in black and white neck-cloth but without clerical collar. He is smoking a pipe.

The Captain rings.

ORDERLY: Sir?

CAPTAIN: Is Happy out there?

ORDERLY: Waiting your orders, sir, in the kitchen.

CAPTAIN: In the kitchen again! Damn! Get him in here right away!

ORDERLY: Yes, sir! (*Exits.*)

CAPTAIN: That son-of-a-gun has been too familiar with the help. Got the kitchen maid pregnant. A hot little devil, isn't he?

PASTOR: You mean Happy? He was in trouble last year! Same thing!

CAPTAIN: Ah, you remember. Why don't you help the cavalry out and talk to him—friendly. Might set him right. I've bawled him out, sworn at him, even thrashed him. Nothing makes an impression.

PASTOR: And you want me to read a sermon to him? What impression do you think God's word makes on a cavalry trooper?

CAPTAIN: Well, as my brother-in-law you know it makes no impression on me.

PASTOR: I do indeed.

CAPTAIN: However, it might on him. Give it a try, hm?

[2]

Happy enters.

CAPTAIN: All right, Happy, out with it!

HAPPY: With your permission, sir, I can't talk about it—I mean with the pastor here.

PASTOR: Don't be embarrassed on my account, my lad.

CAPTAIN: Come on now, let's have it, the whole story. It's that or punishment duty.

HAPPY: Well, you see—well—we went to dance at Gabriel's house, and then—well, then Louis said that—

CAPTAIN: What's Louis got to do with it? Don't go making up stories.

HAPPY: Well, you see, after a while Emma said let's go to the barn.

CAPTAIN: I see. It was Emma who seduced you!

HAPPY: Not exactly, but that ain't far wrong. Let me tell you, if the girl doesn't want to, nothing happens.

CAPTAIN: We're wasting time. Are you or are you not the father of this baby?

HAPPY: How should I know?

CAPTAIN: What! If you don't know, who does?

HAPPY: Well, sir, how can you ever know?

CAPTAIN: You mean you weren't the only one?

HAPPY: Oh, sure, that time I was; but you still can't be certain you're the only one. I mean—

CAPTAIN: Are you trying to implicate Louis in this? Is that your game?

HAPPY: It's hard to know who's at fault.

CAPTAIN: Now just a minute. You told Emma that you wanted to marry her.

HAPPY: Well, you always gotta say that—

CAPTAIN (*to the Pastor*): My God, what's the world coming to?

PASTOR: The same old refrain. —But tell me, Happy, you must be man enough to know if you're the father.

HAPPY: Well, sure I know I got it off with her. But Pastor, you know yourself that don't necessarily mean anything comes of it.

PASTOR: Listen, young man, we are talking about you!—Surely you can't leave the girl to take care of the child by herself. You cannot be forced to marry her, perhaps, but you certainly must help care for the child. I'll see to that.

HAPPY: Then Louis has got to go in with it too!

CAPTAIN: All right! We'll have to let the courts settle it. I can't untangle this mess. I find it rather tedious. That's all. Dismissed.

PASTOR: Happy! Just a second. . . . Don't you think it's a bit unfair to toss the poor girl out into the street like that, with her baby? Don't you? You must realize that conduct like that can only . . . well . . .

HAPPY: Naturally, if I really knew I was the father, but, well, how can you ever know that? Go slaving through life for somebody else's child—I ain't cut out for that. Pastor, you and the captain, sir, you can understand what I mean.

CAPTAIN: Dismissed!

HAPPY: Yes, sir! (*Exits.*)

CAPTAIN: Not that way! Stay out of the kitchen!

[3]

CAPTAIN: Why didn't you whale the daylights out of him?

PASTOR: What do you mean? I thought I really let him have it.

CAPTAIN: Ha! You just sat there sputtering.

PASTOR: Frankly, I don't know what to say. I feel sorry for the girl. And I feel sorry for the boy. Suppose he isn't the father? The girl can put the baby in a maternity hospital, nurse it for four months, and the child is taken care of thereafter. Not the boy—he can't wet-nurse it. The girl can get a good place afterward in some decent home, but the boy's whole future might be ruined— dishonorable discharge and all that.

CAPTAIN: I damn well wouldn't want to sit on the bench and pass judgment in this case. The lad isn't exactly blameless. How can one tell? One thing is certain; the girl is guilty to some extent —if there's any guilt at all.

PASTOR: Yes, that's true. I don't presume to judge any- one. . . . What were we talking about before we got involved in this damned mess? —Bertha and her confirmation.

CAPTAIN: More than her confirmation; it was the question of her whole upbringing. This house is filled with women, and every one of them wants to bring up my little girl. Your step- mother wants her to be a spiritualist; Laura hopes to make an artist out of her; the governess wants her to be a Methodist; old Margaret steers her to the Baptists; and the kitchen help want her to join the Salvation Army. You can't pull a person in several different directions at once without their coming apart. The trouble is that I, who have the primary responsibility for develop- ing her mind and talents, am constantly thwarted. I've got to get her out of this house.

PASTOR: The trouble is you have too many women running things.

CAPTAIN: You can say that again. I live in a cage filled with tigers. If I didn't hold an iron red-hot under their noses, they would tear me to pieces. — All right, laugh, you bastard. It wasn't bad enough that I married your sister; you had to foist your old stepmother on me too.

PASTOR: For heaven's sake, a man can't have his stepmother living in the same house with him.

CAPTAIN: No, you prefer a mother-in-law as a boarder — in somebody else's house.

PASTOR: Yes, well, everyone has his lot in life.

CAPTAIN: Maybe. But I've got a lot too much to bear. I've still got my old nurse, from the time I was a child, and she treats me as if I were still wearing a bib. Oh, she's very kind, Lord knows, but she just doesn't belong here.

PASTOR: You've got to learn to keep the womenfolk in line. You let them run things too much.

CAPTAIN: All right, you old horse, would you be so good as to enlighten me on how women are supposed to be kept in line?

PASTOR: To tell the truth, Laura was always—. She's my own sister, but she certainly could be quarrelsome.

CAPTAIN: Laura? Oh, she can be difficult, but she's not the worst. I can handle her.

PASTOR: Come on, get if off your chest. I know what she's like.

CAPTAIN: She was brought up like a sentimental schoolgirl and she's having a little difficulty getting adjusted. That's all. After all, she's my wife —

PASTOR: And therefore she can do no wrong? No, you don't fool me; she's the one who's putting the screws on you.

CAPTAIN: Anyway, the point is that now the whole house is in an uproar. Laura won't let our child leave, while I can't let her stay in this nuthouse.

PASTOR: Ah, ha, just as I thought: Laura *won't*. In that case, I fear the worst. When she was a child she would lie stiff and still, playing dead, until she got what she wanted. And when she got it, she gave it back, saying it wasn't the thing that she wanted so much, she just wanted to have her own way.

CAPTAIN: Really. Already like that! . . . You know, she gets herself into such a state sometimes, she scares me. I think something's the matter with her.

PASTOR: Now what is it that you and Laura want for Bertha that is so impossible to agree on? Can't you reach a compromise?

CAPTAIN: Don't get the idea that I want to make her into a *Wunderkind* or a prodigy or remake her in my own image. And I don't want to be a matchmaker to my own daughter, bringing her up just so she can get married. If you do that, and things don't work out, she'll turn into a sour old maid. On the other hand, I don't want her to pursue a man's profession, which would take years of study. And all that education would be absolutely wasted if she decided to get married.

PASTOR: So what do you want?

CAPTAIN: I want her to be a teacher. If she doesn't get married, she can still support herself and won't be any worse off than those poor teachers who have to share their salaries with their families. If she gets married, she can use what she's learned to educate her own children. Now what's wrong with that?

PASTOR: Nothing. Nothing's wrong with it. On the other hand, could it be that she has shown such a talent for painting that it would be a crime not to encourage it?

CAPTAIN: No, not at all! I showed some samples of her work to a well-known painter who said it was ordinary, uninspired stuff, the kind of thing one learns in art classes. But then last summer some young whippersnapper, with all the answers—you know the type—comes along and says Bertha has a colossal talent. And that closed the case in favor of Laura.

PASTOR: I suppose he had a crush on Bertha?

CAPTAIN: Of course, what else!

PASTOR: Well then, old boy, God help you. You're going to need His help. Really sad—I mean, Laura has her own faction—in there. (*Pointing to the inner rooms.*)

CAPTAIN: You can bet on that! The whole house is ready to explode. And just between you and me, it isn't exactly what I'd call a fair fight that's being fought on that side.

PASTOR (*rising*): You think I don't know?

CAPTAIN: You know, eh?

PASTOR: Who'd know better?

CAPTAIN: The worst of it is, it seems to me that Bertha's career is being decided in there on the basis of some pretty vile reasons. "This will teach the men." – "Women can do this and women can do that." Man against woman – that's all I hear, all day long. – You're not leaving, are you? No, no, stay for supper. I don't know what we've got in the house; we'll find something. The new doctor is going to drop in. I told you I was waiting for him. Have you seen him?

PASTOR: I caught a glimpse of him as I rode by. Looked like a proper and sensible sort.

CAPTAIN: Good, that's something. Do you think I can find an ally in him?

PASTOR: Who knows? All depends on how long he has lived with women.

CAPTAIN: Oh, come on now, won't you stay?

PASTOR: No, thanks very much, old friend. I promised I'd be home for supper – and the old lady gets so worried if I'm late.

CAPTAIN: Worried? Furious, you mean. Well, as you wish. Here, let me help you with your overcoat.

PASTOR: Must be awfully cold tonight. Ah, thank you, thank you. You should look after yourself, Adolf. You seem so tense and nervous.

CAPTAIN: Do I act nervous?

PASTOR: Well, a little. Are you sure you're feeling all right?

CAPTAIN: What's Laura been telling you? For twenty years now she's been treating me as if I had one foot in the grave.

PASTOR: Laura? No, no, no. It's just that you worry me. Take care of yourself; a bit of free advice. Goodnight, you old horse. —Wait, I thought you wanted to talk about Bertha's confirmation?

CAPTAIN: Not at all. Let me tell you, I'm not going to interfere with the public conscience. Let it run its appointed course. I'm neither a proselytizer nor a martyr. We're beyond all that, right? Say hello to those at home.

PASTOR: Goodnight, Adolf. Say hello to Laura.

[4]

CAPTAIN (*opens the leaf of the secretary and sits down to do the accounts*): Thirty-four, -nine, forty-three, -seven, -eight, fifty-six.

LAURA (*enters through the door at left*): Would you mind telling me —

CAPTAIN: Just a second. —Sixty-six, seventy-one, eighty-four, eighty-nine, ninety-two, one hundred. What did you want?

LAURA: Maybe I'm bothering you.

CAPTAIN: Not at all. The household money, I suppose?

LAURA: That's right. The household money.

CAPTAIN: Put the bills there, and I'll go through them.

LAURA: Bills?

CAPTAIN: Yes.

LAURA: What's this about bills?

CAPTAIN: I've got to have the receipts, obviously. Our financial position isn't too good, and in case of an audit, you've got to produce the bills and receipts; otherwise our creditors could accuse us of negligence.

LAURA: If our finances are that bad, it isn't my fault.

CAPTAIN: That's exactly what we'll find out by going through the accounts.

LAURA: Listen, if that tenant farmer of ours doesn't pay up, it's not my fault.

CAPTAIN: And who gave that tenant farmer the highest recommendation? You did! And why did you recommend this—this—shall we say, wastrel?

LAURA: And why did you give this—this—wastrel a lease?

CAPTAIN: Because you wouldn't let me eat in peace, sleep in peace, or work in peace until you got him here. You wanted him here because your brother wanted to get rid of him. Your mother wanted him because I *didn't* want him. The governess wanted him because he was a Bible-reading pietist. And old Margaret wanted him because she knew his grandmother when they were children. That's why he was hired. And if I hadn't taken him on, by now I'd be raving in the madhouse or pushing up daisies. —Anyway, here's the budget money and your allowance. You can give me the bills and receipts later.

LAURA (*curtseying*): Thank you so much!   . . . What about you? —Do you keep track of what you spend apart from housekeeping expenses?

CAPTAIN: I don't think that's any of your business.

LAURA: No, apparently not—just as little as my child's education is. I see the House and Senate met this evening. What did you and my brother decide?

CAPTAIN: I had already reached my decision, and therefore I had merely to convey it to the only friend I and the rest of my family have in common. Bertha is going to live in town. She will be leaving in two weeks.

LAURA: And where will she be living—if I may ask?

CAPTAIN: She'll be boarding with the Savbergs, the judge advocate.

LAURA: That atheist!

CAPTAIN: A child is to brought up in the faith of its father—that's the law.

LAURA: And the mother has nothing to say about it?

CAPTAIN: Nothing at all. She sold her birthrights in a legal exchange, relinquishing her rights in return for the husband's support of her and her children.

LAURA: So the mother has no rights over her child?

CAPTAIN: None whatsoever. Once you've sold something, you can't take it back and keep the money.

LAURA: What if the father and the mother should come to an agreement . . . ?

CAPTAIN: An agreement?! I want her to live in town, you want her to live out here. Averaging it out arithmetically, she'd move into the railway station, halfway between here and the town. It's a problem without a solution. Do you understand?

LAURA: Then we'll have to invent one, won't we? . . . What did Happy want with you just now?

CAPTAIN: That's a military secret.

LAURA: And the talk of the whole kitchen.

CAPTAIN: Then you must know all about it!

LAURA: I most certainly do!

CAPTAIN: And no doubt you have already handed down your decision.

LAURA: It's in the law books!

CAPTAIN: The law books don't tell who the father of the child is.

LAURA: One usually knows.

CAPTAIN: People with any sense say one can never really know.

LAURA: Isn't that remarkable! You mean you can't know who the father is?

CAPTAIN: So they say.

LAURA: Really remarkable! Then tell me, how can the father have rights over the mother's child?

CAPTAIN: He has them only if he takes on certain responsibilities – or has them forced on him. Besides, in marriage there's no question about who the father is.

LAURA: No question?

CAPTAIN: I should hope not.

LAURA: Not even when the wife has been unfaithful?

CAPTAIN: That doesn't have any application in the present case. Anything else you want to ask?

LAURA: Not a thing.

CAPTAIN: Good. Then I'm going up to my room, and maybe you'll be good enough to inform me when the doctor comes. (*Closes the secretary and stands up.*)

LAURA: Yes, sir, my captain!

CAPTAIN (*opening the wallpapered door at the right*): As soon as he comes, mind you. I don't want to seem rude to him. Understand? (*Exits.*)

LAURA: I understand. Perfectly.

[5]

Laura looks at the money she is holding in her hand.

VOICE OF THE MOTHER-IN-LAW (*from within*): Laura!

LAURA: Yes, what is it?

VOICE OF THE MOTHER-IN-LAW: Where's my tea?

LAURA (*in the doorway to the inner rooms*): Coming—in a moment.

> *Laura is going to the entrance door at the rear when the door is opened, and the Orderly enters, followed by Dr. Eastland.*

ORDERLY: Doctor Eastland.

DR. EASTLAND: How do you do?

LAURA (*going to meet him and offering her hand*): How good of you to come, Doctor. Welcome to our house. The captain is out just now, I'm afraid, but he'll be back soon.

DR. EASTLAND: I beg your pardon for coming so late, but I have already had to make a house call.

LAURA: Please sit down, won't you?

DR. EASTLAND: Thank you.

LAURA: Yes, there seems to be quite a lot of illness in this area right now, but I do hope you'll find everything to your liking here. You know, for us who are rather isolated here in the country it's very important to find a doctor who takes a genuine interest in his patients. I've heard so many good things about you, Doctor. I do hope we shall get along well together.

DR. EASTLAND: Very kind of you, madam. Let me say on my part that I hope my calls here will be social ones and not professional ones. Your family is quite healthy and—

LAURA: Yes, fortunately we haven't had any severe illnesses. Still, things aren't the way they should be.

DR. EASTLAND: Really?

LAURA: Yes, things aren't as good as we might wish.

DR. EASTLAND: I'm sorry to hear that.

LAURA: There are certain situations in family life that, for the sake of propriety and one's conscience, one is compelled to conceal from the world.

DR. EASTLAND: Not from one's doctor, I trust.

LAURA: True. That is why I feel it is my painful duty to let you know right from the start what the true situation is.

DR. EASTLAND: I see. I wonder if we should not put off this discussion until I've met your husband?

LAURA: No! No, you must hear me out *before* you see him.

DR. EASTLAND: So the matter concerns him?

LAURA: Yes, him—my dearly beloved husband.

DR. EASTLAND: How distressing. I assure you, you have my sympathy.

LAURA (*taking out a handkerchief*): My husband is mentally ill. . . . There, I've said it. Now you can judge for yourself.

DR. EASTLAND: I can't believe it! I've read the captain's papers on mineralogy. I've admired them; they reveal a very clear and penetrating intellect.

LAURA: Indeed! You don't know how happy it would make all of us here in the family if we were mistaken.

DR. EASTLAND: Of course it may be that his mind is disturbed in other areas. Perhaps you could tell me—?

LAURA: That's exactly what we fear! You see, sometimes he gets the strangest ideas. He's entitled to them, I suppose—as a scientist, I mean, if only they didn't affect the well-being of the whole family. For instance, he has an absolute mania for buying all sorts of things.

DR. EASTLAND: Oh? What sort of things?

LAURA: Books! Boxes and boxes of them—which he never reads.

DR. EASTLAND: Well, scientists do buy books; that doesn't seem so strange.

LAURA: You don't believe me?

DR. EASTLAND: Madam, I'm convinced that you believe what you say.

LAURA: Then tell me, is it reasonable to think that you can see in a microscope what happens on another planet?

DR. EASTLAND: He says he can do that?

LAURA: That's what he says.

DR. EASTLAND: In a microscope?

LAURA: Yes, in a microscope!

DR. EASTLAND: I must admit that doesn't sound good, if it's true.

LAURA: If it's true! I see you have no confidence in me, Doctor. And here I sit confiding the family secrets to you.

DR. EASTLAND: Now, now, now, madam, what you say will go no further. I'm gratified you feel you can trust me. But as a doctor I have to examine – I have to test things before I can make a diagnosis. Has the captain shown any symptoms of instability, of extreme vacillation?

LAURA: Oh, the stories I could tell you! We've been married for twenty years, and he's never once made up his mind without changing it.

DR. EASTLAND: Is he obstinate? Rigid and difficult to reason with?

LAURA: He always wants his own way, in everything. And once he gets it, he shrugs it off and tells *me* to make the decision.

DR. EASTLAND: Does give one pause, I must say. Perhaps this does need looking into. You see, madam, it's volition, the will, the ability to make decisions, that constitutes the backbone of the psyche; and if that is weakened, the whole mind may collapse.

LAURA: Oh, God knows what I've had to put up with during all these trying years, forcing myself to agree to everything he says. If you only knew how I've struggled with him to keep things going. If you only knew!

DR. EASTLAND: Madam, your misfortune touches me deeply. I assure you I shall do whatever can be done. You have my heartfelt sympathies. I beg you to rely completely on me. From what you tell me there's one thing that I would like to suggest. Avoid bringing up any thoughts with strong emotional associations. In a weak mind they spread like wildfire and turn into obsessions and manias. I think you know what I mean.

LAURA: Yes. You mean anything that would arouse his suspicions.

DR. EASTLAND: Precisely. A sick man can convince himself of anything; he's so susceptible.

LAURA: Yes, of course. . . . Yes, I understand. . . . Yes.

A bell rings from within.

Excuse me, my mother is ringing for me. Could you wait just a moment, please? — Oh, why here's Adolf now —

Laura leaves.

[6]

The Captain enters through the jib door.

CAPTAIN: What, are you already here, Doctor? Welcome, welcome.

DR. EASTLAND: Captain. It's a great pleasure for me to make the acquaintance of such a well-known scientist.

CAPTAIN: Oh, please, please. My military duties don't allow me much time for deep research. Still, I think I may be on the track of an important discovery.

DR. EASTLAND: Really!

CAPTAIN: Yes, yes! I've been subjecting meteor stones to spectroscopy, and I've found carbon, in other words, vestiges of organic life! What do you say to that?

DR. EASTLAND: You can see that in a microscope?

CAPTAIN: No, damnation, man, in the spectroscope!

DR. EASTLAND: Ah, spectroscope! Excuse me, of course, of course. Pretty soon I suppose you'll be telling us what's happening on Jupiter.

CAPTAIN: Not what's happening, but what has happened. If only that damned bookseller in Paris would send me the books. I think all the bookdealers of the world are in a plot against me. For two months I have not had a single reply from any one of them. Imagine, no answers to my orders, my letters, my abusive telegrams, nothing! It's driving me out of my mind. I don't know what's behind it.

DR. EASTLAND: Oh, it's probably just plain ordinary carelessness. You shouldn't get yourself so worked up over that.

CAPTAIN: But, devil take it, I won't be able to get my paper ready in time. And I know that right now in Berlin they're working along the same lines. —But we're not supposed to be talking about this. Forgive me. Now let's get at *your* problem. If you want to live here, we can offer the small flat in the wing of the house. Or do you want to live in the old servants' quarters?

DR. EASTLAND: Just as you wish. Makes no difference to me.

CAPTAIN: No, it's up to you. Take your pick.

DR. EASTLAND: No, I'll let you decide that.

CAPTAIN: No. I'll decide nothing of the sort. It's up to you to say what you want. I have no preference, none at all.

DR. EASTLAND: Well, I can't decide—

CAPTAIN: For Christ's sake man, just say what you want! I don't care. I have no preference, no wish in this matter. What are you, a milksop? Come, come, make up your mind. Infuriating!

DR. EASTLAND: Well, if it's up to me—all right, I'll move in here.

CAPTAIN: Good! That's more like it. Thank you. —I'm sorry, Doctor, but there's nothing that irks me so much as hearing someone say "makes no difference to me." (*He rings.*)

The nurse Margaret enters.

CAPTAIN: Oh, so it's you, Margaret. Say, do you know if the apartment in the wing is ready for the doctor?

MARGARET: Yes, Captain. It's all ready.

CAPTAIN: Good. Then I won't detain you, Doctor. You must be tired. Goodnight. Make yourself at home. I'll see you in the morning, I hope.

DR. EASTLAND: Good evening, Captain.

CAPTAIN: I trust my wife has made things clear to you—given you the lay of the land, as it were.

DR. EASTLAND: Yes, your splendid wife has given me some

pointers that it might be good for an outsider to know. Well, goodnight, Captain.

[7]

CAPTAIN: Ah, dear old Margaret! Now what can I do for you?

MARGARET: My big boy Adolf! Could I speak to you for a moment?

CAPTAIN: My dear old nurse, you go right ahead and say whatever's on your mind. You're the only one I can listen to around here without climbing the walls.

MARGARET: Now Adolf, don't you think you could meet Laura halfway and work out something with her about your child? After all, she's the mother and—

CAPTAIN: After all, I'm the father, Margaret.

MARGARET: Yes, yes, yes. But a father has other things to think about; the mother has only her child.

CAPTAIN: That's exactly it. She's only got one burden to carry, while I have three. And what she carries I also have to carry. Don't you think I would have been something other than an old soldier by now if I didn't have a wife and child?

MARGARET: Well, that isn't what I mean.

CAPTAIN: No, I'm sure it isn't. You're just trying to put me in the wrong.

MARGARET: Oh, Adolf, my boy, don't you believe that I want only the best for you?

CAPTAIN: Of course, I believe it, you dear old girl. But you don't know what is best for me. You see, it isn't enough for me just to have given life to a child; I also want to give it my mind and soul.

MARGARET: Well, I wouldn't know about things like that. I just think that people should make an effort to get along together.

CAPTAIN: You're not my old friend, are you, Margaret?

MARGARET: Me? What are you saying, Adolf? Do you think I can forget you were my baby boy when you were a little tyke?

CAPTAIN: No, old girl. Do you think I can forget? You've been like a mother to me. You've given me aid and comfort—up to now—when everyone else was against me. But now when the chips are down, you betray me and join the enemy.

MARGARET: Enemy?

CAPTAIN: Yes, enemy! You know how things stand in this house. You've seen it all, from beginning to end.

MARGARET: Yes, I've seen—more than enough. For heaven's sake, why should two people torture each other like this—two good people so kind to everybody else? Laura is never like that to me or to the others.

CAPTAIN: No, only to me. I know. But let me tell you, Margaret, if you abandon me now, you'll be doing a bad thing. They're spinning a web around me. And that doctor is no friend of mine.

MARGARET: Oh, Adolf, Adolf, you think the worst of everybody. You know why? Adolf, it's because you don't have the true faith. That's why, Adolf.

CAPTAIN: But you and the Baptists have found the one and only true faith. How fortunate you are.

MARGARET: I am not as unfortunate as you, Adolf, let me tell you. If you would humble your heart you would see that God would make you happy. Thou shalt love thy neighbor.

CAPTAIN: It's remarkable; you just so much as talk of God and love and your voice gets as hard as iron and your eyes glint like steel. No, no, Margaret, you certainly haven't found the true faith.

MARGARET: All right, you be proud and almighty with your books and learning. You'll see how far that gets you when it really counts.

CAPTAIN: How haughtily speak the humble at heart! Of course learning doesn't mean much to cows like you!

MARGARET: You ought to be ashamed! . . . But I still love my boy, my big, silly boy, and he'll come back to his old nurse, like a poor runaway boy, when the winds begin to howl.

CAPTAIN: Margaret! I'm sorry . . . Margaret, you've got to believe me, no one here wants to help me – no one but you. Help me. I know something is going to happen. I don't know what, but whatever it is, it's all wrong.

A sharp cry from within.

What's that? Who's screaming?

[8]

Bertha enters from the right.

BERTHA: Papa, Papa! Help, help! Save me!

CAPTAIN: There, there, my dear child! There, there. What's the matter?

BERTHA: Oh, Daddy, help me! She wants to hurt me!

CAPTAIN: Now, now, who wants to hurt you? Hm? Tell me. Come on now, tell me.

BERTHA: Grandma does. – But it was my fault. I tricked her.

CAPTAIN: All right, now you tell me just what happened.

BERTHA: You've got to promise not to tell. Promise? Promise?

CAPTAIN: Yes, yes. Now what is this all about?

Margaret exits.

BERTHA: It happens at night. Grandma comes in, and turns the lamp down low, and then she sets me down at the table with a pen in my hand over a piece of paper. And then she says the spirits will write.

CAPTAIN: What kind of nonsense –! And you haven't told me about this before?

BERTHA: I'm sorry. I didn't dare. Grandma said the spirits would get back at me if I told on them. And then the pen begins to write, and I don't know if I'm doing it or not. And sometimes it writes a lot, and sometimes nothing comes. But it has to come, she says, it has to. And tonight I thought I was doing good, and then Grandma says it was from Shakespeare, and that I had tricked her. And then she got awfully mad.

CAPTAIN: Do you think there are spirits?

BERTHA: I don't know.

CAPTAIN: But I know that there aren't any.

BERTHA: Grandma says that you don't understand such things, and that you have much worse things that can see what's going on on other planets.

CAPTAIN: Is that what she says? What else does she say?

BERTHA: She says that you really can't do any conjuring.

CAPTAIN: I never said I could. You know what meteor stones are? Stones that have fallen from other heavenly bodies. Well, I can examine them and find out if they contain the same elements as our earth. That's all that I can see.

BERTHA: Grandma says that there are things that she can see but that you can't see.

CAPTAIN: Well, Bertha, that's not true.

BERTHA: Grandma wouldn't tell a lie.

CAPTAIN: Why not?

BERTHA: Then Mama is lying too.

CAPTAIN: Uh huh.

BERTHA: If you say Mama is lying, I'll never believe you again.

CAPTAIN: I haven't said that. And that's why you must believe me when I say that it's best for you, best for your future, that you get away from this house. Do you want to do that? Do you want to go and live in town and learn something practical?

BERTHA: Oh, Daddy, how I want to live in town! Get away

from here, anywhere! As long as I could still see you now and then. Often. Everything here is so gloomy – dark like a long winter night. But when you come home, Daddy, it's like a spring morning.

CAPTAIN: You dear little chatterbox! My dearest little girl!

BERTHA: But, Daddy, if only you could be nice to Mommy, you know. She cries a lot.

CAPTAIN (*murmurs noncommittally, and then says*): So you want to live in town?

BERTHA: Yes, I do, I do!

CAPTAIN: Suppose Mama doesn't want you to?

BERTHA: But she has to want me to!

CAPTAIN: Just suppose she doesn't?

BERTHA: Then I don't know what to do. She has to want me to, she has to!

CAPTAIN: Will you ask her if you can go?

BERTHA: No, you ask her, ask her nice and sweet. She doesn't pay any mind to me.

CAPTAIN: Hmmm. . . . Well now, if you want to go, and I want you to go, and she *doesn't* want you to go, what do we do then?

BERTHA: Oh, no. Then the bickering will start again. Why can't you both – ?

[9]

Laura enters.

LAURA: Ah, so this is where you are, Bertha! This seems to be a good time for hearing what she thinks. We've got to settle the question of her future sooner or later.

CAPTAIN: The child can scarcely have any sound opinion about her future. She doesn't know what lies ahead for a young girl. We on the other hand have a pretty good idea. We've seen a lot of girls grow up and go through life.

LAURA: But since we don't see eye to eye, why not let Bertha's opinion tip the scales?

CAPTAIN: No! I won't allow anyone to usurp my rights, neither women nor children. Bertha, leave us.

Bertha leaves.

LAURA: You were afraid of what she would say. You knew she would come around to me.

CAPTAIN: I know that she herself wants to get away from home. I also know that you have the power to change her mind any way you wish.

LAURA: Really. Am I so strong?

CAPTAIN: You've got the strength of the devil in getting your own way. So has anyone who has no scruples about the means he uses. For example, how did you get rid of Doctor Norling, and how did you get the new doctor out here?

LAURA: Yes, how *did* I manage that?

CAPTAIN: You kept insulting Norling until he left in disgust, and you got your brother to "arrange" the appointment of the new one.

LAURA: What was wrong with that? Very simple and perfectly legal. Is Bertha leaving soon?

CAPTAIN: Yes, in two weeks she'll move into town.

LAURA: That is your decision?

CAPTAIN: Yes!

LAURA: Have you spoken to Bertha about it?

CAPTAIN: Yes.

LAURA: Then I guess I shall have to try to put a stop to it.

CAPTAIN: You can't!

LAURA: Oh, no? Do you suppose a real mother will allow her daughter to go and live with trash and to have the child learn that everything she has implanted in her mind is stupid, so that for the rest of her life she'll be despised by her own daughter?

CAPTAIN: Do you suppose that a real father will allow ignorant superstitious women to teach his daughter that he is a charlatan?

LAURA: It doesn't mean as much in the case of the father.

CAPTAIN: Why not?

LAURA: Because the mother is closer to the child. It's a fact that no one can really know who the father of a child is.

CAPTAIN: I don't see the application in the present case.

LAURA: You don't know if you are Bertha's father.

CAPTAIN: I don't know?

LAURA: Since no one knows, how can you?

CAPTAIN: This is a poor joke.

LAURA: Who's joking? I'm only making use of your teachings. Besides, how do you know I haven't been unfaithful?

CAPTAIN: I can believe you capable of almost anything, but not that. And you wouldn't talk about it if it were true.

LAURA: Suppose I were willing to endure anything, to be shunned, despised, anything to hold on to my child and bring her up as I see fit, and suppose I am sincere when I declare: "Bertha is my child but not yours." Suppose—

CAPTAIN: That's enough!

LAURA: Just suppose. Then your power would be at an end.

CAPTAIN: That is, if you could prove that I was not the father.

LAURA: That shouldn't be difficult. Would you like me to try?

CAPTAIN: I said that's enough!

LAURA: All I would have to do is reveal the name of the real father, specify the time and place. For example—when was Bertha born?—three years after we got married—

CAPTAIN: For the last time I'm telling you—!

LAURA: Telling me what? —You're right, we've had enough. But be very careful what you do and what you decide. And above all, don't make yourself ridiculous.

CAPTAIN: Ridiculous? I think it's tragic.

LAURA: The more you think so, the more comical you become.

CAPTAIN: I get the laughs and you get the tears. Is that it?

LAURA: Yes. Aren't we women clever?

CAPTAIN: That's why we can't fight against you.

LAURA: Then why do you get yourself involved in a fight with a superior enemy?

CAPTAIN: Superior?

LAURA: Yes. It's strange, but I could never look at a man without feeling superior.

CAPTAIN: Well, you'll soon learn who your master is. And you won't forget it.

LAURA: That should be interesting.

MARGARET (*entering*): The table's set. Would you like to have something to eat now?

LAURA: Yes, Margaret, thank you.

> *The Captain hesitates. Sits in the armchair near the table in front of the divan.*

LAURA: Aren't you going to have supper?

CAPTAIN: No thanks. I don't care for anything.

LAURA: What's the matter? Depressed?

CAPTAIN: No, just not hungry.

LAURA: Come, otherwise they'll start asking questions, unnecessary questions. . . . You can have the decency—. . . . All right, if you won't, then sit there! (*She leaves.*)

MARGARET: Adolf, now what's going on here?

CAPTAIN: I don't know what's going on. Can you tell me how you women can handle a grown man as if he were a child?

MARGARET: I don't know. I suppose it's because you are all born of women, all of you, big and small . . .

CAPTAIN: And no woman is born of man. But I've got to be Bertha's father. Tell me, Margaret, you believe that, don't you? You believe it?

MARGARET: Heavens, but you're silly! Of course you're your own child's father. Come on now and get something to eat. Don't sit there putting a face on. There, there. Come on now.

CAPTAIN (*standing up*): Get out of here, you old woman! To hell with all you witches! (*At the door to the hallway.*) Corporal! Orderly!

ORDERLY (*entering*): Yes, sir!

CAPTAIN: Harness up the one-horse sleigh. Immediately!

MARGARET: Adolf! Don't do anything –!

CAPTAIN: Get out, woman! – At once, do you hear!

MARGARET: Lord help us, what are you up to?

CAPTAIN (*putting on his military cap and great coat, etc.*): Don't expect me home. Not before midnight. (*Leaves.*)

MARGARET: God have mercy! Now what's he up to?

ACT II

Same set as first act. The kerosene lamp is burning on the table. Night.

[1]

Dr. Eastland and Laura are in conversation.

DR. EASTLAND: According to what I gathered from our conversation, I'm still not convinced about his condition. In the first place, you were mistaken in saying he had arrived at some astonishing conclusions about the other planets by looking through a microscope. Now that I've found out that it was a spectroscope, I would say that not only is he sane but that he merits the highest praise for his work as a scientist.

LAURA: But, Doctor, I never said anything of the kind!

DR. EASTLAND: Madam, I took notes on our conversation, and I distinctly recall that I asked about this crucial point, fearing that I had not heard you correctly. One has to be extremely scrupulous in making accusations that could lead to a man's being certified and committed.

LAURA: Certified?

DR. EASTLAND: You surely know that a person who is declared insane loses his civil and domestic rights.

LAURA: No, I wasn't aware of that.

DR. EASTLAND: And there's another point that strikes me as questionable. He mentioned that his letters to the booksellers had gone unanswered. Forgive me for asking, but I must know whether you — with the best intentions in the world — have interfered with his correspondence?

LAURA: Yes, I have. I felt it was my duty to look after the best interests of the family. I could not let him ruin us all without doing something.

DR. EASTLAND: Forgive me for saying this, but I don't believe you have seriously considered the possible consequences of your actions. If he finds out that you have been secretly meddling in his affairs, there is no telling what will happen. One confirmed suspicion can set off an avalanche of doubts. Or to put it another way: interfering in his business is like putting a spoke in a wheel, the worst thing for his nervous condition. I'm sure you yourself know how the mind is fretted and torn when your deepest wishes are thwarted, your will paralyzed.

LAURA: Yes, I certainly do.

DR. EASTLAND: Then you know what he must have felt.

LAURA (*rising*): It's midnight and he's still not home. We can fear the worst now.

DR. EASTLAND: Madam, I beg of you to tell me what happened tonight after I left. I must know.

LAURA: He let his imagination run away with him. He had the craziest notions. He was seized with the idea that he was not the father of his own child.

DR. EASTLAND: Strange. Very strange. What brought that up?

LAURA: I can't imagine—unless—well, he was questioning one of his troopers about the parentage of some child, and when I defended the girl in the case, he got all excited and said no one could tell who was the father of a child. God knows I did everything I could to quiet him, but now I think the whole thing's hopeless. (*Cries.*)

DR. EASTLAND: This can't be allowed to continue. Something has to be done—without arousing his suspicions, of course. I wonder if you could tell me if the captain has had such odd notions before?

LAURA: Six years ago there was a similar situation. That time he admitted—in his own letter to his doctor—that he feared for his sanity.

DR. EASTLAND: I see, I see. A case with roots deep in the past. And the sanctity of the family—and now this—I can't pry into everything; I must keep to what meets the eye. What's done can't be undone, unfortunately, and the treatment should have begun at that time. . . . Where do you think he is now?

LAURA: I don't have the slightest notion. I only know he gets the wildest ideas.

DR. EASTLAND: Do you want me to wait up for him? To avoid arousing his suspicions I could say that I was making a call on your mother—some complaint or ailment.

LAURA: Yes, that's excellent. And, Doctor, please don't leave us. If you only knew how upset I am. I wonder, wouldn't it be better if we told him right out what you think of his condition?

DR. EASTLAND: That's something one never tells the mentally disturbed before they themselves bring it up, and only then in exceptional cases. It all depends on how things develop. But we shouldn't be sitting here. Perhaps I should slip into the next room; things would look more natural.

LAURA: Yes, that would be better. And Margaret can sit in here. She always waits up for him. She's the only one who knows how to handle him. (*Goes to the door at left.*) Margaret! Margaret!

MARGARET: Yes, is there something you want? Has the captain come home?

LAURA: No, I want you to sit here and wait for him. And when he comes, you're to tell him that my mother is ill, and that's why the doctor is here.

MARGARET: Yes, yes. All right, I'll tend to it.

LAURA (*opens the door to the inner rooms*): Doctor, would you mind stepping this way?

Dr. Eastland leaves with Laura.

[2]

MARGARET (*sitting at the table. Produces a hymnbook and a pair of spectacles*): Ah, yes, yes. Yes, yes. (*Reading half to herself.*)

"A vale of tears, dark and drear,
Is this our life, and short its span.
Death's angel is ever near
Warning every living man:
    All are mortal, all is vain."

All mortal. If that isn't the truth.

"Yea, all that lives on earth must die
And to the scythe of death succumb.
Only sorrow stays to sigh
And etch with tears the silent tomb:
    All are mortal, all is vain."*

Etch with tears, yes. Yes.

During this Bertha has entered, carrying a tray with a coffee pot and a piece of embroidery on it.

BERTHA (*softly*): Margaret, can I sit here with you? It's so gloomy upstairs.

MARGARET: God in Heaven, are you still up?

BERTHA: I have to work on Daddy's Christmas present. And here's coffee for you.

MARGARET: Ah, you're a sweet child, but this just won't do. You have to get up in the morning, and it's after midnight.

BERTHA: What difference does that make? I don't dare sit alone upstairs. There are ghosts up there, I'm sure there are.

MARGARET: I knew it, I knew it, just what I said! Mark my words, there's no good fairy watching over this house. What did you hear, Bertha?

BERTHA: I—I heard someone singing in the attic.

MARGARET: In the attic! At this time of night!

BERTHA: Such a moaning, mournful song, the most mournful song I've ever heard. And it sounded like it came from the storage

* A hymn by J. O. Wallin, the most prolific of Swedish hymnists.

room up in the attic, where the cradle is, you know, the room to the left —

MARGARET: Hooo, hooo! . . . And Lord what weather tonight!

> "Alas, what is this life we lead on earth?
> Unending toil and pain, and nothing worth.
> Even on the best of days we found
> Cares and tribulations did abound."*

Yes, dear child, may God grant us a happy Christmas.

BERTHA: Margaret, is it true that Daddy is sick?

MARGARET: Yes, I'm afraid he is.

BERTHA: Then we won't be allowed to celebrate Christmas. Why isn't he in bed if he's sick?

MARGARET: Well, Bertha, he has the kind of an illness where he can be up and about. — Shhh! There's someone out in the hall. Now, you be a good girl and go to bed. And take the coffee pot with you; otherwise your daddy will be mad.

BERTHA (*goes out with the serving tray*): Goodnight, Margaret.

MARGARET: Goodnight, child. God bless you.

[3]

CAPTAIN (*enters, covered with snow. Takes off his overcoat*): You still up? Go to bed.

MARGARET: I was only waiting for . . .

> *The Captain lights a candle. Opens the leaf of the secretary. Sits down and takes some letters and newspapers from his pocket.*

MARGARET: Adolf—?

CAPTAIN: What do you want?

* From a hymn by J. Rosenthal.

MARGARET: Laura's mother is sick. And the doctor is here.

CAPTAIN: Anything serious?

MARGARET: No, I don't think so. Only a cold.

CAPTAIN (*standing up*): Who was the father of your child, Margaret?

MARGARET: I've told you the whole story so many times. It was that good-for-nothing Johnson.

CAPTAIN: Are you certain it was him?

MARGARET: Don't be silly – of course I'm certain, since he was the only one.

CAPTAIN: Yes – but was *he* certain he was the only one? No, he couldn't be certain, but you could. There's the difference.

MARGARET: I don't see any difference.

CAPTAIN: No, you can't see it; but it's there all the same. (*He leafs through a photograph album on the table.*) Do you think Bertha looks like me? (*Contemplates a portrait in the album.*)

MARGARET: Why, you're as like as two peas in a pod.

CAPTAIN: Did Johnson admit he was the father?

MARGARET: He had to – what else could he do?

CAPTAIN: Awful! Incredible.

[4]

Dr. Eastland enters.

CAPTAIN: Good evening, Doctor. How is my mother-in-law feeling?

DR. EASTLAND: Oh, it's nothing serious. She sprained her left ankle slightly.

CAPTAIN: I thought I heard Margaret say it was a cold. There seems to be a slight difference of opinion. Go to bed, Margaret.

Margaret exits.

Pause.

CAPTAIN: Sit down, won't you? Sit down, Doctor.

DR. EASTLAND (*seating himself*): Thank you.

CAPTAIN: Is it true that if you cross a zebra with a mare, the foal is striped?

DR. EASTLAND (*taken aback*): Quite true! Absolutely.

CAPTAIN: And is it true that if you continue the breeding with a studhorse, the succeeding foals will also be striped?

DR. EASTLAND: Yes, that's also true.

CAPTAIN: So: under certain conditions a studhorse can be the sire of striped foals, and under other conditions, not.

DR. EASTLAND: Yes, so it would seem.

CAPTAIN: In other words, similarity between offspring and father proves nothing.

DR. EASTLAND: I, ah—

CAPTAIN: In other words, fatherhood cannot be proved.

DR. EASTLAND: Ah, ha . . .

CAPTAIN: You're a widower, aren't you? And have had children?

DR. EASTLAND: Yes, I—

CAPTAIN: Didn't you feel ridiculous at times? Being a father, I mean. I don't know anything so comical as seeing a father parading his children down the street. Or hearing a father talk about *his* children. "My wife's children"—that's what he should say. Didn't you ever sense how false your position was? —Never any little stabs of doubt? —I won't say suspicions; as a gentleman, I presume your wife was above suspicion.

DR. EASTLAND: No, I never had that. But, Captain, you have to accept the parentage of your children in good faith. As Goethe says. I believe it was Goethe.

CAPTAIN: Good faith where a woman is involved? That's taking a big risk, isn't it?

DR. EASTLAND: Well, Captain, there are all kinds of women.

CAPTAIN: No, Doctor! Only three kinds—and only one genus. The latest research has made that clear. When I was young and strong and—let me boast—handsome—I recall now two fleeting impressions that since then have left me apprehensive. I was traveling one time by steamboat. I sat in the forward salon, some friends and I. The young woman who ran the restaurant came and sat down opposite me, sat down sobbing, and told us her fiancé had gone down with his ship. We offered our sympathies, and I ordered champagne. After the second glass, I touched her foot; after the fourth, her knee; and by morning I had completely consoled her.

DR. EASTLAND: We all have our failings and weaknesses. There are spots even on the sun.

CAPTAIN: Yes, and on the leopard, too. You know what they say about them. . . . My second example: I was at a resort, and there was a young wife there who had her children with her while her husband was in town on business. Very religious woman, with the strictest principles, always preaching to me, and utterly honorable, I'm sure. A very plain woman, physically unattractive. I avoided her. I fled from her. But she, on the pretext of borrowing books from me, dogged my heels. I loaned her a book— two books—and when she was about to move, she—strangely enough—returned the books. Have you heard of such a thing! Three months later I found in these selfsame books a visiting card with a sufficiently clear declaration of her feelings. Quite innocent—as innocent as any avowal of love from a married woman to a strange man who has never made any advances to her can be.

DR. EASTLAND: A vulgar, scheming woman, obviously.

CAPTAIN: No, not at all, no! No! She was sincere in her religious beliefs, sincere in her morality, sincere in her marital fidelity. The proof: she actually confided in her husband that she was infatuated with me. You see, therein lies the great peril. This is what fills me with apprehension. They are utterly unconscious of their instinctive deceitfulness. Such is the genus "woman."

DR. EASTLAND: You must not let these morbid thoughts get the better of you, Captain. You'll end up a sick man.

CAPTAIN: Sick? Such an imprecise word for a doctor to use. All steam boilers explode when the manometer goes past one hundred. But one hundred doesn't represent the same pressure on different boilers. Understand? Besides, are you not here to watch over me? If I were not a man, I would have the right to present my case—or to make a case, slyly, out of insinuations. I might in fact provide you with a complete diagnosis, a clinical account of my illness. Alas, and unfortunately, I am only a man, and can do nothing but fold my arms on my chest like an ancient Roman and hold my breath until I die. Goodnight.

DR. EASTLAND: Captain! . . . If you are ill or deeply distrubed, it would do no offense to your honor as a man to tell me all there is to tell. I want to hear the other side of the story, too.

CAPTAIN: Hearing one side of this story is enough, I should think.

DR. EASTLAND: No, Captain. When I saw *Ghosts* and heard Mrs. Alving giving us a postmortem on her husband, I said to myself, "Damned shame the dead can't speak."

CAPTAIN: Do you think he would speak if he were alive? And if *any* dead husband rose up and spoke, do you think he'd be believed? Goodnight, Doctor. You can see I am quite calm. You can go to bed. Go home.

DR. EASTLAND: Very well, Captain, goodnight. I have done all I can do.

CAPTAIN: Do we part as enemies?

DR. EASTLAND: Not at all. I very much regret that we can't be friends. Goodnight. (*Exits.*)

> *The Captain follows Dr. Eastland to the door at rear.*
> *Then he goes to the door at left and opens it halfway.*

CAPTAIN: Come in; let's have a talk. I knew you were eaves-dropping.

[5]

Laura enters, somewhat abashed. The Captain sits down at the secretary, the leaf of which is still down.

CAPTAIN: I know it's late, but we've got to have this out. Sit down. (*Pause.*) I went to the post office tonight and picked up some letters. From them I learn that you have held back both my incoming and outgoing mail. The immediate consequence of this is that, because of the loss of time, others shall rush ahead of me in my research, and I shall fall into the shade.

LAURA: I did what I did for your own good. You were neglecting your military duties for this other work.

CAPTAIN: My good? No! You were quite certain that one day I'd win more honor with my scientific work than with my military duties. And your primary aim was to see to it that I didn't win any honors, because that would emphasize your insignificance. But there's more: I've intercepted some letters addressed to you.

LAURA: What a gentleman you are!

CAPTAIN: From which it appears you have special plans for me. For a long time now you have been gathering my former friends against me by spreading rumors about my mental condition. And you have succeeded in your efforts to the extent that from the colonel down to the cook, there is scarcely anyone who believes I'm not mad. Now as far as my illness is concerned, these are the facts. My mind is clear, as you know, so that I can carry out my duties and my responsibilities as a father. My emotions are still pretty much within my control and will be as long as my willpower remains in working order. But you have gnawed and chewed on it so that the cogs are worn smooth, and soon the gear wheels will slip and the whole mechanism will spin backward and fly to pieces. I won't appeal to your feelings—since you lack them: therein lies your strength. I do, however, appeal to your best interests.

LAURA: What does that mean?

CAPTAIN: Your behavior has succeeded in arousing my suspicions to the point where my acumen is blunted and my thoughts run wild — the onset of madness — what you have been waiting for, and which might come at any moment. Now I put this question to you: is it in your better interest that I am of sound or unsound mind? Think about it. If I collapse, I lose my position in the army, and where would you be? If I die, you get my insurance. However, if I should take my own life, you would receive nothing. So you see, it is in your interest that I live my life out.

LAURA: Is this supposed to be a trap?

CAPTAIN: Of course! It's up to you to set your foot in it or go around it.

LAURA: You say you'll kill yourself. You won't!

CAPTAIN: Can you be sure? Do you think a man can live when he has nothing and no one to live for?

LAURA: So you capitulate?

CAPTAIN: No, I'm suggesting an armistice.

LAURA: On what conditions?

CAPTAIN: That I retain my reason and sanity. Rid me of my suspicions and I lay down my arms.

LAURA: What suspicions?

CAPTAIN: Concerning Bertha's parentage.

LAURA: Are there any suspicions about that?

CAPTAIN: With me there are. Suspicions you have fed and nourished.

LAURA: I? How?

CAPTAIN: You have dropped them like hebona in the porches of my ear, and circumstances have made them doubly poisonous.

Free me from uncertainty. Tell me plainly I'm right, and I shall forgive you in advance.

LAURA: You don't expect me to assume a guilt that's not mine!

CAPTAIN: What difference does that make, since you can be certain that I won't reveal it. A man doesn't go around trumpeting his shame.

LAURA: If I say your suspicions are wrong, you can't be certain; but if I say they are right, then you can be certain. So you want your suspicions to be right.

CAPTAIN: Fantastic, but true. The first instance cannot be proved, you see; only the second.

LAURA: Have you any grounds for these suspicions?

CAPTAIN: Yes and no.

LAURA: I know what you are up to. You want me to admit my guilt so you can get rid of me and keep the child entirely to yourself. No, you won't catch me in that trap.

CAPTAIN: Do you think I'd want to bring up somebody else's child if I were certain of your guilt?

LAURA: I'm confident you wouldn't. And that's why I realize you were lying a moment ago when you said you'd forgive me in advance.

CAPTAIN (*rising*): Laura, save me and my reason. You don't understand what I'm trying to say. If the child isn't mine, I have no rights over it, and want none. Isn't that exactly what you want? Do you want more? What else? You want power over the child, with me on hand to support both her and you? Is that it?

LAURA: Yes, power. What is this whole life-and-death struggle but a struggle for power?

CAPTAIN: For me, since I do not believe in a life in the hereafter, my child was my life in the future. It was my form of immortality, the only form of it that has any basis in reality. Take that from me, and you cut the thread of life.

LAURA: Why didn't we separate before?

CAPTAIN: Because the child held us together. But the child became a chain. How did it happen? IIow? How? . . . I never thought about it before, but now I remember something that happened—a memory that implicates and condemns you. We had been married two years and had no children—you best know why. I fell ill and lay near death. One time when the fever left me, I heard voices in the sitting room. You and the lawyer talking about the money I possessed—at that time. He explained that you couldn't inherit any of it since we didn't have any children, and he asked if you were pregnant. What you said I couldn't hear. I recovered—and we had a child. Who is the father?

LAURA: You!

CAPTAIN: No, not me, not me! There's a crime buried in the past, a crime now coming to light. And what a devilish crime! Your tender consciences made you free the black slaves, but you held on to the white. I have worked and slaved for you, for your child, your mother, your maids. I have sacrificed my career and promotion; I've been whipped from pillar to post, gone without sleep, worried myself sick about taking care of you until my hair has turned gray—gone through hell in order that you might enjoy a trouble-free life and spend your old age enjoying life again through your child. I've endured it all without complaining because I thought I was father of this child. This is the lowest form of theft, the most brutal slavery. I've suffered seventeen years at hard labor as an innocent man; how can you repay me for that?

LAURA: Now you are mad!

CAPTAIN (*sitting down*): That's what you want, isn't it? I've seen how you've worked to conceal your crime. I took pity on you because I didn't understand what was troubling you. I often lulled your troubled conscience, thinking I was chasing away a nightmare. I have heard you cry out in your sleep. I didn't want to listen. I remember now—the other night—the night before Bertha's birthday. Between two and three in the morning, I was still up, reading. You shrieked as if someone were choking you. "Go away, go away—or I'll tell!" I pounded on the wall—I—didn't want to hear more. I've harbored my suspicions a long time, afraid to hear them confirmed. This I have suffered for you; what will you do for me?

LAURA: What can I do? I swear by God and everything that's holy that you are Bertha's father.

CAPTAIN: What good does that do when you've already said that a mother may and should commit any crime for the sake of her child? I beg you, by the memory of all that's past — I beg you like a wounded man asking for the *coup de grace* — tell me all. Don't you see I am as helpless as a child; can't you hear I have come to cry to you as to my mother; can't you forget that I am a man, a soldier commanding man and beast? I ask only for the pity you would show a dying man; I surrender the tokens of my power; I beseech you, have mercy on me. (*He is on his knees.*)

LAURA (*puts her hand on his head*): What! You're crying. A man like you crying!

CAPTAIN: Yes, I am crying. A man and crying. Hath not a man eyes? Hath not a man hands, organs, senses, affections, passions? Is he not fed with the same food, hurt with the same weapons, warmed and cooled by the same summer and winter as a woman is? If you prick us, do we not bleed? If you tickle us, do we not laugh? If you poison us, do we not die? Why should not a man be allowed to wail, a soldier to cry? Because it is unmanly? Why is it unmanly?

LAURA: Cry, cry, my boy, and your mother will comfort you, as she did before. Remember? It was as your second mother that I came into your life. Your big, strong body was a bundle of nerves. You were a giant child who had come into the world too early, or perhaps had come unwanted.

CAPTAIN: It's true. My mother and father did not want me, and so I was born without strength of will. I hoped that I could make myself whole by becoming one with you. And so I let you take charge. I who in the field, who before the troops gave the orders, became with you the one who obeyed. I couldn't do without you. I looked up to you as a higher, more intelligent being, listening to your every word like a stupid child.

LAURA: It's true, it was like that. And I loved you for the child in you. But—oh, you saw it well enough, every time your nature changed and you came to me as my lover, I blushed with shame, and your lovemaking was a joy followed by the anguish of incest. The mother became her boy's lover—. Disgusting!

CAPTAIN: Yes, I felt your disgust but I didn't understand the cause of it. When I saw in you what I thought was your contempt for my unmanliness, I sought to win the woman in you by being a man.

LAURA: That was the mistake. The mother in me was your friend, you see. The woman was your enemy, and love between the sexes is war. And don't think I gave myself. I didn't give, I took—what I wanted. But you had the upper hand, and I always felt it, and longed for the day it would be mine.

CAPTAIN: You always had the upper hand. You could hypnotize me blind and deaf, so that I neither saw nor heard, only obeyed. You could hand me a raw potato and make me believe it was a peach. You could convince me that your silly whims were flashes of genius. You could have induced me to commit a crime —to do the cheapest, most contemptible things. How? Why? Because you didn't think, you didn't reason, you didn't listen to me; you did whatever came into your head. But when I woke from your spell, reflected on what had happened, I saw that my honor was stained, my reputation tarnished. I wanted to restore it by doing something grand—a daring exploit, a great discovery, at least a face-saving suicide. I wanted to fight in the field; I was denied my request. So I turned to science, made it my life. And now when I am about to reach out and pluck the fruit of my endeavors, you hack off my arm. Now I have no honor, and my life is at an end; for a man cannot live without honor.

LAURA: And a woman?

CAPTAIN: Yes. She has her children; but he doesn't. —What are you getting at? Feminism, women's emancipation, Ibsenism? . . . We—all of us—lived our little lives, unconscious as children, full of ideals, illusions, delusions. And then we woke up. Right enough, but we woke up all turned round, with our feet on the pillow, and he who woke us was himself walking in his sleep. When women grow old and cease to be women, they grow beards; I wonder what happens to men when they grow old and cease to be men? Those emanicapators who crowed to make the sun rise were no longer cocks but capons, and those who answered the cockcrow were sexless hens, so that when the sun was to rise we found it was nothing but moonshine, and we were still sitting among ruins, just as in the good old days. It had all been nothing but a little morning nap, a crazy dream, and no waking up at all.

LAURA: You know, you should have been a writer.

CAPTAIN: Who knows?

LAURA: Well, I'm sleepy. If you have any more fantasies, save them for morning.

CAPTAIN: Just one word more about realities. Do you hate me?

LAURA: Yes, sometimes. When you act the man.

CAPTAIN: It's like race hate. If it's true that we are descended from the apes, it must have been from two different species. We're not like each other, are we?

LAURA: What are you getting at?

CAPTAIN: I feel that in this struggle one of us has to go under.

LAURA: Which one?

CAPTAIN: The weaker, naturally.

LAURA: And the stronger is in the right?

CAPTAIN: Always, since he has the power.

LAURA: Then I am in the right.

CAPTAIN: You mean you are already in power?

LAURA: Yes—and legally! As of tomorrow morning when you'll be declared incapable of managing your affairs.

CAPTAIN: Certified?

LAURA: That's right. And I'll be free to bring up my child without having to put up with your wild ideas.

CAPTAIN: And who'll pay for this upbringing when I'm no longer around?

LAURA: Your army pension.

CAPTAIN (*goes toward her threateningly*): How can you have me put under guardianship?

LAURA (*taking out a letter*): With this letter, a certified copy of which is now in the hands of the court.

CAPTAIN: What letter?

LAURA (*moving backward toward the door at the left*): Yours! Your declaration to your doctor that you are insane!

> *The Captain stares at her dumbly.*

LAURA: You have fulfilled your function as an unfortunately indispensable father and family provider. Now you're no longer needed. You're dismissed. You can go. Go – now that you see my mind is as strong as my will. I'm sure you won't want to stay and face up to that!

> *The Captain crosses to the table; takes the burning lamp and throws it at Laura, who has exited backward toward the door.*

ACT III

The same set. A different lamp is on the table. The jib door is barricaded with a chair.

[1]

Laura and Margaret on stage.

LAURA: Did he give you the keys?

MARGARET: Give! No, Lord help me, I took them from the captain's clothes when Happy was brushing them outside.

LAURA: So Happy is on duty today.

MARGARET: Yes, that he is.

LAURA: Give me the keys.

MARGARET: All right, but it's no better than stealing. Listen to him walking up there – back and forth, back and forth.

LAURA: Are you sure he can't get in through that door?

MARGARET: Locked, bolted, barricaded – and Happy on guard outside.

LAURA (*opening the secretary and seating herself at it*): Control yourself, Margaret. We've got to be calm if we want to save ourselves.

A knocking at the hall door.

Who is that?

MARGARET (*opening the door to the hall*): It's Happy.

LAURA: Let him in.

HAPPY (*entering*): A dispatch from the colonel.

183

LAURA: Give it here. (*Reads it.*) I see. . . . Happy, have you removed all the cartridge from all the guns and all the hunting bags?

HAPPY: I did exactly as you ordered.

LAURA: Wait outside until I've answered the colonel's letter.

Happy exits. Laura sits down to write.

MARGARET: Listen! Do you hear that? What do you suppose he's doing up there now?

LAURA: Quiet! Can't you see I'm writing?

The sound of someone sawing can be heard.

MARGARET (*half aloud, to herself*): God have mercy. . . . Where's it all going to end?

LAURA: There. Give this to Happy. And don't breathe a word of this to my mother. Do you hear?

Margaret goes to the door. Laura opens the drawers of the secretary and takes out some papers.

[2]

The Pastor enters and takes a chair. Sits down next to Laura at the secretary.

PASTOR: Good evening, Laura. I've been gone the whole day and just now got back. It's been a bad day for you, hasn't it?

LAURA: The worst night and day I've ever been through.

PASTOR: Well, I see you weren't harmed, in any event.

LAURA: No, thank God. But just think what might have happened.

PASTOR: Tell me, what started it all? I've heard so many different stories.

LAURA: It started with his crazy idea that he wasn't Bertha's father and ended with his throwing a lighted lamp right in my face.

PASTOR: That's appalling! He's completely insane. What are you going to do now?

LAURA: We have to prevent further outbreaks of violence. The doctor has sent for a straitjacket from the hospital. In the meantime I've sent word to the colonel, and I'm trying to familiarize myself with the household finances, which he has completely mismanaged.

PASTOR: What a wretched affair. I can't say I'm surprised though. Fire – water – pressure. Explosion! What have you got in that box?

Laura has taken a drawer from the secretary.

LAURA: Look at this! Here's where he's kept everything.

PASTOR (*going through the contents*): Dear God. . . . He's kept your little doll . . . and here's your christening cap – and Bertha's rattle . . . and all your letters . . . and your locket. . . . (*Drying his eyes.*) He must have held you very dear, Laura, sister. I haven't kept mementos like that.

LAURA: He may have held me dear once upon a time. But time – time brings so many changes.

PASTOR: What's that large piece of paper? – The deed to a cemetery plot. Yes, rather the cemetery than the asylum. Laura – tell me: are you quite blameless in all this?

LAURA: Me? Why blame me because somebody goes insane?

PASTOR: Yes. . . . Well, I shan't say anything. Blood is still thicker than water.

LAURA: Exactly what are you insinuating?

PASTOR (*confronting her*): Listen to me.

LAURA: Well?

PASTOR: You certainly can't deny that this fits in perfectly with your plans to bring up Bertha on your own terms.

LAURA: I don't understand.

PASTOR: I really admire you, Laura.

LAURA: Me? Huh!

PASTOR: I'll be appointed guardian to that atheist! Fact is, I've always regarded him as a weed in our garden.

LAURA (*gives a short laugh, quickly stifled; abruptly serious*): You dare to say this to me, his wife!

PASTOR: God, but you're strong, Laura! Unbelievably strong! Like a fox in a trap, you'd rather bite off your own leg than be caught. Like a master thief—no accomplices, not even your own conscience. —Look at yourself in the mirror. You wouldn't dare.

LAURA: I never use a mirror.

PASTOR: No, you don't dare! —Let me look at your hands. —Not a spot of incriminating blood, not a trace of the secret poison. A little innocent murder, beyond the law's reach. An unconscious crime! Unconscious? Marvelous invention! —Listen to him sawing away up there. —Watch out! If he gets loose, he'll saw you in half.

LAURA: Talk, talk, talk—as if your conscience bothered you. If you think I'm guilty, accuse me—if you can.

PASTOR: I cannot.

LAURA: You see? You cannot. Therefore I am innocent. Now you take charge of your ward, and I'll tend to mine. —Ah, the doctor.

[3]

Dr. Eastland enters.

LAURA (*getting up*): Hello, my dear Doctor. You will help, won't you? Though I'm afraid there isn't much that can be done. Do you hear how he's carrying on upstairs? Are you convinced now?

DR. EASTLAND: I am convinced that an act of violence was

committed. The question is, should this act be regarded as due to an outburst of rage or of insanity?

PASTOR: Putting aside the outburst, you have to admit he was obsessed with certain fixed ideas.

DR. EASTLAND: In my view, Pastor, your ideas are even more fixed. Are they obsessions?

PASTOR: I have definite views regarding higher spiritual matters. They are not —

DR. EASTLAND: Shall we leave our views out of this? . . . Madam, the decision is up to you whether you want to see your husband fined and imprisoned or sent to the asylum. How do you judge his behavior?

LAURA: I can't answer that now.

DR. EASTLAND: In other words, you have no definite views regarding the best interests of the family? Is that right, Pastor?

PASTOR: Either way there will be a scandal. . . . It's difficult to say.

LAURA: If he's only fined for assault and battery, he might become violent again.

DR. EASTLAND: And if he's sent to jail, he'll soon be out again. I take it we're agreed: it's best for all concerned that he be treated as insane. —Where's his old nurse?

LAURA: Why?

DR. EASTLAND: She will have to put the straitjacket on him, after I've spoken to him and given the order. But not before! I have the — the garment out here. (*Goes out into the hall and returns with a large parcel.*) Would you please ask Miss Margaret to step in here?

Laura rings.

PASTOR: I don't like this one bit. "It is a fearful thing to fall into the hands of the living God."

Margaret enters.

DR. EASTLAND (*unwrapping the straitjacket*): Now listen to me carefully. You must slip this jacket on the captain from behind, if and when I think the need should arise, to prevent any violence on his part. As you can see, it's got these unusually long arms, designed to restrain any movement. These arms are to be tied behind his back. Now these two straps go through these buckles and are then fastened to a chair or the sofa, or whatever is convenient. That's all there's to it. Are you willing to do it?

MARGARET: No, Doctor, I can't. Oh, I couldn't, I couldn't.

LAURA: Why don't you do it yourself, Doctor?

DR. EASTLAND: Because he mistrusts me, Madam. You, of course, would be the obvious choice, but I'm afraid he mistrusts you too.

> *Laura gives him a sharp look, then turns away.*

DR. EASTLAND: Perhaps you, Pastor –?

PASTOR: No, I'm afraid I must decline.

[4]

> *Happy enters.*

LAURA: Have you already delivered the message?

HAPPY: As you ordered.

DR. EASTLAND: Ah, my lad. You know the situation here, don't you? The captain is mentally ill, and you've got to help us with him.

HAPPY: Anything I can do to help the captain, sir, I'll be glad to do.

DR. EASTLAND: You've got to get him into this straitjacket –

MARGARET: No. No, he mustn't touch him. I don't want the captain hurt. I'd rather do it myself, gently, very gently. But you can stand outside, Happy, in case I need help. Now that's the way it has to be.

A pounding on the wallpapered door.

DR. EASTLAND: That's him! Hide the straitjacket under your shawl on the chair, and all of you go out—the pastor and I will receive him—that door won't last much longer. Out, out!

MARGARET (*exiting to the left*): Lord help us!

> *Laura closes the secretary and exits to the left. Happy exits at the rear.*

[5]

> *The door is broken in. The lock is torn from its seat, and the chair blocking the door is hurled out into the room. The Captain, wearing a wool shirt, enters with several books under one arm, a saw in one hand, his hair rumpled, a wild expression on his face.*

CAPTAIN (*placing the books on the table*): The same thing in every book! And that proves it—I'm not crazy! The *Odyssey*, first book, line 215. Telemachus talking to Athena: "My mother calls me the son of the man"—meaning Odysseus—"but I myself do not know. No one has ever been certain of his father." And this is the suspicion entertained by Telemachus of Penelope, the most virtuous of all women! Beautiful, eh? Beautiful! . . . And here we have the prophet Ezekiel: "The fool says: Lo here is my father, but who can know whose loins have engendered him?" What could be clearer? —And what have I here? History of Russian literature by Merzlyakov. Alexander Pushkin, Russia's greatest poet, tormented to death by the widespread rumors of his wife's unfaithfulness. That was more the cause of his death than the bullet fired into his chest during a duel. On his deathbed he swore that she was innocent. What an ass! Ass! How could he swear to that? You see I've been doing my homework. —Ah, Jonas, so you are here! And the good doctor, naturally. Have you heard how I replied to an English lady who complained that Irish husbands threw lighted kerosene lamps right in the faces of their wives? "My God, what women!" I said. "W-w-women?" she stammered. "Of course," said I. "When things have gone so far that a man, a man who has loved and adored his woman, takes a lighted lamp and throws it in her face—then you can be sure!"

PASTOR: Sure of what?

CAPTAIN: Nothing. One can't be sure of anything, one can only have faith. Right, Jonas? Believe and you'll be saved. That's the way, isn't it Jonas? No! One is damned for believing! I know that for a fact.

DR. EASTLAND: Captain—!

CAPTAIN: Quiet! I don't wish to talk to you. The human telephone transmitting what they tell you in there. In there! (*Indicates the inner rooms.*) You know. You know. —Tell me, Jonas, do you think you are the father of your children? I seem to remember that you once employed a tutor in your house— pretty face, dimpled cheeks—people talked about him. Oh, yes.

PASTOR: Adolf, that's enough!

CAPTAIN: Feel under your wig and see if there aren't two bumps there. Upon my soul, I do believe he's turning pale. Come, come, it's only tittle-tattle. —But, my God, they tattle so much! Ain't we a lovely bunch of ridiculous rascals, we husbands? Right, Doctor? Right? By the way, how were things in your marriage bed? Wasn't there a lieutenant staying in the house—hmm? Just a minute now, his name—his name was— (*Whispers in Dr. Eastland's ear.*) Look at that! He's turning pale, too. Oh, don't look so upset. She's dead and buried, and what's done cannot be undone. However, I did know the fellow and can tell you that he is now—look at me, Doctor—no, no, right in my eyes—a major in the dragoons! My God, I swear you've got horns, too!

DR. EASTLAND (*irritated*): Captain can't you find something else to talk about?

CAPTAIN: Now look at that! Right away he wants to talk about something else when I want to talk about horns.

PASTOR: Adolf . . . you know that you are mentally ill.

CAPTAIN: I know that well enough. And could I treat your antlered brains some space of time, I would soon have you locked up too. Crazy I may be, but what made me crazy? That doesn't concern you; it doesn't concern anyone. Now let us talk of other things. (*Takes the photograph album from the table.*) My God, there she is! —My child. My? That we cannot know. You know what we should do in order that we might know? First, get married for appearance's sake, get divorced soon after, become lovers, and then adopt the child. That way you can at least be certain that it is your adopted child. Isn't that logical? What good does it do me now—now that you have taken my kind of immortality from me? What good is philosophy and science when I have nothing to live for? What does life mean to me when honor is gone? I grafted my right arm, half my brain, half my spinal cord on another stem. I thought they would grow together, entwine to form a single, more nearly perfect tree. And then someone comes with a knife and cuts just under the graft, leaving me as a mere half-tree. But the other shoots up with my right arm and half my brain, while I wither and die, for those were the best parts of me that I gave away. Now I want to die. Do with me what you will. I no longer exist.

> *Dr. Eastland and the Pastor whisper together. They go into the inner rooms off left. Shortly thereafter Bertha enters.*

[6]

> *The Captain is sitting at the table, hunched over.*

BERTHA (*approaching him*): Are you sick, Daddy?

CAPTAIN (*looking up dully*): I?

BERTHA: You know what you have done? Don't you know that you threw the lamp at Mommy?

CAPTAIN: Did I?

BERTHA: Yes, you did. Suppose she had been hurt?

CAPTAIN: What difference would that make?

BERTHA: You can't be my father if you talk like that!

CAPTAIN: What? Not your father? How do you know? Who told you? And who is your father? Who?

BERTHA: Well, certainly not you!

CAPTAIN: Still not me? Then who? You appear to be well informed. Who informed you? That I should live to see the day when my child comes to me and tells me to my face that I am not her father! Don't you realize that you disgrace your mother when you say this? Don't you understand that if it's true, your mother is shamed?

BERTHA: Don't say anything bad about Mother! I won't have it!

CAPTAIN: No, you all stick together, all against me. And you've done it from the very start!

BERTHA: Daddy!

CAPTAIN: Don't ever use that word again!

BERTHA: Daddy, Daddy!

CAPTAIN (*holding her close*): Bertha, my dearest own child, you are my child! Yes, yes, it's true. It can't be any other way. The rest was only a sick thought brought by the wind like fever or the plague. Look at me so that I may see my soul in your eyes. . . . But I see her soul, too! You have two souls, and you love me with the one and hate me with the other. You must love only me! You must have only one soul, otherwise you will never have peace, nor shall I. You must have only one mind, the child of my mind; you must have only one will, which is my will.

BERTHA: No, I don't want that! I want to be myself.

CAPTAIN: That you may not be! You see, I am a cannibal and I want to eat you. Your mother wanted to eat me, but she couldn't. I am Saturn who ate his own children because it had been prophesied that they would eat him. Eat or be eaten — that is the question! If I don't eat you, you will eat me — and you've already bared your teeth. Don't be afraid now, my dearest girl, I'm not going to hurt you. (*Goes over to the wall where the weapons hang and takes a revolver.*)

BERTHA (*trying to get away, going toward the door*): Help, Mommy! Mommy, help, help! He'll kill me!

MARGARET (*entering*): Adolf, what is going on here?

CAPTAIN (*examining the revolver*): Did you remove the cartridges?

MARGARET: Yes, I've put them away. But if you just sit nice and still here, I'll bring them out again.

> Takes the Captain by the arm and seats him in the chair, where he remains seated, dull and apathetic. She picks up the straitjacket and stands behind the chair. Bertha slips out to the left.

MARGARET: Adolf, do you remember when you were my dear little boy, and I tucked you into bed at night, and we would say, "Now I lay me down to sleep"? Remember how I would get up at night and give you a glass of water? Remember how I would light the candle and tell you lovely fairy tales when you had bad dreams and couldn't sleep. Remember?

CAPTAIN: Go on talking, Margaret; it soothes my head and feels so good. When I was a child and you were my nanny . . .

MARGARET: All right, but you must listen. . . . Remember the time you took the big kitchen knife to carve boats and how I had to trick you into giving it to me. You were being very difficult, and so I had to trick you, because you didn't believe it was for your own good. . . . "Give me that snake," I said, "before it bites you!" And then you let me have the knife. (*Takes the revolver from the Captain's hand.*) And then there were the times you were to get dressed and didn't want to. I had to coax and wheedle and say you were going to have a golden coat and be dressed like a prince. And then I took the little undershirt, which was only green wool, and held it in front of you and said, "Pop in your arms, both arms." And then I would say, "Now you just sit still while I button up the back." (*She has the straitjacket on him by this time.*) And then I would say, "Now stand up and let's see how it looks. Walk across the floor so we can see how it fits." (*She leads him to the sofa.*) And then I would say, "Now it's time to go to bed."

CAPTAIN: Bed? Go to bed when you've just dressed me? —Damn! Damn! What have you done to me! (*Struggles to get loose.*) Oh, you damned deceitful woman! Who would have thought you could be so clever! (*Lying down on the sofa.*) Captured, shorn, outwitted, and not even allowed to die!

MARGARET: Forgive me, Adolf, forgive me, but I couldn't let you kill the child.

CAPTAIN: Why did you not let me kill the child? Life on earth is hell and death is the kingdom of heaven, and the children belong to heaven.

MARGARET: What can you know of what comes after death?

CAPTAIN: That's all we do know. Of life we know nothing. Oh, if we had only known that from the beginning.

MARGARET: Adolf, bow your head, humble your proud heart, and call on God for mercy. It is still not too late. It was not too late for the thief on the cross when the Redeemer said, "Today shalt thou be with me in Paradise!"

CAPTAIN: What, croaking over the corpse already, you old crow!

Margaret takes her hymnbook from her apron pocket.

CAPTAIN (*calling*): Happy! Are you there, Happy? Orderly!

Happy enters.

CAPTAIN: Throw this woman out of here! She wants to suffocate me in the fumes of her psalms. Throw her out the window or up the chimney, wherever you damn please!

HAPPY (*looking at Margaret*): Lord, help me, Captain, really, I mean—I just can't. Honestly, I can't. Six guys, sure, but not a woman.

CAPTAIN: Can't manage one woman, is that what you mean?

HAPPY: Sure I can, but they're something special. I mean, you don't want to do violence to them.

CAPTAIN: Something special? Haven't they done violence to me?

HAPPY: I can't, sir, I mean—well, I can't, sir. It's just like you asking me to hit the pastor here, sir. It's something inside, like religion. I can't.

[7]

Laura enters and signals Happy to leave.

CAPTAIN: Omphale! Omphale! You play with his club while Hercules spins your wool.

LAURA (*crosses to the sofa*): Adolf, look at me. Do you think I am your enemy?

CAPTAIN: Yes, I do believe that. I believe that you are all my enemies. My mother, who didn't want me to come into this world because my birth would cause her pain; she was my enemy. She deprived my first cells of nourishment, stunting and crippling me before I was born. My sister was my enemy when she taught me to be meek and sweet to her. The first woman I made love to was my enemy for she gave me ten years of disease in exchange for the love I gave her. My daughter became my enemy when she had to choose between you and me. And you, my wife, are my mortal enemy, for you would not leave me until I had been cast down lifeless.

LAURA: I don't know that I have ever thought about or intended any of the things you imagine. Perhaps some dim desire to remove you as an obstacle ruled my actions at times. If you see some design in them, it's possible it was there, though I wasn't aware of it. I never laid any plans. Things merely rolled along the rails you yourself laid out. And before God and my conscience I feel that I am innocent, even if I am not. Your presence was like a stone weighing on my breast, pressing and hurting until I had to shake off the burden. That's how it was, and if I have struck you, as a reflex action, I ask you to forgive me.

CAPTAIN: Sounds plausible enough. But what good does it do me? And where does the blame lie? In modern marriage, perhaps, the marriage of minds. One used to marry a wife; now one goes into partnership with a career woman, or sets up housekeeping with a friend. After which one either copulates with the business partner or rapes the friend. What happened to love? Good, sound, carnal love? Died in the process of incorporation. And what about the offspring in this marriage corporation where no one assumes responsibility and love dividends are periodically payable to the stockholder? Who owns the assets when the crash comes? Who is the physical father to the spiritual child?

LAURA: Your suspicions about the child, Adolf—they're completely groundless.

CAPTAIN: That's just what's so terrible. If only there were some grounds for them, there would be something to hang on to—to take hold of. Now there are only goblins hiding in the bushes, sticking their heads out to laugh. It's just shadowboxing, a sham battle fought with blanks. Against something real and deadly one can fight with brain and brawn. But now my thoughts dissolve into nothingness: the grist is gone and my brain grinds on stone until it catches fire. Put a pillow under my head. And throw something over me. I'm freezing. I'm freezing to death.

Laura takes her shawl and spreads it out over him.

Margaret goes out for a pillow.

LAURA: Give me your hand as a friend.

CAPTAIN: My hand! Which you tied behind me. . . . Omphale, Omphale! I feel your soft shawl against my mouth—as warm and soft as your arm. It smells like vanilla, as your hair did when you were young. Laura, when you were young, and we walked among the birch trees—cowslips and thrushes—beautiful, heavenly! How beautiful life was—and look at it now. You didn't want it to be like this; I didn't want it; and still it got to be like this. Who is it makes our lives?

LAURA: God, only God—

CAPTAIN: The god of war, then! Or goddess nowadays. Take away this cat on my chest! Take it away!

Margaret comes in with the pillow; removes the shawl.

CAPTAIN: Give me my army coat. Throw it over me.

Margaret takes his army overcoat from the clothes tree and spreads it over him.

CAPTAIN: Ah, my hard lion skin that you wanted to take from me, Omphale, Omphale! What a cunning woman – the peace lover who invented disarmament. Awaken, Hercules, before they take your club from you! You want to cheat us of our armor, too, and have us believe it is only for show. No, lady, it was iron before it became tassels and braids. The blacksmith used to make the tunic, now it's the seamstress. Omphale, Omphale! Brute strength has fallen before wily weakness. I spit on you, you devil of a woman! To hell with your whole damned sex! (*He raises himself up to spit at her but falls back on the sofa.*) What kind of a pillow have you given me, Margaret? So hard and cold, so cold. Come and sit here on the chair, next to me. Like that, yes. Let me lay my head in your lap. There! . . . That's better. So warm. Lean over me so I can feel your breast. . . . How soft and lovely it is to sleep on a woman's bosom, a mother's or a mistress's, but loveliest a mother's.

LAURA: Do you want to see your child, Adolf? . . . Adolf, do you?

CAPTAIN: My child? A man has no children; only women have children. That's why the future can be theirs, since we die childless. . . . Now I lay me down to sleep, I –

MARGARET: Listen, he's praying to God.

CAPTAIN: No, to you, to lull me to sleep. I'm tired, so tired. . . . Goodnight, Margaret, and blessed be thou among women. (*He raises himself up but falls with a cry back into Margaret's lap.*)

[8]

Crossing to the left, Laura calls in Dr. Eastland, who enters with the Pastor.

LAURA: Help us, Doctor, if it's not too late! He's not breathing.

DR. EASTLAND (*taking the Captain's pulse*): He's had a stroke.

PASTOR: Is he dead?

DR. EASTLAND: No, he may still come to life, but to which life one cannot say.

PASTOR: "Once to die, but after this the judgment."

DR. EASTLAND: No judgment. And no incriminations. You who believe that a god governs our destinies can take the matter up with Him.

MARGARET: Pastor, he prayed to God in his last moment.

PASTOR (*to Laura*): Is that true?

LAURA: Yes, it's true.

DR. EASTLAND: If it is—and I can no more judge of that than of his illness—then my skills can do no more for him. Now try yours, Pastor.

LAURA: Is that all you can find to say at a man's deathbed, Doctor?

DR. EASTLAND: Yes, that's all. I know no more. Let him who knows more speak.

BERTHA (*entering from the left, running to her mother's arms*): Mother, Mother!

LAURA: My child! My own child!

PASTOR: Amen.

Introduction
to
Miss Julie

Through his study of psychology, Strindberg had come to believe that life in the modern age was basically a struggle of minds. Laura in *The Father* is physically weaker than her military husband, but she has a stronger will, and through her strength of will she overcomes brute force and moral scruples.

In presenting this "battle of brains" on stage, the set was relatively unimportant. All that was really needed to stage *The Father* was a table, two chairs, a lamp, and a straitjacket. Strindberg was quite proud of the classic simplicity he had achieved in this modern *Agamemnon* and thought his drama would please Emile Zola, the leader of the naturalistic movement in France, where Strindberg, now the declared enemy of the establishment in Sweden, increasingly placed his literary hopes. Zola had called for a new drama that would be grand, true, and simple, uncluttered with meaningless intrigues meant only to build suspense. Strindberg sent *The Father* to Zola and explained to him that in this play he sought to present "the interior action, dispensing with theatrical tricks, reducing the set decor to a minimum, and preserving the unity of time as far as possible" (29 August 1887). To Strindberg's surprise and disappointment, Zola found *The Father* too simple. He wanted less abstract characters, more description, and more explanation.

In his next play Strindberg took great pains to answer Zola's strictures. Zola's naturalism was predicated on the idea that the methods of physical science and experimental medicine, which had produced miracles in the nineteenth century, should be applied to literature. In practice this meant that characters and their actions should be explained in terms of heredity and environment. In writing *Miss Julie*, Strindberg carefully built up the backgrounds of the two principal characters and placed them in a realistically detailed set. Moreover, he saw to it that the environment, the kitchen, determines what happens to Miss Julie.

Strindberg's theatrical methods, spelled out in his preface, were the result of the success of André Antoine's Théâtre-Libre, which had opened in Paris in March 1887. Antoine had established his theater to give uncommercial and unconventional plays a chance to be seen. Because he began his theater on a gas-clerk's salary, expenses had to be held to a minimum. The actors in his productions were not skilled professionals, the theater he hired was comparatively small, and the sets were often extremely realistic (a real side of beef cost less than a painted one). The very amateurishness of his theater made it the perfect showcase for naturalistic plays.

Reading about its success, Strindberg wrote *Miss Julie* with that kind of theater in mind, a theater that would not cater to the tastes of the general public, that would allow the treatment of unusual, perhaps unsavory, subjects, and that would encourage subtlety in acting. Strindberg's preface to *Miss Julie* reveals the extent to which he was influenced by the Théâtre-Libre.

The preface was written after the play, and although it is undoubtedly the most important manifesto of naturalistic theater, it is remarkable less for its originality than for its comprehensiveness. Strindberg managed to find a place in it for everything that was new or controversial, whether in theater (Antoine), literature (Zola), painting (the impressionists), biology (Darwin), psychology (Ribot, Bernheim), sociology (feminism), politics (the rise of the lower classes), or philosophy (Nietzsche). Fundamental to the play is the Darwinian theory of evolution, which had become the central concern of nineteenth-century intellectual life because it undermined religious faith and pointed to ethical relativism and a world without values. The outcome of the struggle between servant and mistress in the play is an instance of the survival of the fittest. In both the sexual conflict and the class conflict the servant comes out on top.

To keep the plot simple, Strindberg had to find a substitute for the complications that furnished action and suspense in conventional drama. He built his play out of symbols and parallelisms. The songbird and the dog that has got itself pregnant obviously represent aspects of Miss Julie, and the ever-present boots stand for her father. Jean's dream counterbalances Julie's, and Jean's story of how he was caught in the gentry's privy when he was a child becomes the paradigm for Julie's situation in the play itself. She is trapped in the servant's quarters, and also trapped by her own uncontrollable desires. Jean as a child had been forced to crawl through excrement; now the trapped Julie begs Jean to "lift me out of this awful filth I'm sinking in." By such means Strindberg imposes meaning and order on the naturalistic details.

The ending has given actresses and audiences a great deal of trouble, more than it gave Strindberg, who had an actual case in mind. It was clear that Julie had to die, and the manner of her death was determined by what happened to a woman writer who, like Julie, was unhappy in love.

There are motives enough for Julie's suicide. She is bound by the aristocratic code of honor, and she is extremely wrought up by the events of the day. More important, she is filled with shame and self-loathing and knows that she will repeat the episode, knows that, if not today, then tomorrow, she will again seek to degrade herself. By taking her own life, she regains some dignity and claims our sympathy.

The precise manner of her suicide was suggested to Strindberg by the death of the Swedish writer Victoria Benedictsson, a married woman who wrote under the pseudonym Ernst Ahlgren. She was trying to win a place for herself among Scandinavian writers with her realistic short stories, and she had hoped to form an alliance, literary and sexual, with the famous critic Georg Brandes. Strindberg had gotten to know her when he stayed at her hotel in the winter of 1887-88. In January, Victoria, despondent about her career and convinced that Brandes neither respected her as a writer nor loved her as a person, feeling that she was "only a little planet that had come too close to a bigger one," decided to kill herself by taking an overdose of morphine. She confided in her comrade Axel Lundegård, who had collaborated with Strindberg on a play called *Comrades*. Lundegård watched Victoria take the morphine and then, told to leave, he went to Strindberg's room, woke him up, and confided in him. He would always remember Strindberg's response. "He listened," said Lundegård, "with an expression of implacable, cannibal-like interest without the slightest trace of human compassion." Perhaps his interest was not purely that of the objective artist; his own desperate position had often led him to think of killing himself, how seriously it is hard to say, given as he was to self-dramatization.

Victoria Benedictsson did not die on that night. Months later, in July 1888, she made another attempt, this time using a razor. Only after slashing her throat several times did she succeed. Shortly after he heard the news, Strindberg started to write *Miss Julie*. In the meantime, he had learned more about Victoria Benedictsson. Julie blames her neurotic disposition and her unhealthy and self-destructive sexual desires on her upbringing. Victoria's childhood had been much like Julie's.*

The present translation follows the latest scholarly edition of *Fröken Julie*, edited by Gunnar Ollén and printed in *August Strindbergs Samlade Verk*, vol. 27 (Uppsala, 1984). I have also consulted the excellent commentary and critical apparatus in Carl Reinhold Smedmark's edition, *August Strindbergs dramer*, vol. 3 (Stockholm, 1964).

* For more on Victoria Benedictsson, see Evert Sprinchorn, "Ibsen and the Immoralists," in *Comparative Literature Studies*, vol. 9, no. 1 (March 1972), pp. 58–79.

Miss Julie

(Fröken Julie)

A Naturalistic Tragedy
with a preface by the author

Preface

Like the arts in general, the theater has for a long time seemed to me a *Biblia Pauperum*, a picture Bible for those who cannot read, and the playwright merely a lay preacher who hawks the latest ideals in popular form, so popular that the middle classes — the bulk of the audiences — can grasp them without racking their brains too much. That explains why the theater has always been an elementary school for youngsters and the half-educated, and for women, who still retain a primitive capacity for deceiving themselves and for letting themselves be deceived, that is, for succumbing to illusions and responding hypnotically to the suggestions of the author. Consequently, now that the rudimentary and undeveloped mental processes that operate in the realm of fantasy appear to be evolving to the level of reflection, research, and experimentation, I believe that the theater, like religion, is about to be replaced as a dying institution for whose enjoyment we lack the necessary qualifications. Support for my view is provided by the theater crisis through which all of Europe is now passing, and still more by the fact that in those highly cultured lands which have produced the finest minds of our time — England and Germany — the drama is dead, as for the most part are the other fine arts.

Other countries, however, have thought to create a new drama by filling the old forms with new contents. But since there has not been enough time to popularize the new ideas, the public cannot understand them. And in the second place, controversy has so stirred up the public that they can no longer look on with a pure and dispassionate interest, especially when they see their most cherished ideals assailed or hear an applauding or booing majority openly exercise its tyrannical power, as can happen in the theater. And in the third place, since the new forms for the new ideas have not been created, the new wine has burst the old bottles.

In the play that follows I have not tried to accomplish anything new — that is impossible. I have only tried to modernize the form to satisfy what I believe up-to-date people expect and demand of this art. And with that in mind I have seized upon – or let myself be seized by – a theme that may be said to lie outside current party strife, since the question of being on the way up or on the way down the social ladder, of being on the top or on the bottom, superior or inferior, man or woman, is, has been, and will be of perennial interest. When I took this theme from real life – I heard about it a few years ago and it made a deep impression on me – I thought it would be a suitable subject for a tragedy, since it still strikes us as tragic to see a happily favored individual go down in defeat, and even more so to see an entire family line die out. But perhaps a time will come when we shall be so highly developed and so enlightened that we can look with indifference upon the brutal, cynical, and heartless spectacle that life offers us, a time when we shall have laid aside those inferior and unreliable mechanical apparatuses called emotions, which will become superfluous and even harmful as our mental organs develop. The fact that my heroine wins sympathy is due entirely to the fact that we are still too weak to overcome the fear that the same fate might overtake us. The extremely sensitive viewer will of course not be satisfied with mere expressions of sympathy, and the man who believes in progress will demand that certain positive actions be taken for getting rid of the evil, a kind of program, in other words. But in the first place absolute evil does not exist. The decline of one family is the making of another, which now gets its chance to rise. This alternate rising and falling provides one of life's greatest pleasures, for happiness is, after all, relative. As for the man who has a program for changing the disagreeable circumstance that the hawk eats the chicken and that lice eat up the hawk, I should like to ask him why it should be changed. Life is not prearranged with such idiotic mathematical precision that only the larger gets to eat the smaller. Just as frequently the bee destroys the lion (in Aesop's fable) – or at least drives him wild.

If my tragedy makes most people feel sad, that is their fault. When we get to be as strong as the first French Revolutionists were, we shall be perfectly content and happy to watch the forests being cleared of rotting, superannuated trees that have stood too long in the way of others with just as much right to grow and flourish for a while – as content as we are when we see an incurably ill man finally die.

Recently my tragedy *The Father* was censured for being too
unpleasant—as if one wanted merry tragedies. "The joy of life"
is now the slogan of the day. Theater managers send out orders
for nothing but farces, as if the joy of living lay in behaving like
a clown and in depicting people as if they were afflicted with St.
Vitus's dance or congenital idiocy. I find the joy of living in the
fierce and ruthless battles of life, and my pleasure comes from
learning something, from being taught something. That is why
I have chosen for my play an unusual but instructive case, an
exception, in other words—but an important exception of the
kind that proves the rule—a choice of subject that I know will
offend all lovers of the conventional. The next thing that will
bother simple minds is that the motivation for the action is not
simple and that the point of view is not single. Usually an event
in life—and this is a fairly new discovery—is the result of a whole
series of more or less deep-rooted causes. The spectator, however, generally chooses the one that puts the least strain on his
mind or reflects most credit on his insight. Consider a case of
suicide. "Business failure," says the merchant. "Unhappy love,"
say the women. "Physical illness," says the sick man. "Lost
hopes," says the down-and-out. But it may be that the reason lay
in all of these or in none of them, and that the suicide hid his
real reason behind a completely different one that would reflect
greater glory on his memory.

I have motivated the tragic fate of Miss Julie with an abun-
dance of circumstances: her mother's basic instincts, her father's
improper bringing-up of the girl, her own inborn nature, and her
fiancé's sway over her weak and degenerate mind. Further and
more immediately: the festive atmosphere of Midsummer Eve,
her father's absence, her period, her preoccupation with animals,
the erotic excitement of the dance, the long summer twilight, the
highly aphrodisiac influence of flowers, and finally chance itself,
which drives two people together in an out-of-the-way room, plus
the boldness of the aroused man.

As one can see, I have not been entirely the physiologist, not
been obsessively psychological, not traced everything to her
mother's heredity, not found the sole cause in her period, not
attributed everything to our "immoral times," and not simply
preached a moral lesson. Lacking a priest, I have let the cook
handle that.

I am proud to say that this complicated way of looking at things is in tune with the times. And if others have anticipated me in this, I am proud that I am not alone in my paradoxes, as all new discoveries are called. And no one can say this time that I am being one-sided.

As far as the drawing of characters is concerned, I have made the people in my play fairly "characterless" for the following reasons. In the course of time the word *character* has acquired many meanings. Originally it probably meant the dominant and fundamental trait in the soul complex and was confused with temperament. Later the middle class used it to mean an automaton. An individual who once for all had found his own true nature or adapted himself to a certain role in life, who in fact had ceased to grow, was called a man of character, while the man who was constantly developing, who, like a skillful sailor on the currents of life, did not sail with close-tied sheets but who fell off before the wind in order to luff again, was called a man of no character—derogatorily of course, since he was so difficult to keep track of, to pin down and pigeonhole. This middle-class conception of a fixed character was transferred to the stage, where the middle class has always ruled. A character there came to mean someone who was always one and the same, always drunk, always joking, always melancholy, and who needed to be characterized only by some physical defect such as a club foot, a wooden leg, or a red nose, or by the repetition of some such phrase as, "That's capital," or "Barkis is willin'." This uncomplicated way of viewing people is still to be found in the great Molière. Harpagon is nothing but a miser, although Harpagon could have been both a miser and an exceptional financier, a fine father, and a good citizen. Worse still, his "defect"is extremely advantageous to his son-in-law and his daughter who will be his heirs and who therefore should not find fault with him, even if they do have to wait a while to jump into bed together. So I do not believe in simple stage characters. And the summary judgments that writers pass on people—he is stupid, this one is brutal, that one is jealous, this one is stingy, and so on—should not pass unchallenged by the naturalists who know how complicated the soul is and who realize that vice has a reverse side very much like virtue.

Since the persons in my play are modern characters, living in a transitional era more hectic and hysterical than the previous one at least, I have depicted them as more unstable, as torn and divided, a mixture of the old and the new. Nor does it seem improbable to me that modern ideas might also have seeped down through newspapers and kitchen talk to the level of the servants. Consequently the valet may belch forth from his inherited slave soul certain modern ideas. And if there are those who find it wrong to allow people in a modern drama to talk Darwin and who recommend the practice of Shakepeare to our attention, may I remind them that the gravedigger in *Hamlet* talks the then fashionable philosophy of Giordano Bruno (Bacon's philosophy), which is even more improbable, seeing that the means of spreading ideas were fewer then than now. And besides, the fact of the matter is that Darwinism has always existed, ever since Moses' history of creation from the lower animals up to man, but it was not until recently that we discovered it and formulized it.

My souls — or characters — are conglomerations from various stages of culture, past and present, walking scrapbooks, shreds of human lives, tatters torn from old rags that were once Sunday best — hodgepodges just like the human soul. I have even supplied a little source history into the bargain by letting the weaker steal and repeat words of the stronger, letting them get ideas (suggestions as they are called) from one another, from the environment (the songbird's blood), and from objects (the razor). I have also arranged for *Gedankenübertragung** through an inanimate medium to take place (the count's boots, the servant's bell). And I have even made use of "waking suggestions" (a variation of hypnotic suggestion), which have by now been so popularized that they cannot arouse ridicule or skepticism as they would have done in Mesmer's time.

I say Miss Julie is a modern character not because the man-hating half-woman has not always existed but because she has now been brought out into the open, has taken the stage, and is making a noise about herself. Victim of a superstition (one that has seized even stronger minds) that woman, that stunted form of human being, standing with man, the lord of creation, the creator of culture, is meant to be the equal of man or could ever

* Telepathy

possibly be, she involves herself in an absurd struggle with him in which she falls. Absurd because a stunted form, subject to the laws of propagation, will always be born stunted and can never catch up with the one who has the lead. As follows: A (the man) and B (the woman) start from the same point C, A with a speed of let us say 100 and B with a speed of 60. When will B overtake A? Answer: never. Neither with the help of equal education or equal voting rights — nor by universal disarmament and temperance societies — any more than two parallel lines can ever meet. The half-woman is a type that forces itself on others, selling itself for power, medals, recognition, diplomas, as formerly it sold itself for money. It represents degeneration. It is not a strong species for it does not maintain itself, but unfortunately it propagates its misery in the following generation. Degenerate men unconsciously select their mates from among these half-women, so that they breed and spread, producing creatures of indeterminate sex to whom life is a torture, but who fortunately are overcome eventually either by a hostile reality, or by the uncontrolled breaking loose of their repressed instincts, or else by their frustration in not being able to compete with the male sex. It is a tragic type, offering us the spectacle of a desperate fight against nature; a tragic legacy of romanticism, which is now being dissipated by naturalism — a movement that seeks only happiness, and for that strong and healthy species are required.

Miss Julie, however, is also a vestige of the old warrior nobility that is now being superseded by a new nobility of nerve and brain. She is a victim of the disorder produced within a family by a mother's "crime," of the mistakes of a whole generation gone wrong, of circumstances, of her own defective constitution — all of which put together is equivalent to the fate or universal law of the ancients. The naturalists have banished guilt along with God, but the consequences of an act — punishment, imprisonment, or the fear of it — cannot be banished for the simple reason that they remain whether or not the naturalist dismisses the case from his court. Those sitting on the sidelines can easily afford to be lenient; but what of the injured parties? And even if her father were compelled to forgo taking his revenge, Miss Julie would take vengeance on herself, as she does in the play, because of that inherited or acquired sense of honor that has been transmitted to the upper classes from — well, where does it come from? From the age of barbarism, from the first Aryans, from the chivalry of the Middle Ages. And a very fine code it was, but now inimical to the survival of the race. It is the aristocrat's form of hara-kiri, a law of conscience that bids the Japanese to slice his own stomach when someone else dishonors him. The same sort of thing survives, slightly modified, in that exclusive prerogative of the aristocracy, the duel. (Example: the husband challenges his wife's lover to a duel; the lover shoots the husband and runs off with the wife. Result: the husband has saved his *honor* but lost his wife.) Hence the servant Jean lives on; but not Miss Julie, who cannot live without honor. The advantage that the slave has over his master is that he has not committed himself to this defeatist principle. In all of us Aryans there is enough of the nobleman, or of the Don Quixote, to make us sympathize with the man who takes his own life after having dishonored himself by shameful deeds. And we are all of us aristocrats enough to be distressed at the sight of a great man lying like a dead hulk ready for the scrap pile, even, I suppose, if he were to raise himself up again and redeem himself by honorable deeds.

The servant Jean is the beginning of a new species in which noticeable differentiation has already taken place. He began as a child of a poor worker and is now evolving through self-education into a future gentleman of the upper classes. He is quick to learn, has highly developed senses (smell, taste, sight), and a keen appreciation of beauty. He has already come up in the world, for he is strong enough not to hesitate to make use of other people. He is already a stranger to his old friends, whom he despises as reminders of past stages in his development, and whom he fears and avoids because they know his secrets, guess his intentions, look with envy on his rise and with joyful expectation toward his fall. Hence his character is unformed and divided. He wavers between an admiration of high positions and a hatred of the men who occupy them. He is an aristocrat—he says so himself—familiar with the ins and outs of good society. He is polished on the outside, but coarse underneath. He wears his frock coat with elegance but offers no guarantee that he keeps his body clean.

Although he respects Miss Julie, he is afraid of Christine, because she knows his innermost secrets. Yet he is sufficiently hard-hearted not to let the events of the night upset his plans for the future. Possessing both the coarseness of the slave and the toughmindedness of the born ruler, he can look at blood without fainting, shake off bad luck like water, and take calamity by the horns. Consequently he will escape from the battle unwounded, probably ending up as proprietor of a hotel. And if he himself does not get to be a Rumanian count, his son will doubtless go to college and possibly end up as a government official.

Now his observations about life as the lower classes see it, from below, are well worth listening to—that is, they are whenever he is telling the truth, which is not too often, because he is more likely to say what is advantageous to him than what is true. When Miss Julie supposes that everyone in the lower classes must feel greatly oppressed by the weight of the classes above, Jean naturally agrees with her since he wants to win her sympathy. But he promptly takes it all back when he finds it expedient to separate himself from the mob.

Apart from the fact that Jean is coming up in the world, he is also superior to Miss Julie in that he is a man. In the sexual sphere, he is the aristocrat. He has the strength of the male, more highly developed senses, and the ability to take the initiative. His inferiority is merely the result of his social environment, which is only temporary and which he will probably slough off along with his livery.

His slave nature expresses itself in his awe of the count (the boots) and his religious superstitions. But he is awed by the count mainly because the count occupies the place he wants most in life; and this awe is still there even after he has won the daughter of the house and seen how empty that beautiful shell was.

I do not believe that any love in the "higher" sense can be born from the union of two such different souls; so I have let Miss Julie's love be refashioned in her imagination as a love that protects and purifies, and I have let Jean imagine that even his love might have a chance to grow under other social circumstances. For I suppose love is very much like the hyacinth that must strike roots deep in the dark earth *before* it can produce a vigorous blossom. Here it shoots up, bursts into bloom, and turns to seed all at once. Such plants can only be short-lived.

Christine—finally to get to her—is a female slave, spineless and phlegmatic after years spent at the kitchen stove, bovinely unconscious of her own hypocrisy, and with a full quota of moral and religious notions that serve as scapegoats and cloaks for her sins—which a stronger soul does not require since he is able either to carry the burden of his own sins or to rationalize them out of existence. She attends church regularly where she deftly unloads unto Jesus her household thefts and picks up from him another load of innocence. She is only a secondary character, and I have deliberately done no more than sketch her in—just as I treated the country doctor and parish priest in *The Father* where I only wanted to draw ordinary everyday people such as most country doctors and parsons are. That some have found my minor characters one-dimensional is due to the fact that ordinary people while at work are to a certain extent one-dimensional and do lack an independent existence, showing only one side of themselves in the performance of their duties. And as long as the audience does not feel it needs to see them from different angles, my abstract sketches will pass muster.

Now as far as the dialogue is concerned, I have broken somewhat with tradition in refusing to make my characters into interlocutors who ask stupid questions to elicit witty answers. I have avoided the symmetrical and mathematical design of the artfully constructed French dialogue and have let minds work as irregularly as they do in real life, where no subject is quite exhausted before another mind engages at random some cog in the conversation and governs it for a while. My dialogue wanders here and there, gathers material in the first scenes which is later picked up, repeated, reworked, developed, and expanded like the theme in a piece of music.

The action of the play poses no problem. Since it really involves only two people, I have limited myself to these two, introducing only one minor character, the cook, and keeping the unhappy spirit of the father brooding over the action as a whole. I have chosen this course because I have noticed that what interests people most nowadays is the psychological action. Our inveterately curious souls are no longer content to see a thing happen; we want to see how it happens. We want to see the strings, look at the machinery, examine the double-bottom drawer, put on the magic ring to find the hidden seam, look in the deck for the marked cards.

In treating the subject this way I have had in mind the case-

history novels of the Goncourt brothers, which appeal to me
more than anything else in modern literature.

As far as play construction is concerned, I have made a stab
at getting rid of act divisions. I was afraid that the spectator's
declining susceptibility to illusion might not carry him through
the intermission, when he would have time to think about what
he has seen and to escape the suggestive influence of the author-
hypnotist. I figure my play lasts about ninety minutes. Since one
can listen to a lecture, a sermon, or a political debate for that long
or even longer, I have convinced myself that a play should not
exhaust an audience in that length of time. As early as 1872 in
one of my first attempts at the drama, *The Outlaw*, I tried out this
concentrated form, although with little success. I had finished the
work in five acts when I noticed the disjointed and disturbing
effect it produced. I burned it, and from the ashes there arose a
single, complete reworked act of fifty pages that would run for
less than an hour. Although this play form is not completely new,
it seems to be my special property and has a good chance of gain-
ing favor with the public when tastes change. My hope is to educate a public to sit through a full evening's show in one act. But
this whole question must first be probed more deeply. In the
meantime, in order to establish resting places for the audience
and the actors without destroying the illusion, I have made use
of three arts that belong to the drama: the monologue, the pantomime, and the ballet, all of which were part of classic tragedy,
the monody having become the monologue and the choral dance,
the ballet.

The realists have banished the monologue from the stage as
implausible. But if I can motivate it, I make it plausible, and I
can then use it to my advantage. Now it is certainly plausible for
a speaker to pace the floor and read his speech aloud to himself.
It is plausible for an actor to practice his part aloud, for a child
to talk to her cat, a mother to babble to her baby, an old lady to
chatter to her parrot, and a sleeping man to talk in his sleep. And
in order to give the actor a chance to work on his own for once
and for a moment not be obliged to follow the author's directions,
I have not written out the monologues in detail but simply out-
lined them. Since it makes very little difference what is said while
asleep, or to the parrot or the cat, inasmuch as it does not affect
the main action, a gifted player who is in the midst of the situa-

tion and mood of the play can probably improvise the monologue
better than the author, who cannot estimate ahead of time how
much may be said and for how long before the illusion is broken.

Some theaters in Italy have, as we know, returned to the art
of improvisation and have thereby trained actors who are truly
inventive—without, however, violating the intentions of the
author. This seems to be a step in the right direction and possibly
the beginning of a new, fertile form of art that will be genuinely
creative.

In places where the monologue cannot be properly motivated,
I have resorted to pantomime. Here I have given the actor even
more freedom to be creative and win honor on his own. Nevertheless, not to try the audience beyond its limits, I have relied on
music—well motivated by the Midsummer Eve dance—to exercise its hypnotic powers during the pantomime scene. I beg the
music director to select his tunes with great care, so that associations foreign to the mood of the play will not be produced by
reminders of popular operettas or current dance numbers or by
folk music of interest only to ethnologists.

The ballet that I have introduced cannot be replaced by a so-
called crowd scene. Such scenes are always badly acted, with a
pack of babbling fools taking advantage of the occasion to "gag
it up," thereby destroying the illusion. Inasmuch as country
people do not improvise their taunts but make use of material
already to hand by giving it a double meaning, I have not composed an original lampoon but have made use of a little known
round dance that I noted down in the Stockholm district. The
words do not fit the situation exactly, which is what I intended,
since the slave in his cunning (that is, weakness) never attacks
directly. At any rate, let us have no comedians in this serious
story and no obscene smirking over an affair that nails the lid on
a family coffin.

As far as the scenery is concerned, I have borrowed from
impressionistic painting the idea of asymmetrical and open
composition, and I believe that I have thereby gained something
in the way of greater illusion. Because the audience cannot see
the whole room and all the furniture, they will have to surmise
what's missing; that is, their imagination will be stimulated to fill
in the rest of the picture. I have gained something else by this:
I have avoided those tiresome exits through doors. Stage doors

are made of canvas and rock at the slightest touch. They cannot even be used to indicate the wrath of an angry father who storms out of the house after a bad dinner, slamming the door behind him "so that the whole house shakes." (In the theater it sways and billows.) Furthermore, I have confined the action to one set, both to give the characters a chance to become part and parcel of their environment and to cut down on scenic extravagance. If there is only one set, one has a right to expect it to be as realistic as possible. Yet nothing is more difficult than to make a room look like a room, however easy it may be for the scene painter to create waterfalls and erupting volcanos. I suppose we shall have to put up with walls made of canvas, but isn't it about time that we stopped painting shelves and pots and pans on the canvas? There are so many other conventions in the theater that we are told to accept in good faith that we should be spared the strain of believing in painted saucepans.

I have placed the backdrop and the table at an angle to force the actors to play face to face or in half profile when they are seated opposite each other at the table. In a production of *Aida* I saw a flat placed at such an angle, which led the eye out in an unfamiliar perspective. Nor did it look as if it had been set that way simply to be different or to avoid those monotonous right angles.

Another desirable innovation would be the removal of the footlights. I understand that the purpose of lighting from below is to make the actors look more full in the face. But may I ask why all actors should have full faces? Doesn't this kind of lighting wipe out many of the finer features in the lower part of the face, especially around the jaws? Doesn't it distort the shape of the nose and throw false shadows above the eyes? If not, it certainly does something else: it hurts the actor's eyes. The footlights hit the retina at an angle from which it is usually shielded (except in sailors who must look at the sunlight reflected in the water), and the result is the loss of any effective play of the eyes. All one ever sees on stage are goggle-eyed glances sideways at the boxes or upward at the balcony, with only the whites of the eyes being visible in the latter case. And this probably also accounts for that tiresome fluttering of the eyelashes that the female performers are particularly guilty of. If an actor nowadays wants to express something with his eyes, he can only do it looking right at the audience, in which case he makes direct contact with someone outside the proscenium arch—a bad habit known, justifiably or not, as "saying hello to friends."*

I should think that the use of sufficiently strong side lights (through the use of reflectors or something like them) would provide the actor with a new asset: an increased range of expression made possible by the play of the eyes, the most expressive part of the face.

I have scarcely any illusions about getting actors to play for the audience and not directly at them, although this should be the goal. Nor do I dream of ever seeing an actor play through all of an important scene with his back to the audience. But is it too much to hope that crucial scenes could be played where the author indicated and not in front of the prompter's box as if they were duets demanding applause? I am not calling for a revolution, only for some small changes. I am well aware that transforming the stage into a real room with the fourth wall missing and with some of the furniture placed with backs to the auditorium would only upset the audience, at least for the present.

If I bring up the subject of make-up, it is not because I dare hope to be heeded by the ladies, who would rather be beautiful than truthful. But the male actor might do well to consider if it is an advantage to paint his face with character lines that remain there like a mask. Let us imagine an actor who pencils in with soot a few lines between his eyes to indicate great anger, and let us suppose that in that permanently enraged state he finds he has to smile on a certain line. Imagine the horrible grimace! And how can the old character actor wrinkle his brows in anger when his false bald pate is as smooth as a billiard ball?

In a modern psychological drama, in which every tremor of the soul should be reflected more by facial expressions than by gestures and grunts, it would probably be most sensible to experiment with strong side lighting on a small stage, using actors without any make-up or a minimum of it.

And then, if we could get rid of the visible orchestra with its disturbing lights and the faces turned toward the public; if the auditorium floor could be raised so that the spectator's eyes are

* "Counting the house" would be the equivalent in American theater slang. — Trans.

not level with the actor's knees; if we could get rid of the proscenium boxes and their occupants, arriving giggling and drunk from their dinners; and if we could have it dark in the auditorium during the performance; and if, above everything else, we could have a *small* stage and an *intimate* auditorium—then possibly a new drama might arise and at least one theater become a refuge for cultured audiences. While we are waiting for such a theater, we shall have to write for the dramatic stockpile and prepare the repertory that one day shall come.

Here is my attempt. If I have failed, there is still time to try again!

CHARACTERS

MISS JULIE,* twenty-five years old
JEAN, valet, thirty years old
CHRISTINE, cook, thirty-five years old
THE CHORUS, a party of country folk

The scene is a country estate in Sweden.

The time: A Midsummer Night in the 1880s. The hours after midnight, June 24, St. John the Baptist's Day.

* Julie is not a countess; she is the daughter of a count. Her title "fröken" corresponds to the German "Fräulein" and the French "mademoiselle."

THE SET

The scene is the kitchen of the estate belonging to the count, Miss Julie's father. It is a large kitchen, situated along with the servants' quarters in the basement of the manor house. The side walls and the ceiling of the kitchen are masked by the tormentors and borders of the set. The rear wall runs obliquely upstage from the left. On this wall to the left are two shelves with pots and pans of copper, iron, and pewter. The shelves are decorated with goffered paper. A little to the right can be seen three-fourths of a deep arched entry with two glass doors, and through them can be seen a fountain with a statue of a cupid, lilac bushes in bloom, and the tops of some Lombardy poplars.

From the left of the stage the corner of a large, Dutch-tile kitchen stove protrudes with part of the hood showing.

Projecting from the right side of the stage is one end of the servants' dining table of white pine, with a few chairs around it.

The stove is decorated with branches of birch leaves; the floor is strewn with juniper twigs.

On the end of the table is a large Japanese spice jar filled with lilacs.

An icebox, a sink, a washbasin.

Over the door a big old-fashioned bell; and to the left of the door the gaping mouth of a speaking tube.

* * *

Christine is standing at the stove, frying something in a pan. She is wearing a light-colored cotton dress and an apron.

Jean enters, dressed in livery and carrying a pair of high-top boots with spurs. He sets them where they are clearly visible.

JEAN: What a night! She's wild again! Miss Julie's absolutely wild!

CHRISTINE: You sure took your time getting back!

JEAN: I took the count down to the station, and on my way back, I passed the barn and went in for a dance. And there was Miss Julie leading the dance with the game warden. Then she noticed me. And she ran right into my arms and chose me for the ladies' waltz. And she's been dancing ever since like—like I don't know what. Wild, I tell you, absolutely wild!

CHRISTINE: That's nothing new. But she's been worse than ever during the last two weeks, ever since her engagement was broken off.

JEAN: Yes. I never did hear all there was to that. He was a good man, too, even if he wasn't rich. Well, they've got such crazy ideas/(*He sits down at the end of the table.*) Tell me, isn't it strange that a young girl like her—all right, young woman—prefers to stay home here with the servants rather than go with her father to visit her relatives?

CHRISTINE: I suppose she's ashamed to face them after that fiasco with her young man.

JEAN: No doubt. He wouldn't take any nonsense from her. Do you know what happened, Christine? I saw the whole thing. Of course, I didn't let on.

CHRISTINE: You were there? I don't believe it.

JEAN: Well, I was. They were in the stable yard one evening— and she was training him, that's what she called it. Do you know what? She was making him jump over her riding whip—training him like a dog. He jumped over twice, and she whipped him both times. But the third time, he grabbed the whip from her, [scratched her face with it—long scratch on her left cheek;]* then broke it in a thousand pieces—and walked off.

*The passage in brackets was deleted in Strindberg's manuscript, probably by Strindberg himself.

CHRISTINE: I don't believe it! What do you know!

JEAN: Yes, that put an end to that affair. —What have you got for me that's really good, Christine?

CHRISTINE (*serving him from the frying pan*): Just a little bit of kidney. Cut it from the veal roast.

JEAN (*smelling it*): Wonderful! One my special *délices* (*Feeling the plate.*) Hey, you didn't warm the plate!

CHRISTINE: You're more fussy than the count himself when you set your mind to it. (*She rumples his hair affectionately.*)

JEAN (*irritated*): Cut it out! Don't muss up my hair. You know how particular I am!

raising
above.
Christine

CHRISTINE: Oh, don't get mad. Can I help it if I like you?

Jean eats. Christine gets out a bottle of beer.

JEAN: Beer on Midsummer Eve! No thank you! I've got something much better than that. (*He opens a drawer in the table and takes out a bottle of red wine with a gold seal.*) Do you see that? Gold Seal. Now give me a glass.

She hands him a tumbler.

—No, a wineglass of course. This has to be drunk properly. No water.

CHRISTINE (*goes back to the stove and puts on a small saucepan*): Lord help the woman who gets you for a husband. You're an old fussbudget!

JEAN: Talk, talk! You'd consider yourself lucky if you got yourself a man as good as me. It hasn't done you any harm to have people think I'm your fiancé. (*He tastes the wine.*) Very good. Excellent. But warmed just a little too little. (*Warming the glass in his hands.*) We bought this in Dijon. Four francs a liter, unbottled—and the tax on top of that. . . . What on earth are you cooking? It stinks like hell!

CHRISTINE: Some damn mess that Miss Julie wants for her Diana, that damn dog of hers.

JEAN: You should watch your language, Christine. . . . Why do you have to stand in front of the stove on a holiday, cooking for that mutt? Is it sick?

CHRISTINE: Oh, she's sick, all right! She sneaked out to the gatekeeper's pug and—got herself in a fix. And you know Miss Julie, she can't stand anything like that.

JEAN: She's too stuck-up in some ways and not proud enough in others. Just like her mother. The countess felt right at home in the kitchen or down in the barn with the cows, but when she went driving, one horse wasn't enough for her, she had to have a pair. Her sleeves were always dirty, but her buttons had the royal crown on them. As for Miss Julie, she doesn't give a hoot in hell how she looks and acts. I mean, she's not really refined, not really. Just now, down at the barn, she grabbed the game warden right from under Anna's eyes and asked him to dance. You wouldn't see anybody in our class behaving like that. But that's what happens when the gentry try to act like the common people—they become common! . . . However, I'll say one thing for her: she *is* beautiful! Statuesque! Ah, those shoulders—those—and so forth, and so forth!

CHRISTINE: Oh, don't exaggerate. Clara tells me all about her, and Clara dresses her.

JEAN: Clara, pooh! You women are always jealous of each other. I've been out riding with her. . . . And how she can dance . . . !

CHRISTINE: Listen, Jean, you *are* going to dance with me, aren't you, when I'm finished here?

JEAN: Certainly! Of course I am.

CHRISTINE: Promise?

JEAN: Promise! Listen if I say I'm going to do a thing, I do it. . . . Christine, I thank you for a delicious meal. Superb! (*He shoves the cork back into the bottle.*)

> *Miss Julie appears in the entry, talking to someone outside.*

MISS JULIE: I'll be right back. Don't wait for me.

> *Jean slips the bottle into the table drawer quickly and rises respectfully. Miss Julie comes in and crosses over to Christine, who is at the stove.*

MISS JULIE: Did you get it ready?

> *Christine signals that Jean is present.*

JEAN (*polite and charming*): Are you ladies sharing secrets?

MISS JULIE (*flipping her handkerchief in his face*): Don't be nosy!

JEAN: Oh, that smells good! Violets.

MISS JULIE (*flirting with him*): Don't be impudent! And don't tell me you're an expert on perfumes, too. I love the way you dance!–No, mustn't look! Go away!

JEAN (*cocky but pleasant*): What are the ladies cooking up? A witches' brew for Midsummer Eve? So they can tell the future? Read what's in the cards for them, and see who they'll marry?

MISS JULIE (*curtly*): You'd have to have good eyes to see that. (*To Christine.*) Pour it into a small bottle, and seal it tight. . . . Jean, come and dance a schottische with me.

JEAN (*hesitating*): I hope you don't think I'm being rude, but I've already promised this dance to Christine.

MISS JULIE: She can always find someone. Isn't that so, Christine? You don't mind if I borrow Jean for a minute, do you?

CHRISTINE: It ain't up to me. If Miss Julie is gracious enough to invite you, it ain't right for you to say no, Jean. You go on, and thank her for the honor.

JEAN: Frankly, Miss Julie, I don't want to hurt your feelings, but I wonder if it's wise–I mean for you to dance twice in a row with the same partner. Especially since the people around here love to talk.

MISS JULIE (*bridling*): What do you mean? What kind of talk? What are you trying to say?

JEAN (*retreating*): I wish you wouldn't misunderstand me, Miss Julie. It just doesn't look right for you to prefer one of your servants to the others who are hoping for the same unusual honor.

MISS JULIE: Prefer! What an idea! I'm really surprised. I, the mistress of the house, am good enough to come to their dance, and when I feel like dancing, I want to dance with someone who knows how to lead. After all I don't want to look ridiculous.

JEAN: As you wish, Miss Julie. I am at your orders.

MISS JULIE (*gently*): Don't take it as an order. Tonight we're all just having a good time. There's no question of rank. Now give me your arm. —Don't worry, Christine. I won't run off with your boyfriend.

Jean gives her his arm and leads her out.

★ ★ ★

PANTOMIME SCENE

This should be played as if the actress were actually alone. She turns her back on the audience when she feels like it; she does not look out into the auditorium; she does not rush through the scene as if afraid the audience will grow impatient.

Christine alone. In the distance the sound of the violins playing the schottische. Christine, humming in time with the music, cleans up after Jean, washes the dishes, dries them, and puts them away in a cupboard. Then she takes off her apron, takes a little mirror from one of the table drawers, and leans it against the jar of lilacs on the table. She lights a tallow candle, heats a curling iron, and curls the bangs on her forehead. Then she goes to the doorway and stands listening to the music. She comes back to the table and finds the handkerchief that Miss Julie left behind. She smells it, spreads it out, and then, as if lost in thought, stretches it, smooths it out, and folds it in four.

★   ★   ★

Jean enters alone.

JEAN: Wild! I told you she was wild! You should have seen the way she was dancing. Everyone was peeking at her from behind the doors and laughing at her. What's the matter with her, Christine?

CHRISTINE: You might know it's her monthlies, Jean. She always acts peculiar then. . . . Well, are you going to dance with me?

JEAN: You're not mad at me because I broke my promise?

CHRISTINE: Of course not. Not for a little thing like that, you know that. I know my place.

JEAN (*grabs her around the waist*): You're a sensible girl, Christine. You're going to make somebody a good wife—

Miss Julie, coming in, sees them together. She is unpleasantly surprised.

MISS JULIE (*with forced gaiety*): Well, aren't you the gallant beau—running away from your partner!

JEAN: On the contrary, Miss Julie. As you can see, I've hurried back to the partner I deserted.

MISS JULIE (*changing tack*): You know, you're the best dancer I've met. —Why are you wearing livery on a holiday? Take it off at once.

JEAN: I'd have to ask you to leave for a minute. My black coat is hanging right here—(*He moves to the right and points.*)

MISS JULIE: You're not embarrassed because I'm here, are you? Just to change your coat? Go in your room and come right back again. Or else stay here and I'll turn my back.

JEAN: If you'll excuse me, Miss Julie. (*He goes off to the right. His arm can be seen as he changes his coat.*)

MISS JULIE (*to Christine*): Tell me something, Christine. Is Jean your fiancé? He acts so familiar with you.

CHRISTINE: Fiancé? I suppose so. At least we say we are.

MISS JULIE: What do you mean?

CHRISTINE: Well, Miss Julie, you have had fiancés yourself, and you know—

MISS JULIE: But we were properly engaged—!

CHRISTINE: I know, but did anything come of it?

> *Jean comes back, wearing a black cutaway coat and derby.*

MISS JULIE: *Très gentil, monsieur Jean! Très gentil!*

JEAN: *Vous voulez plaisanter, madame.*

MISS JULIE: *Et vous voulez parler français!* Where did you learn to speak French?

JEAN: In Switzerland. I was *sommelier* in one of the biggest hotels in Lucerne.

MISS JULIE: My! but you look quite the gentleman in that coat! *Charmant!* (*She sits down at the table.*)

JEAN: Flatterer!

MISS JULIE (*stiffening*): Who said I was flattering you?

JEAN: My natural modesty would not allow me to presume that you were paying sincere compliments to someone like me, and therefore I could only assume that you were exaggerating, which, in this case, means flattering me.

MISS JULIE: You certainly have a way with words. Where did you learn to talk like that? Seeing plays?

JEAN: And other places. You don't think I stayed in the house for six years when I was a valet in Stockholm, do you?

MISS JULIE: I thought you were born in this district. Weren't you?

JEAN: My father worked as a farmhand on the district attorney's estate, next door to yours. I used to see you when you were little. Of course you didn't notice me.

MISS JULIE: Did you really?

JEAN: Yes. I remember one time in particular—. But I can't tell you about that!

MISS JULIE: Of course you can. . . . Oh, come on. Just this once—for me.

JEAN: No. No, I really couldn't. Not now. Some other time maybe.

MISS JULIE: Some other time? That means never. What's the harm in telling me now?

JEAN: There's no harm. I just don't feel like it. —Look at her.

> *He nods at Christine, who has fallen asleep in a chair by the stove.*

MISS JULIE: Won't she make somebody a pretty wife! I'll bet she snores, too.

JEAN: No, she doesn't. But she talks in her sleep.

MISS JULIE (*archly*): Now how could you know she talks in her sleep?

JEAN (*coolly*): I've heard her . . .

> *Pause. They look at each other.*

MISS JULIE: Why don't you sit down?

JEAN: I wouldn't take the liberty in your presence.

MISS JULIE: Not even if I ordered you?

JEAN: Of course I'd obey.

MISS JULIE: Well then: sit down. —Wait a minute. Could you get me something to drink?

JEAN: I don't know what there is in the icebox. Only beer, I suppose.

MISS JULIE: Only beer?! I have simple tastes. I prefer beer to wine.

> *Jean takes a bottle of beer from the icebox and opens it. He looks in the cupboard for a glass and a plate, and serves her.*

JEAN: At your service, *mademoiselle.*

MISS JULIE: Thank you. What about you?

JEAN: I'm not much of a beer-drinker, thank you, but if it's your wish—

MISS JULIE: My wish! I should think a gentleman would want to keep his lady company.

JEAN: A point well taken! (*He opens another bottle and takes a glass.*)

MISS JULIE: Now drink a toast to me!

> *Jean hesitates.*

You're not shy, are you? A big, strong man like you?

> *Playfully, Jean kneels and raises his glass in mock gallantry.*

JEAN: To my lady's health!

MISS JULIE: Bravo! Now you have to kiss my shoe, too. Then you will have hit it off perfectly.

> *Jean hesitates, then boldly grasps her foot and touches it lightly with his lips.*

Superb! You should have been an actor.

JEAN (*rising*): This has got to stop, Miss Julie! Someone might come in and see us.

MISS JULIE: So what?

JEAN: People would talk, that's what! If you knew how their tongues were wagging out there just a few minutes ago!

MISS JULIE: What did they say? Tell me. Sit down and tell me.

JEAN. I don't want to hurt your feelings. . . . They used expressions that—that hinted at certain—you know what I mean. You're not a child. And when they see a woman drinking, alone with a man—and a servant at that—in the middle of the night— well . . .

MISS JULIE: Well what?! Besides, we're not alone. Christine is here.

JEAN: Sleeping!

MISS JULIE: I'll wake her up. (*She goes over to Christine.*) Christine! Are you asleep? (*Christine babbles in her sleep.*) Christine! —My, how sound she sleeps!

CHRISTINE (*talking in her sleep*): Count's boots are brushed . . . put on the coffee . . . right away, right away, right . . . mm—mm . . . poofff . . .

Miss Julie shakes Christine.

MISS JULIE: Wake up, will you!

JEAN (*sternly*): Let her alone! Let her sleep!

MISS JULIE (*sharply*): What?

JEAN: She's been standing over the stove all day. She's worn out when night comes. Anyone asleep is entitled to some consideration.

MISS JULIE (*changing her tone*): That's a very kind thought. It does you credit, Jean. You're right, of course. (*She offers Jean her hand.*) Now come on out and pick some lilacs for me.

During the following, Christine wakes up and, drunk

*with sleep, shuffles off to the right to go to bed. A polka
can be heard in the distance.*

JEAN: With you, Miss Julie?

MISS JULIE: Yes, with me.

JEAN: That's no good. Absolutely not.

MISS JULIE: I don't know what you're thinking. Aren't you
letting your imagination run away with you?

JEAN: No. Other people are.

MISS JULIE: How? Imagining that I'm — *verliebt* with a servant?

JEAN: I'm not conceited, but it's been known to happen. And to
these people nothing's sacred.

MISS JULIE: "These people!" Why, I do believe you're an aristocrat!

JEAN: Yes, I am.

MISS JULIE: I'm climbing down —

JEAN: Don't climb down, Miss Julie! Take my advice. No one
will believe that you climbed down deliberately. They'll say you
fell.

MISS JULIE: I have a higher opinion of these people than you
do. Let's see who's right! Come on! (*She gives him a long, steady
look.*)

JEAN: You know, you're very strange.

MISS JULIE: Perhaps. But then so are you. . . . Besides,
everything is strange. Life, people, everything. It's all scum,
drifting and drifting on the water until it sinks — drowns. There's
a dream I have every now and then. It's coming back to me now.
I'm sitting on top of a pillar. I've climbed up it somehow and I
don't know how to get back down. When I look down I get dizzy.
I have to get down but I don't have the courage to jump. I can't
hold on much longer and I want to fall; but I don't fall. I know
I won't have any peace until I get down; no rest until I get down,
down on the ground. And if I ever got down on the ground, I'd

desire to reverse M/S relationship

want to go farther down, right down into the earth. . . . Have you ever felt anything like that?

JEAN: Never! I used to dream that I'm lying under a tall tree in a dark woods. I want to get up, up to the very top, to look out over the bright landscape with the sun shining on it, to rob the bird's nest up there with the golden eggs in it. And I climb and I climb, but the trunk is so thick, and so smooth, and it's such a long way to that first branch. But I know that if I could just reach that first branch, I'd go right to the top as if on a ladder. I've never reached it yet, but someday I will—even if only in my dreams.

MISS JULIE: Here I am talking about dreams with you. Come out with me. Only into the park a way. (*She offers him her arm, and they start to go.*)

JEAN: Let's sleep on nine midsummer flowers, Miss Julie, and then our dreams will come true!*

> *Miss Julie and Jean suddenly turn around in the doorway. Jean is holding his hand over one eye.*

MISS JULIE: You've caught something in your eye. Let me see.

JEAN: It's nothing. Just a bit of dust. It'll go away.

MISS JULIE: The sleeve of my dress must have grazed your eye. Sit down and I'll help you. (*She takes him by the arm and sits him down. She takes his head and leans it back. With the corner of her handkerchief she tries to get out the bit of dust.*) Now sit still, absolutely still. (*She slaps his hand.*) Do as you're told. Why, I believe you're trembling—a big, strong man like you. (*She feels his biceps.*) With such big arms!

JEAN (*warningly*): Miss Julie!

MISS JULIE: Yes, *Monsieur Jean?*

* A girl would pick in silence on Midsummer Eve nine different sorts of flowers, make a bouquet of them, and place them under her pillow. The man who appeared in her dreams would be the man she would marry.

JEAN: *Attention! Je ne suis qu'un homme!*

MISS JULIE: Sit still, I tell you! . . . There now! It's out. Kiss my hand and thank me!

JEAN (*rising to his feet*): Listen to me, Miss Julie—Christine has gone to bed!—Listen to me, I tell you!

MISS JULIE: Kiss my hand first!

JEAN: Listen to me!

MISS JULIE: Kiss my hand first!

JEAN: All right. But you'll have no one to blame but yourself.

MISS JULIE: For what?

JEAN: For what! Are you twenty-five years old and still a child? Don't you know it's dangerous to play with fire?

MISS JULIE: Not for me, I'm insured!

JEAN (*boldly*): Oh, no, you're not! And even if you are, there's inflammable stuff next door.

MISS JULIE: Meaning you?

JEAN: Yes. Not just because it's me, but because I'm young and—

MISS JULIE: And irresistibly handsome? What incredible conceit! A Don Juan, maybe! Or a Joseph! Yes, bless my soul, that's it: you're a Joseph!

JEAN: You think so?!

MISS JULIE: I'm almost afraid so!

> *Jean boldly steps up to her, grabs her around the waist, tries to kiss her. She slaps his face.*

None of that!

JEAN: More games? Or are you serious?

MISS JULIE: I'm serious.

JEAN: Then you must have been serious a moment ago, too!

You take your games too seriously; that's dangerous. Well, I'm tired of your games, and if you'll excuse me, I'll return to my work. (*Takes up the boots and starts to brush them.*) The count will be wanting his boots on time, and it's long past midnight.

MISS JULIE: Put those boots down.

JEAN: No! This is my job. It's what I'm here for. I never undertook to be your playmate. That's something I could never be. I consider myself too good for that.

MISS JULIE: You are proud.

JEAN: In some ways. Not in others.

MISS JULIE: Have you ever been in love?

JEAN: We don't use that word around here. But I've hankered after some girls, if that's what you mean. . . . I even got sick once because I couldn't have the one I wanted—really sick, like the princes in the Arabian Nights—who couldn't eat or drink for love.

MISS JULIE: Who was she?

Jean does not reply.

Who was the girl?

JEAN: You can't get that out of me.

MISS JULIE: Even if I ask you as an equal—ask you—as a friend? . . . Who was she?

JEAN: You.

MISS JULIE (*sitting down*): How—amusing . . .

JEAN: Yes, maybe so. Ridiculous. . . . That's why I didn't want to tell you about it before. Want to hear the whole story? . . . Have you any idea what you and your people look like from down below? Of course not. Like hawks or eagles, that's what: you hardly ever see their backs because they're always soaring so high up. I lived with seven brothers and sisters—and a pig—out on the wasteland where there wasn't even a tree growing. But from my window I could see the wall of the count's garden with the apple trees sticking up over it. That was the Garden of Eden for me, and there were many angry angels with flaming swords standing guard over it. But in spite of them, I and the other boys found a way to the Tree of Life. . . . How contemptible, that's what you're thinking.

MISS JULIE: For stealing apples? All boys do that.

JEAN: That's what you say now. All the same, you think me contemptible. Never mind. One day I went with my mother into this paradise to weed the onion beds. Next to the vegetable garden stood a Turkish pavilion, shaded by jasmine and hung all over with honeysuckle. I couldn't imagine what it was used for; I only knew I had never seen such a beautiful building. People went in, and came out again. And then one day the door was left open. I sneaked in. The walls were covered with portraits of kings and emperors, and the windows had red curtains with tassels on them. —Recognize it? Yes, the count's private privy. . . . I— (*He breaks off a lilac and holds it under Miss Julie's nose.*) I had never been inside a castle, never seen anything besides the church. This was more beautiful. And no matter what I tried to think about, my thoughts always came back—to that little pavilion. And little by little there arose in me a desire to experience just for once the whole pleasure of—. *Enfin*, I sneaked in, looked about, and marveled. And just then I heard someone coming! There was only one way out—for the upper-class people. But for me there was one more—a lower one. And I had no other choice but to take it. (*Miss Julie, who has taken the lilac from Jean, lets it fall to the table.*) Then I began to run like mad, plunging through the raspberry bushes, ploughing through the strawberry patches, and came up on the rose terrace. And there I caught sight of a pink dress and a pair of white stockings. You! I crawled under—well, you can imagine what it was like—under thistles that pricked me and wet dirt that stank to high heaven. And all the while I could see you walking among the roses. I said to myself, "If it's true that a thief can enter heaven and be with the angels, isn't it strange that a poor man's child here on God's green earth can't enter the count's park and play with the count's daughter."

MISS JULIE (*sentimentally*): Do you think all poor children have felt that way?

JEAN (*hesitatingly at first, then with mounting conviction*): If all poor ch–? Yes–yes, naturally. Of course!

MISS JULIE: It must be terrible to be poor.

JEAN (*with exaggerated intensity*): Oh, Miss Julie! You don't know! A dog can lie on the sofa with its mistress; a horse can have its nose stroked by the hand of a countess; but a servant–! (*Changing his tone.*) Of course, now and then you meet somebody with guts enough to work his way up in the world, but how often? –Anyway, you know what I did afterward? I threw myself into the millstream with all my clothes on. Got fished out and spanked. But the following Sunday, when Pa and everybody else in the house went to visit Grandma, I arranged things so I'd be left behind. Then I washed myself all over with soap and warm water, put on my best clothes, and went off to church–just to see you there once more. I saw you, and then I went home determined to die. But I wanted to die beautifully and comfortably, without pain. I remembered some stories I had heard about how fatal it was to sleep under an elderberry bush. And we had a big one that had just blossomed out. I stripped it of every leaf and blossom it had and made a bed of them in a bin of oats. Have you ever noticed how smooth oats are? As smooth to the touch as human skin. . . . So I pulled the lid of the bin shut and closed my eyes. Fell asleep. And when they woke me I was really very sick. However, I didn't die, as you can see. –What was I trying to prove? I don't know. There was no hope of winning you. It was just that you were a symbol of the absolute hopelessness of my ever getting out of the class I was born in.

MISS JULIE: You know, you have a real gift for telling stories. Did you go to school?

JEAN: A little. But I've read a lot of novels and gone to the theater. And I've also listened to educated people talk. That way I learned the most.

MISS JULIE: You mean to tell me you stand around listening to what we're saying!

JEAN: Certainly! And I've heard an awful lot, I can tell you–sitting on the coachman's seat or rowing the boat. One time I heard you and a girlfriend talking–

MISS JULIE: Really? . . . And just what did you hear?

JEAN: Well, now, I don't know if I can repeat it. I can tell you I was a little amazed. I couldn't imagine where you had learned such words. Maybe at bottom there isn't such a big difference as you might think, between people and people.

MISS JULIE: How vulgar! At least people in my class don't behave like you when we're engaged.

JEAN (*looking her in the eye*): Are you sure? —Come on now, it's no use playing the innocent with me.

MISS JULIE: He was a beast. The man I offered my love was a beast.

JEAN: That's what you all say—afterward.

MISS JULIE: All?

JEAN: I'd say so. I've heard the same expression used several times before in similar circumstances.

MISS JULIE: What kind of circumstances?

JEAN: The kind we're talking about. I remember the last time I—

MISS JULIE (*rising*): That's enough! I don't want to hear any more.

JEAN: How strange! Neither did she! . . . Well, now if you'll excuse me, I'll go to bed.

MISS JULIE (*softly*): Go to bed on Midsummer Eve?

JEAN: That's right. Dancing with that crowd up there really doesn't amuse me.

MISS JULIE: Jean, get the key to the boathouse and row me out on the lake. I want to see the sun come up.

JEAN: Do you think that's wise?

MISS JULIE: You sound as if you were worried about your reputation.

JEAN: Why not? I don't particularly care to be made ridiculous, or to be kicked out without a recommendation just when I'm trying to establish myself. Besides, I have a certain obligation to Christine.

MISS JULIE: Oh, I see. It's Christine now.

JEAN: Yes, but I'm thinking of you, too. Take my advice, Miss Julie. Go up to your room.

MISS JULIE: When did you start giving me orders?

JEAN: Just this once. For your own sake! Please! It's very late. You're so tired, you're drunk; you don't know what you're doing. Go to bed, Miss Julie. —Besides, if my ears aren't deceiving me, they're coming this way, looking for me. If they find us here together, you're done for!

THE CHORUS (*is heard coming nearer, singing*):

> Said Jill to Jack, "Soil needs a tilling."
> Tri-di-ri-di-ralla, tri-di-ri-di-ra.
> Said Jack to Jill, "Time's a-spilling."
> Tri-di-ri-di-ralla-la.
> Said Jill to Jack, "Gold's a-hoarding."
> Tri-di-ri-di-ralla, tri-di-ri-di-ra.
> Said Jack to Jill, "Tell not my lording."
> Tri-di-ri-di-ralla-la.
> Said Jill to Jack, "Hair is for plaiting."
> Tri-di-ri-di-ralla, tri-di-ri-di-ra.
> "But Jill for Jack is not waiting."
> Tri-di-ri-di-ralla-la!*

MISS JULIE: I know these people. I love them just as they love me. Let them come. You'll see.

JEAN: Oh, no, Miss Julie, they don't love you! They take the food you give them, but they spit on it as soon as your back is turned. Believe me! Just listen to them. Listen to what they're singing. —No, you'd better not listen.

MISS JULIE (*listening*): What are they singing?

JEAN: A nasty song—about you and me!

*The Swedish original of this song appears on p. 238.

238 MISS JULIE

BONDFOLKETS DANSVISA

Allegretto.

Det kom-mo två fru - ar från sko-gen

Tri di- ri- di ral - la Tri - di - ri - di - ra

Den en - a var våt om fo - o - ten

Tri di - ri - di ral - la - la.

De talte om hundra riksdaler
Tri (etc.)
Men ägde knappast en daler
Tri (etc.)

Och kransen jag dig skänker
Tri (etc.)
En annan jag påtänker
Tri (etc.)

The melody of the peasants' song was not printed in the first
Swedish edition, but it did appear in Charles de Casanove's
French translation of the play in 1893.

MISS JULIE: How disgusting! Oh, what cowardly, sneaking—

JEAN: That's what the mob always is—cowards! You can't fight them; you can only run away.

MISS JULIE: Run away? Where? There's no way out of here. And we can't go in to Christine.

JEAN: What about my room? What do you say? Rules don't count in a situation like this. You can trust me. —You said, let's be friends. Remember? Well, I'm your friend—your true, devoted, respectful friend.

MISS JULIE: But suppose—suppose they looked for you there?

JEAN: I'll bolt the door. If they try to break it down, I'll shoot. Come, Miss Julie! (*On his knees.*) Please, Miss Julie!

MISS JULIE (*meaningfully*): You promise me that you won't—

JEAN: I swear to you!

> *Miss Julie goes out quickly to the right. Jean follows her impetuously.*

★　★　★

THE BALLET

> *The country people enter in festive costumes, with flowers in their hats. The fiddler is in the lead. A keg of small beer and a little keg of liquor, decorated with greenery, are set up on the table. Glasses are brought out. They all drink. Then they form a circle and sing "Said Jill to Jack," dancing the round dance as they sing. At the end of the dance, they all leave singing.*

★　★　★

> *Miss Julie comes in alone; looks at the devastated kitchen; clasps her hands together; then takes out a powder puff and powders her face. Jean enters. He is in high spirits.*

JEAN: You see! You heard them, didn't you? You've got to admit it's impossible to stay here.

MISS JULIE: No, I don't. But even if I did, what could we do?

JEAN: Go away, travel, get away from here!

MISS JULIE: Travel? Yes—but where?

JEAN: Switzerland, the Italian lakes. You've never been there?

MISS JULIE: No. Is it beautiful?

JEAN: Eternal summer, oranges, laurel trees, ah . . . !

MISS JULIE: What do we do when we get there?

JEAN: I'll set up a hotel—a first-class hotel with a first-class clientele.

MISS JULIE: Hotel?

JEAN: I tell you that's the life! Always new faces, new languages. Not a minute to think about yourself or worry about your nerves. No looking for something to do. The work keeps you busy. Day and night the bells ring, the trains whistle, the buses come and go. And all the while the money comes rolling in. I tell you it's the life!

MISS JULIE: Yes, that's the life. But what about me?

JEAN: The mistress of the whole place, the star of the establishment! With your looks—and your personality—it can't fail. It's perfect! You'll sit in the office like a queen, setting your slaves in motion by pressing an electric button. The guests will file before your throne and timidly lay their treasures on your table. You can't imagine how people tremble when you shove a bill in their face! I'll salt the bills and you'll sugar them with your prettiest smile. Come on, let's get away from here—(*He takes a timetable from his pocket.*)—right away—the next train! We'll be in Malmö at six-thirty, Hamburg eight-forty in the morning; Frankfurt to Basle in one day, and to Como by way of the Gotthard tunnel in—let me see—three days! Three days!

MISS JULIE: You make it sound so wonderful. But, Jean, you have to give me strength. Tell me you love me. Come and put your arms around me.

JEAN (*hesitates*): I want to . . . but I don't dare. Not anymore, not in this house. I do love you—without a shadow of a doubt. How can you doubt that, Miss Julie?

MISS JULIE (*shyly, very becomingly*): You don't have to be formal with me, Jean. You can call me Julie. There aren't any barriers between us now. Call me Julie.

JEAN (*agonized*): I can't! There are still barriers between us, Miss Julie, as long as we stay in this house! There's the past, there's the count. I've never met anyone I feel so much respect for. I've only got to see his gloves lying on a table and I shrivel up. I only have to hear that bell ring and I shy like a frightened horse. I only have to look at his boots standing there so stiff and proud and I feel my spine bending. (*He kicks the boots.*) Superstitions, prejudices that they've drilled into us since we were children! But they can be forgotten just as easily! Just we get to another country where they have a republic! They'll crawl on their hands and knees when they see my uniform. On their hands and knees, I tell you! But not me! Oh, no. I'm not made for crawling. I've got guts, backbone. And once I grab that first branch, you just watch me climb. I may be a valet now, but next year I'll be owning property; in ten years, I'll be living off my investments. Then I'll go to Rumania, get myself some decorations, and maybe—notice I only say maybe—end up as a count!

MISS JULIE: How wonderful, wonderful.

JEAN: Listen, in Rumania you can buy titles. You'll be a countess after all. My countess.

MISS JULIE: But I'm not interested in that. I'm leaving all that behind. Tell me you love me, Jean, or else—or else what difference does it make what I am?

JEAN: I'll tell you a thousand times—but later! Not now. And not here. Above all, let's keep our feelings out of this or we'll make a mess of everything. We have to look at this thing calmly and coolly, like sensible people. (*He takes out a cigar, clips the end, and lights it.*) Now you sit there and I'll sit here, and we'll talk as if nothing had happened.

MISS JULIE (*in anguish*): My God, what are you? Don't you have any feelings?

JEAN: Feelings? Nobody's got more feelings than I have. But I've learned to control them.

MISS JULIE: A few minutes ago you were kissing my shoe—and now—!

JEAN (*harshly*): That was a few minutes ago. We've got other things to think about now!

MISS JULIE: Don't speak to me like that, Jean!

JEAN: I'm just trying to be sensible. We've been stupid once; let's not be stupid again. Your father might be back at any moment, and we've got to decide our future before then. —Now what do you think about my plans? Do you approve or don't you?

MISS JULIE: I don't see anything wrong with them. Except one thing. For a big undertaking like that, you'd need a lot of capital. Have you got it?

JEAN (*chewing on his cigar*): Have I got it? Of course I have. I've got my knowledge of the business, my vast experience, my familiarity with languages. That's capital that counts for something, let me tell you.

MISS JULIE: You can't even buy the railway tickets with it.

JEAN: That's true. That's why I need a backer—someone to put up the money.

MISS JULIE: Where can you find him on a moment's notice?

JEAN: You'll find him—if you want to be my partner.

MISS JULIE: I can't. And I don't have a penny to my name.

     Pause.

JEAN: Then you can forget the whole thing.

MISS JULIE: Forget—?

JEAN: And things will stay just the way they are.

MISS JULIE: Do you think I'm going to live under the same roof with you as your mistress? Do you think I'm going to have people sneering at me behind my back? How do you think I'll ever be able to look my father in the face after this? No, no! Take me away from here, Jean—the shame, the humiliation. . . . What have I done? Oh, my God, my God! What have I done! (*She bursts into tears.*)

JEAN: Now don't start singing that tune. It won't work. What have you done that's so awful? You're not the first.

MISS JULIE (*crying hysterically*): Now you think me contemptible—I'm falling, falling!

JEAN: Fall down to me, and I'll lift you up again!

MISS JULIE: What awful hold did you have over me? What drove me to you? The weak to the strong? The falling to the rising! Or maybe it was love? Love? This? You don't know what love is!

JEAN: Want to bet? Did you think I was a virgin?

MISS JULIE: You're coarse—vulgar! The things you say, the things you think!

JEAN: That's the way I was brought up. It's the way I am! Now don't get hysterical. And don't play the fine lady with me. We're eating off the same platter now. . . . That's better. Come over here and be a good girl and I'll treat you to something special. (*He opens the table drawer and takes out the wine bottle. He pours the wine into two used glasses.*)

MISS JULIE: Where did you get that wine?

JEAN: From the wine cellar.

MISS JULIE: My father's burgundy!

JEAN: Should be good enough for his son-in-law.

MISS JULIE: I was drinking beer and you—!

JEAN: Shows I have better taste than you.

MISS JULIE: Thief!

JEAN: You going to squeal on me?

MISS JULIE: Oh, God! Partner in crime with a petty house thief! I must have been drunk; I must have been walking in my sleep. Midsummer Night! Night of innocent games —

JEAN: Yes, very innocent!

MISS JULIE (*pacing up and down*): Is there anyone here on earth as miserable as I am?

JEAN: Why be miserable? Look at the conquest you've made! Think of poor Christine in there. Don't you think she's got any feelings?

MISS JULIE: I thought so a while ago; I don't now. A servant's a servant —

JEAN: And a whore's a whore!

MISS JULIE (*falls to her knees and clasps her hands together*): Oh, God in heaven, put an end to my worthless life! Lift me out of this awful filth I'm sinking in! Save me! Save me!

JEAN: I feel sorry for you, I have to admit it. When I was lying in the onion beds, looking up at you on the rose terrace, I — I'm telling you the truth now — I had the same dirty thoughts that all boys have.

MISS JULIE: And you said you wanted to die for me!

JEAN: In the oat bin? That was only a story.

MISS JULIE: A lie, you mean.

JEAN (*getting sleepy*): Practically. I think I read it in a paper about a chimney sweep who curled up in a wood-bin with some lilacs because they were going to arrest him for nonsupport of his child.

MISS JULIE: Now I see you as you really are.

JEAN: What did you expect me to do? It's always the fancy talk that gets the women.

MISS JULIE: You dog!

JEAN: You bitch!

MISS JULIE: Well, now you've seen the eagle's back —

JEAN: Wasn't exactly its back—!

MISS JULIE: I was going to be the window dressing for your hotel—!

JEAN: And I the hotel—!

MISS JULIE: Sitting at the desk, attracting your customers, padding your bills—!

JEAN: I could manage that myself—!

MISS JULIE: How can a human soul be so dirty and filthy?

JEAN: Then why don't you clean it up?

MISS JULIE: You lackey! You shoeshine boy! Stand up when I talk to you!

JEAN: You lackey lover! You bootblack's tramp! Shut your mouth and get out of here! Who do you think you are telling me I'm coarse? I've never seen anybody in my class behave as crudely as you did tonight. Have you ever seen any of the girls around here grab at a man like you did? Do you think any of the girls of my class would throw themselves at a man like that? I've never seen the like of it except in animals and prostitutes!

MISS JULIE (*crushed*): That's right! Hit me! Walk all over me! It's all I deserve. I'm rotten. But help me! Help me to get out of this—if there is any way out for me!

JEAN (*less harsh*): I'd be doing myself an injustice if I didn't admit that part of the credit for this seduction belongs to me. But do you think a person in my position would have dared to look twice at you if you hadn't asked for it? I'm still amazed—

MISS JULIE: And still proud.

JEAN: Why not? But I've got to confess the victory was a little too easy to give me any real thrill.

MISS JULIE: Go on, hit me again!

JEAN (*standing up*): No. . . . I'm sorry I said that. I never hit a person who's down, especially a woman. I can't deny that, in one way, it was good to find out that what I saw glittering up above was only fool's gold, to see that the eagle's back was as gray as its belly, that the smooth cheek was just powder, and that there could be dirt under the manicured nails, that the handkerchief was soiled even though it smelled of perfume. But, in another way, it hurts to find that everything I was striving for wasn't very high above me after all, wasn't even real. It hurts me to see you sink far lower than your own cook. Hurts, like seeing the last flowers cut to pieces by the autumn rains and turned to muck.

MISS JULIE: You talk as if you already stood high above me.

JEAN: Well, don't I? Don't forget I could make you a countess but you can never make me a count.

MISS JULIE: I have a father for a count. You can never have that!

JEAN: True. But I might father my own counts—that is, if—

MISS JULIE: You're a thief! I'm not!

JEAN: There are worse things than being a thief. A lot worse. And besides, when I take a position in a house, I consider myself a member of the family—in a way, like a child in the house. It's no crime for a child to steal a few ripe cherries when they're falling off the trees, is it? (*He begins to feel passionate again.*) Miss Julie, you're a beautiful woman, much too good for the likes of me. You got carried away by your emotions and now you want to cover up your mistake by telling yourself that you love me. You don't love me. Maybe you were attracted by my looks—in which case your kind of love is no better than mine. But I could never be satisfied to be just an animal for you, and I could never make you love me.

MISS JULIE: How do you know that for sure?

JEAN: You mean there's a chance? I could love you, there's no doubt about that. You're beautiful, you're refined—(*He goes up to her and takes her hand.*)—educated, lovable when you want to be, and once you set a man's heart on fire, I'll bet it burns forever. (*He puts his arm around her waist.*) You're like hot wine with strong spices. One of your kisses is enough to—

> He attempts to lead her out, but she rather reluctantly breaks away from him.

MISS JULIE: Let me go. You don't get me that way.

JEAN: Then how? Not by petting you and not with pretty words, not by planning for the future, not by saving you from humiliation! Then how, tell me how?

MISS JULIE: How? How? I don't know how! I don't know at all! —I hate you like I hate rats, but I can't get away from you.

JEAN: Then come away with me!

MISS JULIE (*pulling herself together*): Away? Yes, we'll go away! —But I'm so tired. Pour me a glass of wine, will you?

Jean pours the wine, Miss Julie looks at her watch.

Let's talk first. We still have a little time. (*She empties the glass of wine and holds it out for more*)

JEAN: Don't overdo it. You'll get drunk.

MISS JULIE: What difference does it make?

JEAN: What difference? It looks cheap. —What did you want to say to me?

MISS JULIE: We're going to run away together, right? But we'll talk first—that is, I'll talk. So far you've done all the talking. You've told me your life, now I'll tell you mine. That way we'll know each other through and through before we become . . . traveling companions.

JEAN: Wait a minute. Are you sure you won't regret this afterward—surrendering your secrets to me?

MISS JULIE: I thought you were my friend.

JEAN: I am—sometimes. Just don't count on it.

MISS JULIE: You don't mean that. Anyway, everybody knows my secrets. —My mother's parents were very ordinary people, just commoners. She was brought up, according to the theories of her time, to believe in equality, the independence of women, and all that. And she had a strong aversion to marriage. When my father proposed to her, she swore she would never become his wife but that she might possibly consent to become his mistress. So he told her he didn't want to see the woman he loved enjoy less respect than he did. But she said she didn't care what the world thought—and he, believing that he couldn't live without her, accepted her conditions. That did it. From then on he was cut off from his old circle of friends and left without anything to do in the house, which couldn't have kept him occupied anyway. Then I came into the world—against my mother's wishes, as far as I can make out. My mother decided to bring me up as a nature child. And on top of that I had to learn everything a boy learns, so I could be living proof that women were just as good as men. I had to wear boy's clothes, learn to handle horses—but not to milk the cows! Girls did that! I was made to groom the horses and harness them, and learn farming and go hunting—I even had to learn how to slaughter the animals. It was disgusting. Awful! And on the estate all the men were set to doing women's chores, and the women to doing men's work— with the result that the whole place fell to pieces, and we became the local laughing-stock. Finally, my father must have come out of his trance. He rebelled, and everything was changed according to his wishes. They got married—very quietly. Then my mother got sick. I don't know what kind of sickness it was, but she often had convulsions, and she would hide herself in the attic or in the garden, and sometimes she would stay out all night. Then there occurred that big fire you've heard about. The house, the stables, the cowsheds, all burned down—and under very peculiar circumstances that led one to suspect arson. You see, the accident occurred the day after the insurance expired, and the premiums on the new policy, which my father had sent in, were delayed through the messenger's carelessness, and didn't arrive in time. (*She refills her glass and drinks.*)

JEAN: You've had enough.

MISS JULIE: Who cares! —We were left without a penny to our name. We had to sleep in the carriages. My father didn't know where to turn for money to rebuild the house. Then Mother suggested to him that he might try to borrow money from an old friend of hers, who owned a brick factory not far from here. Father took out a loan, but there wasn't any interest charged, which surprised him. So the place was rebuilt. (*She drinks some more.*) Do you know who set fire to the place?

JEAN: Your honorable mother!

MISS JULIE: Do you know who the brick manufacturer was?

JEAN: Your mother's lover?

MISS JULIE: Do you know whose money it was?

JEAN: Let me think a minute. . . . No, I give up.

MISS JULIE: It was my mother's!

JEAN: The count's, you mean. Or was there a marriage settlement?

MISS JULIE: There wasn't a settlement. My mother had a little money of her own which she didn't want under my father's control, so she invested it with her—friend.

JEAN: Who pinched it!

MISS JULIE: Right! He kept it for himself. Well, my father found out what happened. But he couldn't go to court, couldn't pay his wife's lover, couldn't prove that it was his wife's money. That was how my mother got her revenge because he had taken control of the house. He was on the verge of shooting himself. There was even a rumor that he tried and failed. But somehow he took a new lease on life and he forced my mother to pay for her mistakes. Can you imagine what those five years were like for me? I loved my father, but I took my mother's side because I didn't know the whole story. She had taught me to hate all men—I'm sure you've heard how she hated men—and I swore to her that I'd never be slave to any man.

JEAN: You got engaged to the attorney, didn't you?

MISS JULIE: Only to make him my slave.

JEAN: I guess he didn't go for that, did he?

MISS JULIE: Oh, he wanted to well enough. I didn't give him the chance. I got bored with him.

JEAN: Yes, so I noticed—in the stable yard.

MISS JULIE: What did you notice?

JEAN: I saw how he—. [Still see it on your cheek.

MISS JULIE: What!

JEAN: The stripe on your cheek.]* He broke it off.

MISS JULIE: It's a lie! I broke it off! Did he tell you that? He's beneath contempt!

JEAN: Come on now, as bad as that? So you hate men, hm?

MISS JULIE: Yes, I do. . . . Most of the time. But sometimes, when I can't help myself—oh . . . (*She shudders in disgust.*)

JEAN: Then you hate me, too?

MISS JULIE: You have no idea how much! I'd like to see you killed like an animal—

JEAN: Like when you're caught having sex with an animal: you get two years at hard labor and the animal is killed. Right?

MISS JULIE: Right.

JEAN: But there's no one to catch us—and *no animal!*—So what are we going to do?

MISS JULIE: Go away from here.

JEAN: To torture ourselves to death?

MISS JULIE: No. To enjoy ourselves for a day or two, or a week, for as long as can—and then—to die—

JEAN: Die? That's stupid! I've got a better idea: start a hotel!

MISS JULIE (*continuing without hearing Jean*): —on the shores of Lake Como, where the sun is always shining, where the laurels bloom at Christmas, and the golden oranges glow on the trees.

JEAN: Lake Como is a stinking wet hole, and the only oranges I saw there were on the fruit stands. But it's a good tourist spot with a lot of villas and cottages that are rented out to lovers. Now there's a profitable business. You know why? They rent the villa for the whole season, but they leave after three weeks.

---

* The passage in brackets was deleted in Strindberg's manuscript, probably by Strindberg himself.

MISS JULIE (*naively*): Why after only three weeks?

JEAN: Because that's about as long as they can stand each other. Why else? But they still have to pay the rent. You see? Then you rent it out again to another couple, and so on. There's no shortage of love — even if it doesn't last very long.

MISS JULIE: Then you don't want to die with me?

JEAN: I don't want to die at all! I enjoy life too much. And moreover, I consider taking your own life a sin against the Providence that gave us life.

MISS JULIE: You believe in God? You?

JEAN: Yes, certainly I do! I go to church every other Sunday —. Honestly, I've had enough of this talk. I'm going to bed.

MISS JULIE: Really? You think you're going to get off that easy? Don't you know that a man owes something to the woman he's dishonored?

JEAN (*takes out his purse and throws a silver coin on the table*): There you are. I don't want to owe anybody anything.

MISS JULIE (*pretending not to notice*): Do you know what the law says —?

JEAN: Lucky for you the law says nothing about women who seduce men!

MISS JULIE (*as before*): What else can we do but go away from here, get married, and get divorced?

JEAN: Suppose I refuse to enter into this *mésalliance*?

MISS JULIE: *Mésalliance*?

JEAN: For me! I've got better ancestors than you. I don't have a female arsonist in my family.

MISS JULIE: You can't prove that.

JEAN: You can't prove the opposite — because we don't have any family records — except in the police files. But I've read the whole history of your family in that peerage book in the drawing room. Do you know who the founder of your family line was? A miller — who let his wife sleep with the king one night during the

Danish war. I don't have any ancestors like that. I don't have any ancestors at all! But I can become an ancestor myself.

MISS JULIE: This is what I get for baring my heart and soul to someone too low to understand, for sacrificing the honor of my family —

JEAN: Dishonor! — I warned you, remember? Drinking makes one talk, and talking's bad.

MISS JULIE: Oh, how sorry I am! . . . If only it had never happened! . . . If only you at least loved me!

JEAN: For the last time — what do you want me to do? Cry? Jump over your whip? Kiss you? Lure you to Lake Como for three weeks and then —? What am I supposed to do? What do you want? I've had more than I can take. This is what I get for involving myself with women. . . . Miss Julie, I can see that you're unhappy; I know that you're suffering; but I simply cannot understand you. My people don't behave like this. We don't hate each other. We make love for the fun of it, when we can get any time off from our work. But we don't have time for it all day and all night like you do. If you ask me, you're sick, Miss Julie. Your mother's mind was affected, you know. There are whole counties affected with pietism. That was your mother's trouble — pietism. It's spreading like the plague.

MISS JULIE: You can be understanding, Jean. You're talking to me like a human being now.

JEAN: Well, be human yourself. You spit on me, but you don't let me wipe it off — on you.

MISS JULIE: Help me, Jean. Help me. Tell me what I should do, that's all — which way to go.

JEAN: For Christ's sake, if only I knew myself!

MISS JULIE: I've been crazy — I've been out of my mind — but does that mean there's no way out for me?

JEAN: Stay here as if nothing had happened. Nobody knows anything.

MISS JULIE: Impossible! Everybody who works here knows. Christine knows.

JEAN: They don't know a thing. Anyhow they'd never believe it.

MISS JULIE (*slowly, significantly*): But . . . it might happen again.

JEAN: That's true!

MISS JULIE: And one time there might be . . . consequences.

JEAN (*stunned*): Consequences!! What on earth have I been thinking of! You're right. There's only one thing to do: get away from here! Immediately! I can't go with you – that would give the whole game away. You'll have to go by yourself. Somewhere – I don't care where!

MISS JULIE: By myself? Where? – Oh, no, Jean, I can't. I can't!

JEAN: You've got to! Before the count comes back. You know as well as I do what will happen if you stay here. After one mistake, you figure you might as well go on – the damage is already done. Then you get more and more careless until – finally you're exposed. I tell you, you've got to get out of the country. Afterward you can write to the count and tell him everything – leaving me out, of course. He'd never figure it was me. He wouldn't even let himself think it was me.

MISS JULIE: I'll go – if you'll come with me!

JEAN: Lady, are you out of your mind? "Miss Julie elopes with her footman." The day after tomorrow it would be in all the papers. The count would never live it down.

MISS JULIE: I can't go away. I can't stay. Help me. I'm so tired, so awfully tired. . . . Tell me what to do. Order me. Start me going. I can't think anymore, can't move anymore . . .

JEAN: Now do you realize how weak you all are? What gives you the right to go strutting around with your noses in the air as if you owned the world? All right, I'll give you your orders. Go up and get dressed. Get some traveling money. And come back down here.

MISS JULIE (*almost in a whisper*): Come up with me!

JEAN: To your room? . . . You're going crazy again! (*He hesitates a moment.*) No! No! Go! Right now! (*He takes her hand and leads her out.*)

MISS JULIE (*as she is leaving*): Don't be so harsh, Jean.

JEAN: Orders always sound harsh. You've never had to take them.

> *Jean, left alone, heaves a sigh of relief and sits down at the table. He takes out a notebook and a pencil and begins to calculate, counting aloud now and then. The pantomime continues until Christine enters, dressed for church, and carrying Jean's white tie and shirtfront in her hand.*

CHRISTINE: Lord in Heaven, what a mess! What on earth have you been doing?

JEAN: It was Miss Julie. She dragged the whole crowd in here. You must have been sleeping awfully sound if you didn't hear anything.

CHRISTINE: I slept like a log.

JEAN: You already dressed for church?

CHRISTINE: Yes, indeed. Don't you remember you promised to go to communion with me today?

JEAN: Oh, yes. Of course, I remember. I see you've brought my things. All right. Come on, put it on me. (*He sits down, and Christine starts to put the white tie and shirtfront on him. Pause.*)

JEAN (*yawning*): What's the lesson for today?

CHRISTINE: The beheading of John the Baptist, what else? It's Midsummer. It's his feast day.

JEAN: My God, that will go on forever. —Hey, you're choking me! . . . Oh, I'm so sleepy, so sleepy.

CHRISTINE: What were you doing up all night? You look green in the face.

JEAN: I've been sitting here talking with Miss Julie.

CHRISTINE: That girl! She doesn't know how to behave herself!

Pause.

JEAN: Tell me something, Christine . . .

CHRISTINE: Well, what?

JEAN: Isn't it strange when you think about it? Her, I mean.

CHRISTINE: What's so strange?

JEAN: Everything!

> *Pause. Christine looks at the half-empty glasses on the table.*

CHRISTINE: Have you been drinking with her?

JEAN: Yes!

CHRISTINE: Shame on you! — Look me in the eyes! You haven't . . . ?

JEAN: Yes!

CHRISTINE: Is it possible? Is it really possible?

JEAN (*thinking about it*): Yes. It is.

CHRISTINE: Oh, how disgusting! I could never have believed anything like this would happen! No. No. This is too much!

JEAN: Don't tell me you're jealous of her?

CHRISTINE: No, not of her. If it had been Clara — or Sophie — I would have scratched your eyes out! But her — ? That's different. I don't know why. . . . But it's still disgusting!

JEAN: You're not mad at her?

CHRISTINE: No. Mad at you. You were mean and cruel to do a thing like that, very mean. The poor girl! . . . Let me tell you, I'm not going to stay in this house a moment longer, not when I can't have any respect for my employers.

JEAN: Why do you want to respect them?

CHRISTINE: Don't try to be smart. You don't want to work for people who behave like pigs, do you? Well, do you? If you ask me, you'd be lowering yourself by doing that.

JEAN: Oh, I don't know. I think it's rather comforting to find out that they're not one damn bit better than we are.

CHRISTINE: Well, I don't. If they're not any better, there's no point in us trying to be like them. —And think of the count. Think of all the sorrows he's been through in his time. My God! I won't stay in this house any longer. . . . Imagine! You, of all people! If it had been the attorney fellow; if it had been somebody respectable—

JEAN: Now just a minute—!

CHRISTINE: Oh, you're all right in your own way. But there's a big difference between one class and another. You can't deny that. —No, this is something I can never get over. She was so proud, and so sarcastic about men, you'd never believe she'd go and throw herself at one. And at someone like you! And she was going to have Diana shot because the poor thing ran after the gatekeeper's mongrel! —Well, I tell you, I've had enough! I'm not going to stay here any longer. When my term's up, I'm leaving.

JEAN: Then what'll you do?

CHRISTINE: Well, since you brought it up, it's about time that you got yourself a decent place, if we're going to get married.

JEAN: Why should I go looking for another place? I could never get a job like this if I'm married.

CHRISTINE: Well, I know that! But you could get a job as a porter, or maybe try to get a government job as a caretaker somewhere. A square deal and a square meal, that's what you get from the government—and a pension for the wife and children.

JEAN (*wryly*): Fine, fine! But I'm not the kind of guy who thinks about dying for his wife and children this early in the game. Let me tell you, I've got slightly bigger plans than that.

CHRISTINE: Plans! Ha! What about your obligations? You'd better start giving them a little thought!

JEAN: Don't start nagging me about obligations! I know what I have to do without you telling me. (*He hears a sound upstairs.*)

Anyhow, we'll have plenty of chance to talk about this later. You just go and get yourself ready, and we'll be off to church.

CHRISTINE: Who is that walking around up there?

JEAN: I don't know. Clara, I suppose. Who else?

CHRISTINE (*starting to leave*): It can't be the count, can it? Could he have come back without anybody hearing him?

JEAN (*frightened*): The count? No, it can't be. He would have rung.

CHRISTINE (*leaving*): God help us! I've never heard the like of this.

> *The sun has now risen and strikes the tops of the trees in the park. As the scene progresses, the light shifts gradually until it is shining very obliquely through the windows. Jean goes to the door and signals. Miss Julie enters, dressed for travel, and carrying a small birdcage, covered with a towel. She sets the cage down on a chair.*

MISS JULIE: I'm ready now.

JEAN: Shh! Christine's awake.

MISS JULIE (*extremely tense and nervous during the following*): Did she suspect anything?

JEAN: She doesn't know a thing. —My God, what happened to you?

MISS JULIE: What do you mean? Do I look so strange?

JEAN: You're white as a ghost, and you've—excuse me—you've got dirt on your face.

MISS JULIE: Let me wash it off. (*She goes over to the washbasin and washes her face and hands.*) There! Do you have a towel? . . . Oh, look, the sun's coming up!

JEAN: That breaks the magic spell!

MISS JULIE: Yes, we were spellbound last night, weren't we? Midsummer madness . . . Jean, listen to me! Come with me. I've got the money!

JEAN (*suspiciously*): Enough?

MISS JULIE: Enough for a start. Come with me, Jean. I can't travel alone today. Midsummer Day on a stifling hot train, packed in with crowds of people, all staring at me – stopping at every station when I want to be flying. I can't, Jean, I can't! . . . And everything will remind me of the past. Midsummer Day when I was a child and the church was decorated with leaves – birch leaves and lilacs . . . the table spread for dinner with friends and relatives . . . and after dinner, dancing in the park, with flowers and games. Oh, no matter how far you travel, the memories tag right along in the baggage car . . . and the regrets and the remorse.

JEAN: All right, I'll go with you! But it's got to be now – before it's too late! This very instant!

MISS JULIE: Hurry and get dressed! (*She picks up the birdcage.*)

JEAN: No baggage! It would give us away.

MISS JULIE: Nothing. Only what we can take to our seats.

JEAN (*as he gets his hat*): What in the devil have you got there? What is that?

MISS JULIE: It's only my canary. I can't leave it behind.

JEAN: A canary! My God, do you expect us to carry a birdcage around with us? You're crazy. Put that cage down!

MISS JULIE: It's the only thing I'm taking with me from my home – the only living thing who loves me since Diana was unfaithful to me! Don't be cruel, Jean. Let me take it with me.

JEAN: I told you to put that cage down! – And don't talk so loud. Christine can hear us.

MISS JULIE: No, I won't leave it with a stranger. I won't. I'd rather have you kill it.

JEAN: Give it here, the little pest. I'll wring its neck.

MISS JULIE: Oh, don't hurt it. Don't –. No, I can't do it!

JEAN: Don't worry, I can. Give it here.

Miss Julie takes the bird out of the cage and kisses it.

MISS JULIE: Oh, my little Serena, must you die and leave your mistress?

JEAN: You don't have to make a scene of it. It's a question of your whole life and future. You're wasting time!

> *Jean grabs the canary from her, carries it to the chop-
> ping block, and picks up a meat cleaver. Miss Julie
> turns away.*

You should have learned how to kill chickens instead of shooting revolvers — (*He brings the cleaver down.*) — then a drop of blood wouldn't make you faint.

MISS JULIE (*screaming*): Kill me too! Kill me! You can kill an innocent creature without turning a hair — then kill me. Oh, how I hate you! I loathe you! There's blood between us. I curse the moment I first laid eyes on you! I curse the moment I was conceived in my mother's womb.

JEAN: What good does your cursing do? Let's get out of here!

MISS JULIE (*approaches the chopping block, drawn to it against her will*): No, I don't want to go yet. I can't. — I have to see. — Shh! (*She listens but keeps her eyes fastened on the chopping block and cleaver.*) You don't think I can stand the sight of blood, do you? You think I'm so weak, don't you? Oh, how I'd love to see your blood, your brains on that chopping block. I'd love to see the whole of your sex swimming in a sea of blood just like that. I could drink blood out of your skull. Use your chest as a foot bath, dip my toes in your guts! I could eat your heart roasted whole! — You think I'm weak! You think I loved you because my womb hungered for your semen. You think I want to carry your brood under my heart and feed it with my blood? Bear your child and take your name? — Come to think of it, what is your name? I've never even heard your last name. I'll bet you don't have one. I'd be Mrs. Doorman or Madame Garbageman. You dog with *my* name on your collar — you lackey with *my* initials on your buttons! Do you think I'm going to share you with my cook and fight over you with my maid?! Ohh! – You think I'm a coward who's going to run away! No, I'm going to stay – come hell or high water. My father will come home – find his desk broken into – his money gone. He'll ring – on that bell – two rings for the valet. And then he'll send for the sheriff – and I'll tell him everything. Everything! Oh, what a relief it'll be to have it all over . . . over and done with . . . if only it will be over. . . . He'll have a stroke and die . . . and there'll be an end to all of us. There'll be peace . . . and quiet . . . forever. . . . The coat of arms will be broken on his coffin; the count's line will be extinct – while the valet's breed will continue in an orphanage, win triumphs in the gutter, and end in jail!

> *Christine enters, dressed for church and with a hymn-book in her hand. Miss Julie rushes over to her and throws herself into her arms as if seeking protection.*

MISS JULIE: Help me, Christine! Protect me against this man!

CHRISTINE (*cold and unmoved*): This is a fine way to behave on a holy day! (*She sees the chopping block.*) Just look at the mess you've made there! How do you explain that? And what's all this shouting and screaming about?

MISS JULIE: Christine, you're a woman, you're my friend! I warn you, watch out for this – this monster!

JEAN (*feeling awkward*): If you ladies are going to talk, you won't want me around. I think I'll go and shave. (*He slips out to the right.*)

MISS JULIE: You've got to understand, Christine! You've got to listen to me!

CHRISTINE: No, I don't. I don't understand this kind of she-nanigans at all. Where do you think you're going dressed like that? And Jean with his hat on? – Well? – Well?

MISS JULIE: Listen to me, Christine! If you'll just listen to me, I'll tell you everything.

CHRISTINE: I don't want to know anything.

MISS JULIE: You've got to listen to me –!

CHRISTINE: What about? About your stupid behavior with Jean? I tell you that doesn't bother me at all, because it's none of my business. But if you have any silly idea about talking him into skipping out with you, I'll soon put a stop to that.

MISS JULIE (*extremely tense*): Christine, please don't get upset. Listen to me. I can't stay here, and Jean can't stay here. So you see, we have to go away.

CHRISTINE: Hm, hm, hm.

MISS JULIE (*suddenly brightening up*): Wait! I've got an idea! Why couldn't all three of us go away together?—out of the country—to Switzerland—and start a hotel? I've got the money, you see. Jean and I would be responsible for the whole affair— and Christine, you could run the kitchen, I thought. Doesn't that sound wonderful! Say you'll come, Christine, then everything will be settled. Say you will! Please! (*She throws her arms around Christine and pats her.*)

CHRISTINE (*remaining aloof and unmoved*): Hm. Hm.

MISS JULIE (*presto tempo*): You've never been traveling, Christine. You have to get out and see the world. You can't imagine how wonderful it is to travel by train—constantly new faces, new countries. We'll go to Hamburg, and stop over to look at the zoo—it's famous, has everything—you'll love that. And we'll go to the theater and the opera. And then when we get to Munich, we'll go to the museums, Christine. They have Rubenses and Raphaels there—those great painters, you know. Of course you've heard about Munich where King Ludwig lived—you know, the king who went mad. And then we can go and see his castles—they're just like the ones you read about in fairy tales. And from there it's just a short trip to Switzerland— with the Alps. Think of the Alps, Christine, covered with snow in the middle of summer. And oranges grow there, and laurel trees that are green the whole year round—

> *Jean can be seen in the wings at the right, sharpening his straight razor on a strop held between his teeth and his left hand. He listens to Miss Julie with a satisfied expression on his face, now and then nodding approvingly. Miss Julie continues tempo prestissimo.*

—and that's where we'll get a hotel. I'll sit at the desk while Jean stands at the door and receives the guests, goes out shopping, writes the letters. What a life that will be! The train whistle blowing, then the bus arriving, then a bell ringing upstairs, then the bell in the restaurant rings—and I'll be making out the bills—and I know just how much to salt them—you can't imagine how timid tourists are when you shove a bill in their face! —And you, Christine, you'll run the whole kitchen—there'll be not standing at the stove for you—of course not. If you're going to talk to the people, you'll have to dress. And with your looks—I'm not trying to flatter you, Christine—you'll run off with some man one fine day—a rich Englishman, that's who it'll be, they're so easy to—(*Slowing down*)—to catch. —Then we'll all be rich. —We'll build a villa on Lake Como. —Maybe it does rain there sometimes, but—(*More and more lifelessly.*)—the sun has to shine sometimes, too—even if it looks cloudy. —And—then . . . or else we can always travel some more—and come back . . . (*Pause.*)—here . . . or somewhere else . . .

CHRISTINE: Do you really believe a word of that yourself, Miss Julie?

MISS JULIE (*completely beaten*): Do I believe a word of it myself?

CHRISTINE: Do you?

MISS JULIE (*exhausted*): I don't know. I don't believe anything anymore. (*She sinks down on the bench and lays her head between her arms on the table.*) Nothing. Nothing at all.

CHRISTINE (*turns to the right and faces Jean*): So! You were planning to run away, were you?

JEAN (*taken aback, lays his razor down on the table*): We weren't exactly going to run away! Don't exaggerate. You heard Miss Julie's plans. Even if she's tired now after being up all night, her plans are perfectly practical.

CHRISTINE: Well, just listen to you! Did you really think you could get me to cook for that little—!

JEAN (*sharply*): You keep a respectful tongue in your mouth when you talk to your mistress! Understand?

CHRISTINE: Mistress!

JEAN: Yes, mistress!

CHRISTINE: Well of all the—! I don't have to listen—

JEAN: Yes, you do! You need to listen more and blabber less. Miss Julie is your mistress. Don't you forget that! And if you're going to despise her for what she did, you ought to despise yourself for the same reason.

CHRISTINE: I've always held myself high enough to—

JEAN: High enough to make you look down on others!

CHRISTINE: —enough to keep from lowering myself beneath my station. Don't you dare say that the count's cook has ever had anything to do with the stable groom or the swineherd. Don't you dare!

JEAN: Yes, you got yourself a decent man. Lucky you!

CHRISTINE: What kind of a decent man is it who sells the oats from the count's stables?

JEAN: Listen to who's talking! You get the gravy on the groceries and take bribes from the butcher!

CHRISTINE: How dare you say a thing like that!

JEAN: And you say you can't respect your employers. You of all people! You!

CHRISTINE: Are you going to church or aren't you? You need a good sermon after your great exploits.

JEAN: No, I'm not going to church! Go yourself. Go tell God how bad you are.

CHRISTINE: Yes, I'll do just that. And I'll come back with enough forgiveness for your sins, too. Our Redeemer suffered and died on the cross for all our sins, and if we come to Him in faith and with a penitent heart, He will take all our sins upon Himself.

JEAN: Rake-offs included?

MISS JULIE: Do you really believe that, Christine?

CHRISTINE: With all my heart, as sure as I'm standing here. It was the faith I was born into, and I've held on to it since I was a little girl, Miss Julie. Where sin aboundeth, there grace aboundeth also.

MISS JULIE: If I had your faith, Christine, if only—

CHRISTINE: But you see, that's something you can't have without God's special grace. And it is not granted to everyone to receive it.

MISS JULIE: Then who receives it?

CHRISTINE: That's the secret of the workings of grace, Miss Julie, and God is no respecter of persons. With Him the last shall be first—

MISS JULIE: In that case, he does have respect for the last, doesn't he?

CHRISTINE (*continuing*): —and it is easier for a camel to go through the eye of a needle than for a rich man to enter the kingdom of God. That's how things are, Miss Julie. I'm going to leave now—alone. And on my way out I'm going to tell the stable boy not to let any horses out, in case anyone has any ideas about leaving before the count comes home. Goodbye. (*She leaves*)

JEAN: She's a devil in skirts! —All because of a canary!

MISS JULIE (*listlessly*): Never mind the canary. . . . Do you see any way out of this, any end to it?

JEAN (*after thinking for a moment*): No.

MISS JULIE: What would you do if you were in my place?

JEAN: In your place? Let me think. . . . An aristocrat, a woman, and—fallen. . . . I don't know. —Or maybe I do.

MISS JULIE (*picks up the razor and makes a gesture with it*): Like this?

JEAN: Yes. But I wouldn't do it, you understand. That's the difference between us.

MISS JULIE: Because you're a man and I'm a woman? What difference does that make?

JEAN: Just the difference that there is—between a man and a woman.

MISS JULIE (*holding the razor in her hand*): I want to! But I can't do it. My father couldn't do it either, that time when he should have.

JEAN: No, he was right not to. He had to get his revenge first.

MISS JULIE: And now my mother is getting her revenge again through me.

JEAN: Didn't you ever love your father, Miss Julie?

MISS JULIE: Yes, enormously. But I must have hated him too. I must have hated him without knowing it. It was he who brought me up to despise my own sex, to be half woman and half man. Who's to blame for what has happened? My father, my mother, myself? Myself? I don't have a self that's my own. I don't have a single thought I didn't get from my father, not an emotion I didn't get from my mother. And that last idea—about all people being equal—I got that from him, my fiancé. That's why I say he's beneath contempt. How can it be my own fault? Put the blame on Jesus, like Christine does? I'm too proud to do that— and too intelligent, thanks to what my father taught me. . . . A rich man can't get into heaven? That's a lie. But at least Christine, who's got money in the savings bank, won't get in. . . . Who's to blame? What difference does it make who's to blame? I'm still the one who has to bear the guilt, suffer the consequences—

JEAN: Yes, but—

> The bell rings sharply twice. Miss Julie jumps up. Jean
> changes his coat.

JEAN: The count's back! What if Christine—(*He goes to the speaking tube, taps on it, and listens.*)

MISS JULIE: Has he looked in his desk yet?

JEAN: This is Jean, sir! (*Listens. The audience cannot hear what the count says.*) Yes, sir! (*Listens.*) Yes, sir! Yes, as soon as I can.

(*Listens.*) Yes, at once, sir! (*Listens.*) Very good, sir! In half an hour.

MISS JULIE (*trembling with anxiety*): What did he say? For God's sake, what did he say?

JEAN: He ordered his boots and his coffee in half an hour.

MISS JULIE: Half an hour then! . . . Oh, I'm so tired. I can't bring myself to do anything. Can't repent, can't run away, can't stay, can't live . . . can't die. Help me, Jean. Command me, and I'll obey like a dog. Do me this last favor. Save my honor, save his name. You know what I ought to do but can't force myself to do. Let me use your willpower. You command me and I'll obey.

JEAN: I don't know—. I can't either, not now. I don't know why. It's as if this coat made me—I can't give you orders in this. And now, after the count has spoken to me, I—I can't really explain it—but—I've got the backbone of a damned lackey! If the count came down here now and ordered me to cut my throat, I'd do it on the spot.

MISS JULIE: Then pretend you're him. Pretend I'm you. You were such a good actor just a while ago, when you were kneeling before me. You were the aristocrat then. Or else—have you been to the theater and seen a hypnotist?

> *Jean nods.*

He says to his subject, "Take this broom!" and he takes it. He says, "Now sweep!" and he sweeps.

JEAN: The person has to be asleep!

MISS JULIE (*ecstatic, transported*): I'm already asleep. The whole room has turned to smoke. You seem like an iron stove, a stove that looks like a man in black with a high hat. Your eyes are glowing like fading coals in a dying fire. Your face is a white smudge, like ashes.

> *The sun is now shining in on the floor and falls on Jean.*

It's so good and warm—(*She rubs her hands together as if warming them at a fire.*)—and so bright—and so peaceful.

JEAN (*takes the razor and puts it in her hand*): There's the broom. Go now, when the sun is up—out into the barn—and—(*He whispers in her ear.*)

MISS JULIE (*waking up*): Thanks! I'm going to get my rest. But tell me one thing. Tell me that the first can also receive the gift of grace. Tell me that, even if you don't believe it.

JEAN: The first? I can't tell you that. —Wait a moment, Miss Julie. I know what I can tell you. You're no longer one of the first. You're one of—the last.

MISS JULIE: That's true! I'm one of the last. I am the very last! —Oh! —Now I can't go! Tell me just once more, tell me to go!

JEAN: Now I can't either. I can't!

MISS JULIE: And the first shall be the last . . .

JEAN: Don't think—don't think! You're taking all my strength from me. You're making me a coward. . . . What?! I thought I saw the bell move. No. . . . Let me stuff some paper in it. —Afraid of a bell! But it isn't just a bell. There's somebody behind it. A hand that makes it move. And there's something that makes the hand move. —Stop your ears, that's it, stop your ears! But it only rings louder. Rings louder and louder until you answer it. And then it's too late. Then the sheriff comes—and then—(*There are two sharp rings on the bell. Jean gives a start, then straightens himself up.*) It's horrible! But there's no other way for it to end. —Go!

Miss Julie walks resolutely out through the door.

Introduction
to
Creditors

There are indications that *Miss Julie* first took shape in Strindberg's mind as a three-act drama, like *The Father*. But he probably soon realized that he could enhance the effectiveness of his naturalistic, Darwinian tragedy if he imitated the form of ancient Greek drama. All the plays of the Greek tragedians conformed to the same pattern: no more than three actors, a playing time of ninety minutes, and the use of music, of song and dance. The element of intrigue was kept to a minimum, with the stage action centering on one crucial event. By adhering to this formula, which had withstood the test of time, Strindberg was able to fashion a drama that was a mixture of the very old and the very new, a drama that compressed into a ninety-minute span the whole course of sexual love, from the initial sexual attraction, through the game-playing, the sexual teasing, the adopting of roles, through the sex act itself, and on to the falling out of love, the sexual disgust of the woman, and her death – the whole process shown step by step, with every step explained and motivated. No other play in the history of drama had ever done that.

At this time in his career, Strindberg was obsessed and fascinated by the power of drama to concentrate action and ideas. He wanted to surpass the Greeks in this respect. He explained to Georg Brandes that

> in every play there is one real scene. That's the one I want. Why should I bother with the left-overs and give six or eight actors the trouble learning that stuff?
>
> In France I always ordered five mutton chops, to the astonishment of the autochthons. A mutton chop has 1/2 pound of bone and 2 inches of fat. Within was a ball – *la noix* – the nut that I ate. "Give me the nut" – that's what I tell playwrights.
>
> (Letter of 29 November 1888.)

Creditors, written immediately after *Miss Julie*, carries the process of concentration a step further and relies even more on the power of suggestion. In it, Strindberg eliminated the dance that provided a respite in *Miss Julie* and examined the lives and psychological constitutions of three people, not just two, in the same ninety-minute span of time. The result, he said, was "better than *Miss Julie*, with three persons, one table, two chairs, and no sunrise." (Letter of 21 August 1888.)

The most difficult of the three roles is Adolph's. If he is made too weak and pathetic, there will be no tension in his scenes with Gustav. Like Miss Julie, he is, in Strindberg's eyes, a neurotic and unhealthy type. Although he surely put a great deal of himself into the character, he also drew the type from the medical books and psychological studies that he read voraciously. In Henry Maudsley's standard text, *The Pathology of Mind* (London, 1879), there are descriptions of cases similar to Adolph's, people who have convulsions, an unsteady walk, and great artistic talent. Whereas Julie was sexually abnormal, partly because of her upbringing and education, Adolph suffers from what Maudsley refers to as a "morbid hereditary taint." Sexual excess has also taken its toll on Adolph and made him a nervous wreck, and in this weakened condition he quickly falls under the spell of the strong-willed, purposeful creditor Gustav, who has come to claim restitution for his lost honor.

In *Miss Julie*, the heroine lets herself succumb to the stronger will of Jean. She goes to her death in a hypnotic trance. The death of Adoph in *Creditors* is the result of a psychic shock administered by Gustav, who has made the hysterical and epileptic Adolph subservient to his will through the power of suggestion. At the time the play was written, the most hotly debated question in psychology concerned the part that suggestion and hypnotism played in patients suffering from hysteria. In the 1880s, nearly 800 books and articles dealing with hypnosis were published. The most eminent investigator of hysteria, Dr. Charcot in Paris, had demonstrated to his own satisfaction that hypnosis was a form of hysterical or neurotic behavior that could be divided into three phases: catalepsy, lethargy, somnambulism. In Nancy, Dr. Bernheim challenged this idea, arguing that the three phases were induced in the patients by the doctors. The patients went through the three phases because they knew subconsciously what was expected of them. Furthermore, Dr. Bernheim amassed a great deal of evidence showing that suggestibility operated not only on those who were under hypnosis but often also on those who were wide awake. Far from being a purely pathological symptom, suggestibility was a phenomenon of everyday life. "The study of suggestibility," wrote Bernheim in his book *De la suggestion* (1888), "opens new horizons in the fields of medicine, psychology, and sociology. The impoverished human imagination is open to all sorts of impressions, good and bad, salutary and pernicious."

As the author of *The Father*, in which suggestibility plays an important role, Strindberg was entranced by these new horizons, and he broadened them by arguing that suggestibiliy was continually at work in every sphere of life. "All political, religious, and literary conflicts appear to me," he wrote, "as deriving from the struggles of individuals and parties to transmit suggestions, that is, to form opinions, which is nothing more than the struggle for power, at present a battle of brains, since the battle of brawn has gone out of style." ("The Battle of Brains," 1888.)

Gustav, in *Creditors*, is able to undo Adolph simply through the power of suggestion. Tekla is, however, not so suggestible, and Gustav must use cunning and deceit to avenge himself on her.

Although the manner of Adolph's death may seem absurd to modern readers, it, like everything else in the play, was grounded in the scientific and medical knowledge of the time. Hysteria and epilepsy were thought to be basically similar illnesses, and some doctors described intense sexual orgasm as being a genuine epileptiform seizure. Even the extravagant idea mentioned in the play that a child born to a woman who has taken a second husband or lover would quite likely resemble her first sexual partner was accepted by learned men. It was expounded by the eminent historian Jules Michelet in his widely read moral tract, *l'Amour*, and the factually minded Emile Zola made it central to the plot of his novel *Madeleine Férat*.

Like *Miss Julie*, *Creditors* is a naturalistic play, but its tone is different, so different that Strindberg called it a tragicomedy. In Paris there had sprung up a type of play known as *comédie rosse*, brutal, rough, cynical, and often sexually frank—not unlike the *film noir* of more recent times. Still hopeful that Paris would prove more hospitable than Stockholm to his examinations of the psychology of sex, Strindberg meant *Creditors* to be his contribution to the new genre.

In giving advice on how the play should be performed, Strindberg suggested (in a letter to his second wife, September 1896) that it should be acted in the manner of French boulevard comedy: delicately, softly, elegantly; that the inner life be brought to light; that Tekla be portrayed as acting out of her unconscious, not as a fury destroying her man but as a bewitching coquette who destroys without knowing what she is doing; that Gustav carry out his assassination of Adolph with a tender hand, acting out of a complex of intentions, calculations, impulses, and chance; and that above all a sense of Greek fate should hover over the action, so that the poor human creatures play their parts as puppets, criminal in their deeds but still guiltless. He also gave some special advice to an actor about to undertake the role of Gustav, telling him to portray Gustav as "playful and good-natured, which he as the superior person can afford to be. He plays with Adolph as cat with mouse. Never gets angry, never moralizes, never preaches." (Letter of 3 March 1889.) This is perfectly in keeping with Strindberg's conception of Gustav as a Darwinian evolutionist and Nietzschean superman, for whom morality is an invention of the ruling order and emotions merely instincts that must be subordinated to intellect.

Creditors

(Fordringsägäre)

A Tragicomedy

CHARACTERS

TEKLA, a novelist
ADOLPH, her husband, a painter
GUSTAV, her first husband, a teacher at a university, traveling
under an alias

Non-speaking parts:
TWO LADIES
WAITER

The parlor or common room in a small hotel at a seaside resort. At the rear a door opens onto a veranda with a view of the land and water. Just right of center, a table with newspapers on it. A chair to the left of the table, a sofa to the right. At right a door leads to another room.

Adolph and Gustav are at the table, right. Adolph is sculpting a wax figure on a small stand. Propped up near him are his crutches.

ADOLPH: —and for all this I have you to thank.

GUSTAV (*puffing on a cigar*): Nonsense.

ADOLPH: No, it's true. During those first few days when my wife was away, I lay on a sofa, helpless, longing for her. I couldn't move. It was as if she had taken my crutches with her. All I could do was sleep. But after a few days I woke up, pulled myself together. My fever-maddened head cooled off. Old projects, ideas I'd nearly forgotten, popped back into my head. I felt like working, felt the itch to create again. Once again I had vision. Could see the shapes hidden in things. And then you showed up.

GUSTAV: Yes, you were in rotten shape—hobbling on your crutches—no denying that. But that doesn't mean it was my presence that brought you back to health. You needed a rest, obviously. In fact, what you really needed was some masculine company.

ADOLPH: I think you've hit it. You're always right, you know. I had men friends before, of course; but when I got married, they seemed superfluous. I had my dearly beloved; and she was all I needed. Oh, I hung around with other people, got to know a lot of them. But my wife was jealous of them. Wanted me all to herself. Worse than that, she wanted my friends, too—all to herself. Which left me all alone and feeling jealous.

GUSTAV: Well, Adolph, face the fact: you have a jealous constitution.

ADOLPH: I was afraid of losing her and I tried to circumvent it. What normal man wouldn't do the same? I never feared she was being unfaithful to me, you understand—

GUSTAV: No, the doting husband never does.

ADOLPH: No. Remarkable, isn't it? What I really feared was that her friends would influence her, her mind, her tastes; and in that way indirectly exercise a power over me. That's what I couldn't stand.

GUSTAV: Simply put: you and your wife had a difference of opinion.

ADOLPH: Maybe. I've told you so much already, you might as well hear the rest. . . . My wife likes to be independent. —What are you smiling at?

GUSTAV: Don't mind me. She "likes to be independent" . . .

ADOLPH: Yes, so independent that she wouldn't accept anything I had to offer.

GUSTAV: Only what others had to offer!

ADOLPH (*mulling that over*): Y-e-s. . . . How to explain it? She abhorred my ideas not because they were so screwy but because they were mine. I mean, she would grab one of my old ideas and push it as one of hers. Had to be hers, see? Even if she got it from one of my friends who had got it from me. She got a kick out of that. She got a kick out of everything, except what came from me.

GUSTAV: I gather from this that you aren't too happy.

ADOLPH: I wouldn't say that. . . . No, I'm happy. I married the woman I loved, and I've never wanted anyone else.

GUSTAV: Never wanted to be a free man?

ADOLPH: No, I can't say I have. Of course I've sometimes imagined how peaceful things would be if I were single again. But whenever she left me, I felt how much I needed her, like I need my arms, legs. I know it's strange, but sometimes I think of her not as somebody else but as a part of me. She's my heart and guts./In her is my will to live and my lust for life. It's as if I had deposited in her all my gray matter, what the anatomy books call the cerebral cortex.

GUSTAV: That may be pretty close to the truth, when all is said and done.

ADOLPH: No, that doesn't make any sense. After all, she's an independent person with lots of ideas of her own. And when I met her, I was nothing—a painter in diapers—and she brought me up, educated me.

GUSTAV: However, you subsequently developed her mind, didn't you, and brought her up?

ADOLPH: No, she just stopped growing, and I shot up past her.

GUSTAV: Yes, it's a remarkable fact that she never wrote anything better than her first book. Of course, that time she had a good subject. Rumor has it that she put her first husband into that book. Did you ever know him? An absolute idiot, from what I hear.

ADOLPH: I never knew him. He had left Tekla six months before I met her. But it did sound like he was a horse's ass. That is, from Tekla's description of him. (*Pause.*) And her description was right on the mark, you can be sure of that.

GUSTAV: Oh, I am, I am. . . . Odd. What possible reason could she have had for marrying him, I wonder?

ADOLPH: A good reason: she didn't know what he was like. You never get to know each other until afterward.

GUSTAV: For which reason one shouldn't get married until— afterward. He must have been a bully, that's obvious.

ADOLPH: Why is that obvious?

GUSTAV: All husbands are. (*Feeling his way.*) You're no exception, you know.

ADOLPH: Me?! I let my wife come and go as she pleases.

GUSTAV: That's not saying much. After all, you can't keep her under lock and key, now can you? —Does it bother you if she stays out all night, runs around with other men?

ADOLPH: Of course it does.

GUSTAV: See what I mean? (*Suddenly changing his tone.*) Frankly speaking, it only makes you look ridiculous.

ADOLPH: Ridiculous? How can I look ridiculous if I show everybody that I trust my wife?

GUSTAV: Well, you can. In fact, you do. Look ridiculous. Like a horse's ass.

ADOLPH (*exploding convulsively*): Me? Ridiculous?! I won't have it! There'll be some changes made! God, will there not!

GUSTAV: Easy, easy! You'll have another one of your attacks.

ADOLPH: I don't get it. Why doesn't she look like a fool if I stay out all night and carry on?

GUSTAV: Who knows? That's beside the point. It just happens to be a fact. And while you're trying to figure it out, disaster strikes!

ADOLPH: What disaster?

GUSTAV: As I was saying: her husband was a bully, but she married him to be independent and live her own life. Now how can that be? you ask. Simple: how does a girl get to be free and independent? Answer: by having a cover—a blind. Then she can go anywhere. And who is the cover? Her husband.

ADOLPH: Exactly.

GUSTAV: And now you're the cover, aren't you?

ADOLPH: Me?

GUSTAV: Well, you are her husband.

Adolph is lost in thought.

GUSTAV: Am I right, or am I right?

ADOLPH (*troubled*): I don't know. . . . You live with a woman for years, never thinking too much about her, or about your life together. And then something happens—you begin to reflect— and that's the beginning of the end. . . . Gustav, you're my friend. The only man I can call a friend. You've given me a new lease on life this past week. It's as if your personality galvanized me. You've been my repairman. You took this clockwork brain of mine, fixed the mainspring, and set it going again. Can't you see how I'm thinking more clearly, talking more logically? I even think my voice has recovered its timbre.

GUSTAV: I think so too. How do you explain that?

ADOLPH: A man talks more softly to a woman. After a while, it gets to be a habit. Tekla always bawled me out for yelling at her. *reversal*

GUSTAV: So you made your voice small and let her wear the pants in the family.

ADOLPH: That's not how it was! (*After a moment's thought.*) It was worse. . . . Let's not talk about that now. —Where was I? Oh, yes. You arrived on the scene; you showed me what was wrong with my painting. For a long time I had been losing interest in painting. It didn't offer me the scope I needed. I couldn't express what I had to say. And you understood why that was. You explained why a painter today couldn't be the artistic conscience of our times. That was an eye-opener for me. I saw that from here on I could not possibly produce anything worthwhile in oils and colors on a flat surface.

GUSTAV: And are you certain now that you can't paint anymore? Certain that you won't fall back into the old ways?

ADOLPH: Absolutely! I've already put it to the test. That evening after our long chat, when I lay in bed, I went over your argument point by point. I could tell it was right. However, after a good night's sleep and waking up with a clear head, it struck me like a bolt of lightning that you might be wrong. So I ran to my easel, took brushes and palette in hand and—you know what? Nothing. No sense of illusion. Nothing but daubs of pigments. It made me sick to think that I could make myself believe—make others believe—that that painted canvas was anything more than painted canvas. The veil had dropped from my eyes, and I could no more go back to painting than I could become a newborn child again.

GUSTAV: That's when you came to understand that if realism

is the tendency of our times, then the only way to achieve the true illusion of reality—its palpableness, its concreteness—is through sculpture—the physical body, the filling of space in all three dimensions.

ADOLPH (*faltering*): The three dimensions . . . yes . . . the body, the physical body.

GUSTAV: And so you became a sculptor. Which is to say, you had always been one, but you had lost your way, and all you needed was a guide to steer you in the right direction. . . . Tell me, Adolph, do you feel that lust for life now when you're at work?

ADOLPH: It's the only time I really feel alive.

GUSTAV: Let me look at it. Do you mind?

ADOLPH: A female nude.

GUSTAV: And no model? Striking! So alive!

ADOLPH (*dully, his mind drifting*): Yes. And so much like her. That woman lives in my body, just as I do in hers. It's strange.

GUSTAV: The latter isn't strange at all. Do you know what a transfusion is?

ADOLPH: Blood transfusion? Yes.

GUSTAV: Well, you've given too much of yours. Looking at this statue, I understand a lot that I only suspected before. You've loved her deeply, madly.

ADOLPH: So madly I couldn't tell whether she was I or I was she. When she smiles, I smile; when she cries, I cry. And when—I swear it's true—when she gave birth to our child, I felt the labor pains.

GUSTAV (*shaking his head*): You are in a bad way, my dear fellow. But I'm not surprised. I'm sorry to tell you this, but you're already displaying the symptoms of a nervous breakdown, of convulsive epilepsy.

ADOLPH (*shaken*): I am? How can you tell?

GUSTAV: I know them. Emotional explosions, flying off the handle, convulsions, and worse. I know what they are and what brings them on. Saw them in my younger brother. His problem was sex. Addicted to it.

ADOLPH: What were they like—the symptoms?

> *Gustav gives a vivid demonstration. Adolph observes intently and involuntarily begins to imitate Gustav's gestures and grimaces.*

GUSTAV: I tell you it was horrible to see. If you feel the least bit weak, I won't torture you with a description.

ADOLPH (*in anguish, but fascinated*): No, no, no, don't stop. Don't stop.

GUSTAV: All right. My little brother got himself married to a sweet little thing—bangs on her forehead, the eyes of a dove, the face of a child, the soul of an angel. Nonetheless, she contrived to arrogate to herself the prerogative of the male.

ADOLPH: The prerogative of the male? You mean—?

GUSTAV: The sexual initiative. What else? She made the advances. And the result was that the insatiable little angel nearly succeeded in sending my innocent little brother to heaven. First, however, he had to be crucified. Nailed to the cross. God, it was horrible!

ADOLPH (*hanging on every word*): Yes, horrible. What happened?

GUSTAV (*slowly, deliberately*): We might be sitting and talking, just he and I—and after I had been talking awhile, his face would become white—like chalk. His arms and legs grew stiff. And his thumbs would turn inward like this.

> *Gestures, and Adolph imitates him.*

Then his eyes became bloodshot, and he began working his jaws, like this.

> *Chews. Adolph imitates him.*

The saliva rattled in his throat. His chest contracted, as if in a vise. His pupils flickered, like the flames in a gas lamp. His tongue whipped the saliva into a froth. He began to slip down . . . slowly . . . backward . . . in his chair. As if he were drowning. The next thing—

ADOLPH (*in a hoarse whisper*): Stop, that's enough!

GUSTAV: The next thing—. Something the matter? Not feeling well?

ADOLPH: No.

GUSTAV (*fetches a glass of water*): Here, drink this. We'll talk about something else

ADOLPH (*weakly*): Thanks. . . . Let me hear the rest.

GUSTAV: You sure you want to? When he came to, he didn't remember anything that had happened. He had completely lost consciousness. Ever had that experience?

ADOLPH: Yes, I've had fainting spells sometimes. The doctor says it's because I'm anemic.

GUSTAV: Of course. That's how it begins. But, believe me or not, it turns into epilepsy if you don't take care of yourself.

ADOLPH: What should I do?

GUSTAV: Stop having sex. That's the first thing.

ADOLPH: For how long?

GUSTAV: Half a year. At least.

ADOLPH: I couldn't! What kind of married life would that be?

GUSTAV: Then it's curtains for you, I'm afraid.

ADOLPH (*as he drapes the cloth over the wax figure*): I couldn't, not possibly.

GUSTAV: Not even to save your life? . . . Very well. . . . I was wondering—since you have put me so much in your confidence—if there might not be some other sore spot in your life, something that secretly troubles you. Life is so complicated—there are so many causes of misunderstandings—it's very rare for there to be only one source of friction. There must be some skeleton in the closet that only you know about. That child you mentioned, for instance. Why isn't the child here with you?

ADOLPH: My wife wanted it that way. Didn't want it around.

GUSTAV: There must have been a reason. . . . Come on, let's hear it.

ADOLPH: Reason? Because the child, when it got to be three years old, began to look like him—the first husband.

GUSTAV: Indeed! . . . Have you ever seen him—the first husband?

ADOLPH: No, never have. Once I cast a glance at a portrait of him, a poor picture. I couldn't see any resemblance.

GUSTAV: Portraits always lie. Besides, he might have changed a lot. Anyway, you couldn't have any reason to be suspicious, now could you?

ADOLPH: Absolutely not. Our child was born a full year after we were married. And her first husband was traveling abroad when I met Tekla here. This is where I met her, you know, at this resort. This very house. That's why we come here every summer.

GUSTAV: So there weren't any grounds for suspecting any hanky-panky. Not even the resemblance. The child of a widow who remarries often resembles the dead husband. It's a fact, annoying but true. That's why in India they burn the widows. —Tell me honestly, haven't you ever been jealous of him, of her memory of him? Suppose you and Tekla met him on the street. Wouldn't it make you feel sick to hear him say, with his eyes on her, "we" instead of "I"? Not "I"—"We."

ADOLPH: The thought has occurred to me. Often. I can't deny it.

GUSTAV: You see! It will haunt you forever. It'll become an obsession, a discord that you can't resolve, a jarring note always ringing in your ears. All you can do is stuff cotton in them, and work. Work; grow older and wiser; gather experiences, lots of new experiences to pile on top of the coffin and lay to rest the ghost that haunts you.

ADOLPH: It's funny—forgive me for interrupting—it's remarkable how much you resemble Tekla at times. When you talk, you have the habit of squinting one eye, as if taking aim. And you look at me just as she does sometimes. Hypnotically.

GUSTAV: Not really.

ADOLPH: There! You even said "Not really" with that same nonchalant tone. She's always saying "Not really" like that.

GUSTAV: Perhaps we're distantly related. Everybody is, one way or another. Still it is odd. It might be amusing to meet your wife and see for myself.

ADOLPH: You know, she never picks up anything from me. No, she carefully avoids my vocabulary, and I've never seen her use one of my gestures. Married couples are supposed to take after each other, to have telltale habits; that's how you know they're married.

GUSTAV: Yes, I'm sure. —Now let me tell you something. That woman has never loved you.

ADOLPH: What?

GUSTAV: Forgive me, but it's true. Listen: a woman in love is a receptacle. She takes. And if she doesn't take from a man, she doesn't love him. I tell you, she has never loved you.

ADOLPH: You don't think it's possible for her to fall in love a second time?

GUSTAV: No. You only allow yourself to be cheated once. After that, you keep your eyes peeled. Your trouble is that you've never been cheated. Watch out for those who have. They're dangerous, very dangerous.

ADOLPH: Your words are like knives; I feel I'm being slashed. But I can't do anything about it. In fact, I need it. It's like boils that have to be lanced because they would never ripen and burst by themselves. . . . Never loved me? —Then why did she take me? Why?

GUSTAV: You tell me first *how* she came to take you. And did she take you, or did you take her?

ADOLPH: God knows! I don't. —How it happened? It didn't happen all at once.

GUSTAV: With a little guesswork I can work out how it happened. Let me have a stab at it.

ADOLPH: A waste of time. You can't even imagine.

GUSTAV: My dear fellow, with what you've told me about your wife, I can reconstruct the whole episode. Listen, my child, and you shall hear. (*Factually, almost as if telling a funny story.*) The husband is away doing research, and his wife is left alone. At first she feels happy, being free. Then comes the emptiness. I think I can assume she did feel rather empty—two weeks without a husband. Now, enter the other man, and gradually the emptiness is filled up. In comparison, the absent husband fades into insignificance—simply because he is so far away. You know, the law of sexual attraction: inversely proportional to the square of the distance. But now their passions flare up, and they begin to feel queasy about themselves, their consciences, and about him. They want to conceal their embarrassment—with fig leaves; they play at being brother and sister. And the more physical their relationship becomes, the more spiritual they pretend it is.

ADOLPH: Brother and sister! How do you know that?

GUSTAV: A hunch. Little children play husband and wife; when they're bigger, they play brother and sister—to hide what has to be hidden. . . . So now they take a solemn vow of chastity, which means they play "I spy" with each other. Until one day, neither one wants to be "it," and they both hide in a dark corner where they are certain no one can see them. (*Putting on a severe air.*) However, they know in their hearts that someone, someone in particular, sees them even in the dark. And that frightens them. And in their fear, the absent one begins to haunt them, looms up before their eyes, becomes a bogeyman, a nightmare disturbing their nights of love. A creditor, knocking at the door, come to collect. In bed, about to pluck the fruit of paradise, they see his black hand on it. They hear his piercing voice stabbing the quiet of the night, which should be throbbing with the beating of their blood. Maybe he can't stop them from having each other, but he can make them miserable. And when they feel his invisible presence destroying their happiness, when they finally run away—ah, but run away in vain—can't escape the memories that pursue them, the debts they can't pay, the public opinion that unnerves them. —And since they haven't the strength to assume the responsibility for what they've done, a scapegoat has to be found and slaughtered. Oh, they are free-thinking, liberated people, but they haven't the courage to go to him and tell him frankly, "We love each other." No, they are cowards. And therefore the tyrant has to be got rid of, done away with, disposed of. —How am I doing?

ADOLPH: Fine. But you forgot something. She taught me, inspired me, fed me new ideas.

GUSTAV: I didn't forget. Now you tell me, how was it that she couldn't teach her first husband also, couldn't inspire him—make him a freethinker?

ADOLPH: That's easy. He was an idiot.

GUSTAV: Of course! I had forgotten: he was an idiot. Still, what's an idiot? A rather imprecise term. In that novel she wrote, her husband is supposed to be an idiot because he couldn't under-stand her. Forgive me for asking, but is your wife really so pro-found? I haven't discovered any great depths in her novels. Have you?

ADOLPH: No. —In fact, I have to admit that I don't find it easy to understand her either. It's as if the cogs and wheels in my brain don't mesh with hers. When I try to grasp her meaning, the wheels just spin madly.

GUSTAV: Oh, dear! It couldn't be that you're an idiot, too?

ADOLPH: No. At least, I don't think so. In fact, I almost always think she's wrong. Look at this letter; you'll see what I mean. It came today. (*He takes a letter from his wallet.*)

GUSTAV (*scanning the letter*): Hmm. It's a hand that I think I've seen before.

ADOLPH: A man's handwriting, wouldn't you say?

GUSTAV: I might. I know of one man, at least, who has a similar hand. —She calls you "Brother." Are you still playing games, the two of you? Still wearing fig leaves?—albeit a little withered. —"Brother?" Aren't you on a first-name basis? No pet names?

ADOLPH: I don't like pet names. We respect each other.

GUSTAV: Is that so? You mean that she wins your respect by calling herself your sister?

ADOLPH: I respect her as being above me. I want her to be my better self.

GUSTAV: Come off it! Be your own better self. More of a bother, admittedly, than letting somebody else be it. —You really want to be inferior to your wife? I don't believe it!

sick; anti-Darwinist

ADOLPH: That's exactly what I want. I enjoy being a little less clever than she is. Look: I taught her how to swim, and now I think it's fun to hear her brag that she's better at it than I am— faster—takes more chances. At first I pretended I couldn't keep up with her, said I was afraid, just to give her courage. And then, somehow, one day I actually was less strong, more afraid. It struck me that she had taken my courage and made it hers— literally.

more reversal.

GUSTAV: What else, I wonder, have you taught her?

ADOLPH: Well—strictly between ourselves—I taught her how to write. She couldn't spell worth a damn. And you know what happened? After I taught her, she took charge of all the correspondence; I didn't have to write at all. So for years I didn't keep in practice, and—well you can imagine. Now I've even forgotten my grammar. But do you suppose she remembers who it was that taught her how to write? Not a bit! Now *I'm* the idiot, naturally.

GUSTAV: Ah ha! You're the idiot, so soon!

ADOLPH: That's a joke, you understand.

GUSTAV: Of course I understand. —It's cannibalism, wouldn't you say? I mean, savages eat their enemies to acquire their outstanding qualities. She has eaten you, this woman—your heart, your courage, your knowledge—

ADOLPH: —My belief in myself. . . . I was the one who encouraged her to write her first book.

GUSTAV (*making a wry face*): Did you now?

ADOLPH: I was the one who praised her writing to the skies, even when I thought it was pretty shabby stuff. It was I who introduced her into literary circles, so she could buzz around and gather honey from all the beautiful people. It was I who spoke to the critics and asked them to go easy on her. And when she lost inspiration, I gave it to her. But in inspiring her, I expired. I gave and gave and gave for her sake—until there was nothing left of me to give. —Here I am, baring my soul to you, but so what! You know, right now it seems to me—oh, the ways of the soul are strange!—when my success as a painter threatened to overwhelm her success and overshadow her reputation, I attempted to enhearten her by reducing my own significance, telling her my art was inferior to hers. I told her so often that painting was a relatively unimportant art, and invented so many reasons to convince her, that I ended up believing it myself. My faith in painting was only a house of cards, Gustav. All you had to do was blow on it.

GUSTAV: Forgive me, but I must remind you that at the beginning of our little chat you said she never takes anything from you.

ADOLPH: It's true. She doesn't. Not now. There's nothing left for her to take.

GUSTAV: The python is sated. Now it regurgitates.

ADOLPH: Perhaps she has taken more from me—things I don't know about.

GUSTAV: That you can be sure of. She took when you weren't looking. I call that theft.

ADOLPH: Maybe I never learned anything from her.

GUSTAV: And she everything from you? In all probability. But she was clever enough to make you think the opposite. Let me ask you: how did she go about teaching you?

ADOLPH: Well, in the beginning . . . (*Hesitates.*)

GUSTAV: Yes? In the beginning—?

ADOLPH: Well—well, I—I—

GUSTAV: No. *She—she.*

ADOLPH: I don't want to talk about it now.

GUSTAV: Ah, ha, you see!

ADOLPH: Well, it's just that—. My faith in myself, my work— she had eaten that, too. I went into a decline, until you came and gave me something I could throw myself into, heart and soul.

GUSTAV (*smiling*): Sculpture?

ADOLPH (*unsure of himself*): Well . . . yes.

GUSTAV: And you put your heart in that! An abstract, out- moded form of art? Sculpture dates back to primitive times, when people were like children. You don't really believe that pure form—in three dimensions, no less—can mean anything to people nowadays, who want realism—that you can create realism without color? Good heavens! Without color! You don't really—

ADOLPH (*crushed*): No, I don't.

GUSTAV: Nor do I.

ADOLPH: Then why did you tell me you did?

GUSTAV: I felt sorry for you.

ADOLPH: I feel sorry for myself. And well I may! I'm finished, bankrupt, done for! Nothing's left. Not even her.

GUSTAV: What on earth do you want her for?

ADOLPH: Some people have God. I had her. What God was to me before I became an atheist, she was to me: something to worship. She was the object of my veneration.

GUSTAV: Bury your idol, and let something better grow out of it. Like good, healthy contempt.

ADOLPH: I can't live without something to look up to—

GUSTAV: Slave!

ADOLPH: A woman whom I can adore, revere.

GUSTAV: Jesus Christ! Go back to God! Better Him than her if you have a need to cross yourself and genuflect. An atheist who

still believes in the feminine mystique! A freethinker who thinks
what you're told to think about the dames. What's so profound,
so sphinxlike, so unfathomable about that wife of yours? You
know what she really is? Stupid. Dumb. Look! (*Points to the
letter.*) She can't even tell the difference between i-e and e-i. She
doesn't know whether she's coming or going. She's all mixed up.
She's like a cheap watch: the case looks expensive, but it can't
give you the right time. . . . It's all in the skirts, my boy. Put
a pair of pants on her; take a piece of burnt cork and draw a
moustache under her nose. Then lend a sober ear to her prattle;
you'll hear the real sound of her. A phonograph, that's all, playing back your words—or somebody else's—just a little tin-
nier. . . . Have you ever seen a naked woman? Sorry! Of course
you have. A teenager with tits, an undeveloped man, a kid who
shot up and stopped short. A chronic anemic, who spews blood
like clockwork thirteen times a year. —What can such a creature
possibly amount to?

ADOLPH: All right, suppose I accept all that, for the sake of
argument—then what is it that makes me believe she's my equal?

GUSTAV: It's a hallucination. I told you: it's all in the skirts;
they've bewitched you. —Or—who knows?—maybe you have
become equal. Like water seeking its own level. Her capillary
tubes have sucked up your manhood, and now you're both on the
same level. —Listen, old boy (*Taking out his watch.*), we've been
talking for six hours. Your wife should be back any minute now.
Haven't we had enough? You should get some sleep.

ADOLPH: No, no, don't go away. I don't dare to be left alone.

GUSTAV: Buck up; it's only for a short while. She'll soon be
here.

ADOLPH: Yes, she'll be here. . . . It's strange. Although I
yearn for her, I'm afraid of her. She fondles me, she's tender; but
there's something in her kisses that suffocates me, sucks my
strength, paralyzes me. Reminds me of the child who works in
the circus. The clown pinches him offstage so his cheeks look
pink and rosy for the public.

GUSTAV: My friend, I'm truly sorry for you. I don't have to be a doctor to see that you're ill, a dying man. You only have to look at your last paintings. It's all there.

ADOLPH: What do you mean, it's all there?

GUSTAV: The colors! Pale, washed out. You can see the canvas through them—yellow like a corpse. When I look at them, I see your hollow, clay-colored cheeks showing through.

ADOLPH: All right! Enough!

GUSTAV: It's not just my opinion, you know. Have you read this morning's paper?

ADOLPH (*startled*): No!

GUSTAV: It's right here on the table.

ADOLPH (*reaches for the paper, but dares not take it*): It's in the paper?

GUSTAV: Go ahead. Or should I?

ADOLPH: No . . .

GUSTAV: I'll go, if you want me to.

ADOLPH: No, no, no. —I don't know what I—. I think I'm beginning to hate you but still can't let you go. I'm drowning; you haul me up, and when I'm up, you hit me on the head and dunk me again. As long as I kept my secrets to myself, I had some guts. Now I'm empty. There's a painting by an Italian master—a scene of torture. There's a saint, and his intestines are being pulled out and wound on a windlass. The martyr lies there, looking at what's happening to him. He's getting thinner and thinner, and the roll on the wheel is getting thicker and thicker. I can see how much bigger you've grown since you began digging into my life; and when you leave me, you'll take my innards with you and leave behind an empty shell.

GUSTAV: You do have an imagination, Adolph. Anyway, your wife will be bringing your heart back to you, won't she?

ADOLPH: Oh, no. Not now. You put the torch to her. You've turned everything to ashes—my art, my love, my hope, my faith.

GUSTAV: Somebody else had already done that—and done it well.

ADOLPH: Maybe. But there was still time to save something. Now it's too late. Arsonist!

GUSTAV: Come on, we've only scorched the ground a little. Now we'll sow seeds in the fertile ashes.

ADOLPH: I detest you! Damn you!

GUSTAV: A good sign. There's still some spunk left in you. And now I'm going to haul you up again. Listen to me. . . . Will you listen to me? And will you do as I tell you?

ADOLPH: Do with me as you wish. I'll obey.

GUSTAV (*standing up*): Look at me.

ADOLPH (*fastening his eyes on Gustav*): Now you're looking at me again with those eerie eyes that draw me to you.

GUSTAV: Now listen to me.

ADOLPH: All right, I'm listening. But talk about yourself. Not about me. I'm one big open wound, and I can't bear being touched.

GUSTAV: Myself? There's nothing to talk about. I'm a classicist, a teacher of dead languages; and a widower. That's the whole of it. —Now take my hand.

ADOLPH (*takes his hand*): What terrible power you must have! It's like plugging into a socket.

GUSTAV: Then consider: I was once as weak as you. —Get up!

ADOLPH (*stands up; starts to fall; grabs Gustav by the neck*): I'm like a baby. My bones haven't grown together yet, and my brains are slipping through them.

GUSTAV: Take a few steps. Cross the floor.

ADOLPH: I can't.

GUSTAV: You can't?! I'll slap your face!

ADOLPH (*rears up*): What!

GUSTAV: I'll slap your silly face!

ADOLPH (*jumps back, furious*): You'll what?

GUSTAV: Ah, ha! You see! Now the blood rose to your head. Some of the old confidence came back, didn't it? Now I'll give you another jolt of electricity. —Where's your wife?

ADOLPH: Where's my wife?

GUSTAV: Yes. Where is your wife?

ADOLPH: She's at a—at a meeting.

GUSTAV: You're sure?

ADOLPH: Absolutely.

GUSTAV: What kind of meeting?

ADOLPH: Trustees' meeting for an orphanage.

GUSTAV: When she went off to the meeting, it was a friendly parting?

ADOLPH (*hesitating*): Not exactly.

GUSTAV: In other words you'd had a tiff. —What did you say that riled her?

ADOLPH: You're terrible. You really scare me. How could you know?

GUSTAV: I have three known quantities. It's simple to calculate the unknown one. —Now what did you say to her?

ADOLPH: I said—. They were just three words. They were awful words. I regret them, oh, how I regret them!

GUSTAV: You shouldn't. Now what were they?

ADOLPH: I said: "You old whore."

GUSTAV: That's all?

ADOLPH: Not a word more.

GUSTAV: Yes, you did. Only you've forgotten it—because you don't dare remember. You've tucked it away in a secret drawer in that brain of yours, and now it's time to open it.

ADOLPH: I tell you I can't bring it to mind.

GUSTAV: But I can. What you said was this: "You ought to be ashamed. Flirting at your age, when you're too old to attract a lover."

ADOLPH: Is that what I said? I must have. —But how could you know?

GUSTAV: She told the whole story on the steamship that I took coming here. That's how I heard it—overheard it.

ADOLPH: Told it to whom?

GUSTAV: To four young men she was keeping company with. She's already infatuated with innocent young boys, just like—

ADOLPH: There's nothing wrong in that.

GUSTAV: No, of course not. It's like playing sister and brother when you're really mommy and daddy.

ADOLPH: So you've seen her, actually seen her?

GUSTAV: Yes, I have. Which you never have. Seen her when you weren't looking at her. I mean, when you weren't present. And that's why a man can't possibly get to know his wife. —Do you have a photograph of her?

> *Adolph takes a photograph from his wallet; wonders what Gustav is up to.*

GUSTAV: You weren't there when this picture was taken?

ADOLPH: No.

GUSTAV: Look at it. Is it like the portrait you painted? No. The features are the same, but the expression is different. You can't see that because you superimpose on it your own image of her. Now try to look at it as a painter, without thinking of the original. . . . Who is the person in that picture? All I can see is a flirt, with lots of makeup, and a saucy wink in her eye. Look at that brazen smile. *You* never get to see that. Look at the way her eyes are prowling for some man. And it isn't you. Look at the low cut of her dress—the hair done up differently—her sleeves pushed up, the bared arms. Do you see?

ADOLPH: Yes. I see. Now.

GUSTAV: Take care, my friend. Watch out!

ADOLPH: For what?

GUSTAV: Revenge! —You have hit her where it hurts, don't forget that. You told her she couldn't attract a man. Now if you had said that what she writes in her books is crap, she would only have laughed at your lack of taste and discrimination. But now—believe me—if she hasn't already gotten even with you, it isn't for want of trying.

ADOLPH: I've got to know.

GUSTAV: That's right. You've got to find out.

ADOLPH: Yes. Find out.

GUSTAV: See to it. Now. I can help if you want me to.

ADOLPH: Why not? I'm going to die anyway. As well now as later. What do you have in mind?

GUSTAV: First, some information. Doesn't your wife have a single vulnerable spot?

ADOLPH: Hardly. She's got nine lives like a cat.

A steamship's whistle is heard.

GUSTAV: That's the steamer coming in to dock. She'll be here soon.

ADOLPH: I have to go to the dock to meet her!

GUSTAV: No! You're going to stay right here. You're going to be rude and impolite. No currying. If her conscience is clear, you'll get a bawling out that will make your ears ring. However, if she's feeling guilty, she'll be sweetness itself, and coo and cuddle up to you.

ADOLPH: You're sure this will really work?

GUSTAV: Not really. Rabbits sometimes double back and run rings around the dogs. Not to worry, old boy, I'll take care of it. —My room is next to this one. (*Points to the door at right, behind the chair.*) I'll post myself there and keep an eye on you while you play games with her in here. And when you've had your fun, we'll change places. I'll go into the lion cage, and you'll be at the keyhole. Afterward we'll meet in the park and compare notes. But hold your ground. If I see you weakening, I'll pound twice on the floor with a chair.

ADOLPH: Agreed! But don't abandon me. I've got to know that you're in that room.

GUSTAV: Rest assured. —A warning, however: don't get sick when you see me dissecting a human soul and laying the pieces out on this table. An autopsy is a horrible experience for the novice. But nobody who's seen one regrets it. —Oh, one thing more. Not a word about meeting me. You never met anybody while she was away. Not anybody, understand? —And leave it to me to find her Achilles' heel. —Quiet! She's already here. She's in her room. I can hear her humming to herself. That means she's mad as a hornet. —All right! Straighten up! Shoulders back! Sit down in your chair—there, so she'll have to sit in mine. That way I can see you both at once.

ADOLPH: It's an hour till dinnertime. I haven't heard the desk bell ring, and that means no new guests have arrived. So we're alone. Unfortunately.

GUSTAV: Feeling weak?

ADOLPH: Feeling nothing. —No, I'm afraid of what's going to happen. But I can't stop it from happening. The stone has started to roll. Wasn't the last drop of water that set it going, and not the first. It was all of them together.

GUSTAV: So let it roll! You won't have any peace until it does. —I'll see you soon. (*He exits.*)

> *Adolph nods. Looks at the photograph in his hands. He tears it to pieces and throws them under the table. Sits down in his chair, fusses with his tie, runs his fingers through his hair, nervously adjusts the lapels on his coat, and so on.*
>
> *Tekla enters. Goes straight to him and kisses him. She is friendly, frank, cheerful, and charming.*

TEKLA: Hello, Adolph! How's my little brother?

ADOLPH (*succumbing to her charm in spite of himself; resistingly, jokingly*): What have you been up to that entitles me to a kiss?

TEKLA: What do you think? I've been spending money like mad!

ADOLPH: Have any fun doing it?

TEKLA: A lot! But certainly not at that awful foundling home! What a lot of shit! – if you'll pardon my French. – Now tell me what Little Brother has been up to while Pussycat was away. (*She looks around the room, trying to find some clue to what has been going on.*)

ADOLPH: Boring myself to death.

TEKLA: No company?

ADOLPH: No. All alone.

> *Tekla scrutinizes him. Sits in the sofa.*

TEKLA: Who's been sitting here?

ADOLPH: Sitting there? No one.

TEKLA: How odd! The seat's still warm. And there's a depression here in the arm made by somebody's elbow. Oh ho! I do believe Little Brother has been entertaining a lady.

ADOLPH: Me?! You don't believe that at all.

TEKLA: You're blushing! Don't tell me Little Brother is trying to play games with me. Come over here and tell Pussycat all about it. Little Brother has something on his conscience, hasn't he?

> *She pulls him toward her. He sinks down and puts his head in her lap.*

ADOLPH (*smiling*): You're a little devil; you know that, don't you?

TEKLA: No. I don't know a thing about myself.

ADOLPH: You mean you never think about yourself?

TEKLA (*looks around, suspecting something, still trying to find a clue*): I think only *of* myself. I'm a frightful egotist. —My! haven't you become analytical!

ADOLPH: Put your hand on my forehead.

TEKLA (*babytalking*): Has my little boy got bugsy-wugsy in his head? Shall I make them go away? Hmm? Hmm? (*She kisses his forehead.*) There now! Isn't that better?

ADOLPH: Yes. Much better.

Pause.

TEKLA: Now my little boy is going to tell me what he's been doing while I've been away, isn't he? Has he been painting?

ADOLPH: No. I've had it with painting. I'm through.

TEKLA: What? Through painting?

ADOLPH: Finished! Don't bawl me out! It's not my fault that I can't paint anymore.

TEKLA: What on earth are you going to do with yourself?

ADOLPH: I'm taking up sculpture.

TEKLA: Oh, God! Always something new!

ADOLPH: I said, don't start bawling me out! I mean it. —Take a look at what I've done.

TEKLA (*removes the cloth from the wax figure*): Well, I declare! Who is it supposed to be?

ADOLPH: Guess!

TEKLA (*breezily*): Is that supposed to be your Pussycat? Have you no shame?

ADOLPH: It's like you, isn't it?

TEKLA: How should I know? It's got no face.

ADOLPH: It's got a lot else—(*Indicating her breasts.*) those big brown eyes here—another bunch of delicacies there . . .

TEKLA (*playfully slapping his face*): Shut your mouth—or I'll close it for you—with a kiss.

ADOLPH (*avoiding her*): Cut it out! Someone might come in!

TEKLA: What do I care! Isn't a wife allowed to kiss her husband? I want to exercise my legal rights.

ADOLPH: Fine, fine! Except that here at the hotel they don't believe we're married: we're always kissing each other. And our little spats don't convince them otherwise. Lovers' quarrels, that's what they think.

TEKLA: Then let's not quarrel. Why can't you always be as sweet as you are now? Why? . . . Don't you—? Don't you want us to be happy together? Hm?

ADOLPH: If you only knew how much! But—but . . .

TEKLA: Now what's the matter with you? . . . Whoever told you you should give up painting?

ADOLPH: Why should it be anybody? You're always suspecting somebody behind what I do and what I think. As if I couldn't act on my own. —You know what? You're jealous!

TEKLA: Of course I am, you silly! I'm afraid somebody will come and take Little Brother away from me.

ADOLPH: How can you be? You know that no woman on earth could take your place. I can't live without you.

TEKLA: It's not the women I'm afraid of. It's your male friends—the ones who put crazy ideas into your head.

ADOLPH (*studying her closely*): You *are* afraid. Afraid of what?

TEKLA (*standing up*): Someone has been here, I know it. Who was it?

ADOLPH: Why can't you look me in the eye?

TEKLA: Not like that. You never used to look at me like that.

ADOLPH: I'm just looking into your eyes.

TEKLA: No, your eyes are veiled. You're looking through your eyelids.

ADOLPH: Through yours, you mean. I want to see what's going on behind them.

TEKLA: Go ahead; take a good look! I've got nothing to hide. . . . There's something funny going on. You're talking different—using expressions. . . . (*Searchingly.*) Analyzing. . . . What's going on? (*Advancing on him threateningly.*) I want to know who's been here!

ADOLPH: No one—except my doctor.

TEKLA: Your doctor! You don't have a doctor here.

ADOLPH: My doctor from Rivertown.

TEKLA: What's his name?

ADOLPH: Seaberg.

TEKLA: What did he have to say?

ADOLPH: He said . . . he said a lot of things. . . . He said . . . that I was in danger of having an epileptic attack.

TEKLA: A lot of things? What else?

ADOLPH: Something pretty . . . distressing.

TEKLA: Well, out with it!

ADOLPH: He forbade us to have sex together for a while.

TEKLA: Forbade—! I knew it! Oh, I knew that was coming! They want to separate us. I've seen that coming for a long time.

ADOLPH: You couldn't possibly have seen it coming. It's never once happened!

TEKLA: I tell you I've seen it coming!

ADOLPH: You couldn't see what wasn't there—unless you were afraid. Your imagination made you see what never existed. What are you afraid of? That I would get to see you with someone else's eyes? See you for what you are—and not for what I took you to be?

TEKLA: Don't let your imagination run away with you, Adolph. Imagination is the monster that dwells in man's soul, Adolph.

ADOLPH: Oh, God! Where on earth did you hear that? From the innocent adolescents on the steamboat? — Right?

TEKLA (*unflustered, without skipping a beat*): That's right. Even the young have something to teach us.

ADOLPH: My, my! I do believe you've fallen in love with youth. Already!

TEKLA: Haven't I always? Why do you think I loved you? What have you got against youth?

ADOLPH: Nothing. I just prefer to be loved alone, and not as part of a group.

TEKLA (*babytalking playfully*): Pussycat has a great big heart. Little Brother knows what a big heart she has. There's room in it for many besides him.

ADOLPH: Maybe Little Brother doesn't want any brothers.

TEKLA: Come here to Big Sister. What you need is a spanking. It isn't good to be jealous. No, you're envious; that's what you are. Tut, tut.

> *The sound of two raps with the chair in Gustav's room are heard.*

ADOLPH: Cut it out! I'm not in the mood for games. I want a serious talk.

TEKLA (*as if to a child*): Heaven's to betsy! Does the little man want a serious talk? Gracious, hasn't he become the somber one! (*She takes his head in her hands and kisses him.*) Now let me see a little smile. A little chuckle.

ADOLPH (*smiling in spite of himself*): You damned witch! You can charm the pants off a man!

TEKLA: There, there. Of course I can. You know I can. That's why you shouldn't quarrel. Because I'll charm you right out of your skin.

ADOLPH (*getting to his feet*): Tekla! Sit there with your profile toward me. I want to put a face on my statue.

TEKLA: Happy to oblige. (*Poses.*) How's that?

ADOLPH (*studies her; pretends to model*): Good. Now put me out of your thoughts. Think of someone else.

TEKLA: All right. My most recent conquest. Will that do?

ADOLPH: The innocent young boy?

TEKLA: Yes, exactly. Oh, he had such a darling little moustache, and his cheeks were all peaches and cream. So soft and tender, I wanted to bite into them.

ADOLPH (*frowning*): That's it! That expression around your mouth—hold it!

TEKLA: Which expression?

ADOLPH: Cynical, brazen. An expression I've never seen on you before.

TEKLA (*making a face*): You mean this one?

ADOLPH: Precisely. (*Stands up.*) Do you know how Bret Harte describes an adulteress?

TEKLA (*smiling*): His name's Harte and he writes about women? How quaint. Never read him.

ADOLPH: He says an adulteress is a pale woman who can never blush.

TEKLA: Never? Oh, come on, when she meets her lover, I'm sure she blushes. Only her husband—or Mr. Harte—isn't there to see it.

ADOLPH: Are you sure?

TEKLA (*sweetly*): Yes. The husband isn't man enough to make the blood rush to her head, so he never gets to see that enchanting sight.

ADOLPH (*furious*): Damn you!

TEKLA: Silly nincompoop!

ADOLPH: Tekla!

TEKLA: Little Brother should call me Poodycat, and I'll blush–all over–just for you. You want me to? Do you?

ADOLPH (*defenseless*): I'm so mad at you, you monster, I could bite you!

TEKLA (*playfully*): Come on! Come and bite me! Come!

> *She stretches out her arms to him. Adolph embraces her and kisses her.*

ADOLPH: I'll bite and bite until you die.

TEKLA (*teasingly, recalling his earlier words*): Careful! Someone might come in!

ADOLPH: What the hell do I care! I don't give a damn about anything as long as I have you!

TEKLA: And when you don't have me–?

ADOLPH: I'll die.

TEKLA: No fear of that, is there? Since I'm so old no one wants me.

ADOLPH: Oh, Tekla, you can't forget I said that, can you? I'm sorry. I take back those words.

TEKLA: You're so jealous, and at the same time so cocksure of yourself. How do you explain that?

ADOLPH: I can't explain anything. Possibly the thought that someone else has possessed you, maybe that thought lies and rankles in me. Sometimes I think that our love is an act of self-defense, a story we've had to invent to save our self-respect, an affair of the heart that has become a point of honor. Because I know that nothing torments me more than the thought that *he* might see I'm unhappy. Oh, God, I've never seen him, but the mere idea that there is someone out there who is praying I'll be miserable, who every day calls down curses on my head, who will laugh himself sick when I fall–just that thought is like an incubus riding me, compulsively driving me into your arms, obsessing me, paralyzing me.

TEKLA: Do you suppose I'd give him that pleasure? Do you think I'd want to make his dreams come true?

ADOLPH: I don't want to believe it, no.

TEKLA: Then why can't you settle down and forget about it?

ADOLPH: How can I when you carry on like a flirt? Why do you play your idiotic little games?

TEKLA: They're not games. I want to be liked and admired, that's all.

ADOLPH: Yes, but only by men.

TEKLA: Naturally. Women don't like each other; they envy each other.

ADOLPH: Tell me something. . . . Have you heard—from him—recently?

TEKLA: Not for half a year.

ADOLPH: Don't you ever think of him?

TEKLA: No. Since our child died, there's been no connection between us.

ADOLPH: You've never bumped into him—on the street?

TEKLA: No. He's living somewhere on the west coast. Why do you worry yourself about that?

ADOLPH: I don't know. These last few days, when I've been alone here, I couldn't help wondering how he must have felt when he found himself all alone, when you left him.

TEKLA: Dear me? Don't tell me your conscience is bothering you.

ADOLPH: Well, it is.

TEKLA: You feel like a thief, don't you?

ADOLPH: Something like that.

TEKLA: That's lovely! What does that make me? You think you can steal women like you steal chickens or kidnap children? You think I'm his personal property—chattel goods? Thanks a lot!

ADOLPH: No. I think of you as his wife. That's not the same as a piece of furniture. You can't buy another one.

TEKLA: Of course you can! Let me tell you, if you heard he had married again, you wouldn't have these silly quirks. — Look, you've replaced him for me, haven't you?

ADOLPH: Is that what I've done? Didn't you ever love him?

TEKLA: I most certainly did!

ADOLPH: And what happened?

TEKLA: I got bored with him.

ADOLPH: Suppose you got bored with me?

TEKLA: I won't. I won't.

ADOLPH: If someone else came along, someone who had what you're looking for — *now* — in a man — I say *suppose* — you'd toss me aside.

TEKLA: Never!

ADOLPH: Even if he fascinated you? — swept you off your feet? — so you couldn't live without him — of course you'd live without me.

TEKLA: No. That doesn't follow.

ADOLPH: You don't mean you could love two at once?

TEKLA: Sure. Why not?

ADOLPH: That's beyond me.

TEKLA: There are things in heaven and earth, darling, that are not dreamt of in your philosophy. All people are not created alike.

ADOLPH: I think I'm beginning to understand.

TEKLA: Not really.

ADOLPH (*imitating her inflection*): "Not really." (*Adolph tries to remember something but cannot quite bring it into focus.*) Tekla, your frankness is beginning to give me a pain.

TEKLA: Frankness is the highest virtue. That's what you used to preach.

ADOLPH: I know I did. But now I have the distinct impression that you're hiding out in the open.

TEKLA: The latest thing in camouflage. Didn't you know?

ADOLPH: No, I didn't. I only know that it's getting to be unpleasant here. What do you say we leave for home – tonight!

TEKLA: Now what are you up to? I just arrived! I have no desire to leave.

ADOLPH: Well, I want us to.

TEKLA: All right, it's a free country. Go on, leave, if that's what you want.

ADOLPH: I'm telling you to leave with me on the next boat.

TEKLA: Telling me! Who do you think you are?!

ADOLPH: I'll have you know that you are my wife!

TEKLA: I'll have you know that you are my husband!

ADOLPH: Exactly! And there's a difference between those two things.

TEKLA: Ah ha! So you've sunk to that level! . . . I knew you never loved me.

ADOLPH: Never loved you?!

TEKLA: No. Because to love means to give.

ADOLPH: To love like a man means to give. To love like a woman means to take. And, God knows, I have given – *given* – *given*!

TEKLA: Pooh! What have you given?

ADOLPH: Everything!

TEKLA: A hell of a lot that was! – Even if it's true, I was good enough to accept it. Are you going to send me bills for your gifts? If I took what you gave, it proves I loved you. A woman only accepts gifts from her lover.

ADOLPH: Lover! That's it! That's the truth. I've been your lover, never your husband.

TEKLA: How convenient for you. You never had to be a cover for me. —However, if you're not content to be a lover, off you go! I certainly don't need a husband hanging around.

ADOLPH: So I've noticed. These past few months when I saw how you wanted to sneak away like a thief in the night, saw how you sought out your own kind, with whom you could parade around in borrowed feathers — my feathers — and sparkle with my brilliant wit, that's when I tried to remind you of what you owed me. And in an instant I was transformed into the troublesome creditor, who wouldn't go away. You wanted to tear up the IOU's. And to avoid going deeper into debt, you stopped dipping into my wallet: you went to others. I became your husband — without wanting to. And as soon as I played the husband, you hated me. But now I'm going to *be* your husband, whether you like it or not — since I can't be your lover.

TEKLA (*playfully*): You're talking nonsense, you know that, you darling idiot!

ADOLPH: A word of advice, Tekla. It's dangerous to go around thinking everyone's an idiot except yourself.

TEKLA: Doesn't everybody?

ADOLPH: I'm beginning to suspect that possibly he — your first husband — wasn't an idiot.

TEKLA: Heaven help us! Don't tell me you're beginning to feel sorry for him!

ADOLPH: What if I am?

TEKLA: Well, what *do* you know! You want to meet him — perhaps pour out your heart to him. What a pretty picture that would make. —Funnily enough, even I'm beginning to feel attracted to him, now that I've gotten bored being your nurse-maid. At least he was a real man. The only thing wrong with him was that he was mine.

ADOLPH: I knew it. —For God's sake, don't talk so loud! We can be overheard.

TEKLA: So what! They'd only take us for a married couple.

ADOLPH: So you've got a hankering for real he-men—and for pure young men—both at the same time.

TEKLA: My hankerings have no limit. It's simple. I open my heart to all, for all—the short and the tall, the pretty and the plain, what's old, what's new. I love the whole world. *Mother*

ADOLPH: You know what that means?

TEKLA: I don't know what anything means. I only feel.

ADOLPH: It means you're getting old.

TEKLA: Harping on that again? Watch out, sonny!

ADOLPH: You watch out!

TEKLA: What for?

ADOLPH: The knife!

TEKLA (*babytalking*): Little Brother shouldn't play with such things. He might hurt himself.

ADOLPH: Who says I'm playing?

TEKLA: You want to be serious? Dead serious? All right, I'll show you what a mistake you're making. But you'll never know what I'll do to you, never really know. The whole world will be in on it—everybody except you. You'll suspect it, sense it always, and you'll never have a moment's peace. You'll feel in your bones what a fool you are, how I'm being unfaithful to you, but you'll never get your hands on a shred of evidence. The husband never does. Oh, I'm going to make you pay!

ADOLPH: You really hate me, don't you?

TEKLA: No, I don't hate you. I won't ever come to hate you. How could I? You're such a child.

ADOLPH: *Now* I am, yes. But what about the time when we had it rough. You cried like a baby in diapers. You sat in my lap, and I had to kiss your eyes until you fell asleep. I was your nurse then. Had to comb your hair and straighten you up so you wouldn't go out looking a mess. Get your shoes repaired. Cook something on the stove. I had to sit by your side for hours, holding your hand. You were afraid, afraid of the whole world. Didn't have a friend. The critics, the public, everybody was against you. You were crushed, and I had to give you the courage to go on, talking to you through the night until my tongue withered and cracked, and my head ached. I had to convince myself that I was strong—force myself to believe that tomorrow would be better. And finally I succeeded in breathing life into you, when you lay as if dead. I astonished you then, and you admired me. Then I was the man, the real man, not that sexual athlete you had left but a man with a strength of spirit—the hypnotist who stroked his energy into your slack muscles and recharged your empty brain with his electricity. I rehabilitated you. Made friends for you. Provided you with a little court of admirers who, out of friendship to me, let themselves be talked into fawning over you. I set you above myself and my home. I portrayed you in my most beautiful paintings—in rose and azure against a gilt background; and there wasn't an exhibition in which you didn't occupy the best spot. Sometimes you were St. Cecelia, or you might be Mary Stuart, or Maria Walewska. I advertised you, made you the focus of attention. I got the whole braying mob of asses to see you through my adoring eyes. I drilled your personality into their lives, forced you down their throats. Finally everybody knew who you were, liked you. You were a celebrity. Then you were on your own. . . . But it was I who made you, and, having made you, I had no strength left. The effort had been too much for me. In making you, I had undone myself. I was in the dumps and you were riding high. I became ill, and my illness embarrassed you. Sometimes I felt that what was behind it was a desire to get rid of me, the creditor, the man who knew too much about you. Your love for me changed. You became the grown-up sister, always acting uppity. I didn't have much choice. I learned my new part: Little Brother. You were so tender—even more so than before. But all that sweetness had a thin coating of pity, and that pity contained a large amount of disrespect, and that disrespect grew into contempt as my talent withered on the vine while yours blossomed in the sun. . . . But then something happened. Unforeseen. Your well of inspiration seemed to go dry when I wasn't there to replenish it. Or rather, when you tried to prove that you didn't have to dip into it. The result was that we both dried up. And now you want someone to blame. Somebody new. Because you're weak. Because you can never blame yourself or pay your own debts. I became the scapegoat to be sacrificed. You cut me up. But you didn't realize that when you cut my tendons, you crippled yourself—because by then we had grown together like Siamese twins. I was the plant and you were the shoot taken from me, but you tried to grow on your own before you had taken root. You couldn't survive—and the plant couldn't live without its main branch. So we both died.

TEKLA: What you're trying to say is that *you* wrote *my* books!

ADOLPH: That's what you want me to say—to make me out a liar. I carefully avoided expressing myself as coarsely as that. I've been talking for five minutes because I wanted to render all the nuances, all the shadings, all the modulations. You keep harping on one note. I'm an orchestra and you're a tin whistle.

TEKLA: Talk, talk! In one word, you're saying you wrote my books!

ADOLPH: No! I'm saying that you can't put what I'm saying into one word. You can't break up a chord of music and play it as one note. You can't reduce a lifetime of experiences to one number. I never said anything so stupid as that I wrote your books.

TEKLA: It's what you meant!

ADOLPH (*furious*): It's not what I meant!

TEKLA: It was the sum total of what you said, the bottom line!

ADOLPH (*in a wild rage*): There can't be a bottom line if you don't add! You get a quotient, a long quotient with an endless number of decimal places when you divide and it doesn't come out even. I tell you I wasn't adding!

TEKLA: No? Well, I was!

ADOLPH: I just bet you were! But I wasn't!

TEKLA: But you wanted to! Didn't you? Didn't you?

ADOLPH (*giving up; closing his eyes*): No, no, no, I tell you. . . . Don't talk to me. You're giving me convulsions. Just shut up and go away. You're prying my brain apart with that crowbar tongue of yours. . . . Your nails claw into my thoughts and tear them to shreds. (*He seems to fall into a stupor. Stares vacantly, rolls his thumbs inward against his palms.*)

TEKLA (*solicitously*): What's the matter? Adolph—are you ill? Adolph?

Adolph waves her away.

TEKLA: Adolph!

Adolph shakes his head.

TEKLA: Adolph?

ADOLPH: What?

TEKLA: Now do you admit you were unfair?

ADOLPH: Yes, yes, yes. I admit it.

TEKLA: And are you going to ask my forgiveness?

ADOLPH: Yes, yes, yes. I beg you to forgive me. Just stop talking to me!

TEKLA: Now give me a kiss.

Adolph kisses her.

TEKLA: Kiss my hand.

ADOLPH (*kisses her hand*): There. I kiss your hand. Just stop talking to me.

TEKLA: Now go outside and get some fresh air before dinner.

ADOLPH: I certainly need it. Then we'll pack our bags and leave.

TEKLA: We'll do nothing of the sort!

ADOLPH (*rising to his feet*): Why not? You must have a good reason.

TEKLA: My good reason is that I have promised to partake in the *soirée* this evening.

ADOLPH: So that's it! I knew it!

TEKLA: Yes, that's it. I promised I'd be there.

ADOLPH: No you didn't. You said you'd think about it. That's not going to prevent you from saying you've thought about it and decided not to go.

TEKLA: That's how you might act. I stick to my word.

ADOLPH: A person sticks to his promises, but he doesn't have to stick to every word he says. Did you *promise* anyone that you'd go?

TEKLA: Yes.

ADOLPH: All right. Then you can be released from your promise. You can tell them that your husband is not feeling good.

TEKLA: I'll do nothing of the sort! Besides, you're not so sick you can't come too.

ADOLPH: Why do you always want me tagging along? Does my presence make you more comfortable?

TEKLA: I don't know what you mean.

ADOLPH: That's what you always say when you know exactly what I mean and don't like what I mean.

TEKLA: Is that so? And just what is it that I don't like?

ADOLPH: Enough, enough! Don't let's start again. —Go on, goodbye. —Only for God's sake, think what you're doing. (*He leaves by the door at rear and turns right.*)

> *Tekla is alone for a few moments.*

> *Gustav enters. He goes directly to the table and picks up a newspaper, pretending not to see Tekla.*

> *Seeing him, she is visibly shaken. Gets control of herself.*

TEKLA: I don't believe it!

GUSTAV (*recognizing her*): I'm afraid it's true. Sorry.

TEKLA: How did you get here?

GUSTAV: By land. —Don't fret. I won't be staying here, since—you—

TEKLA: Don't let that stop you. . . . Well, well, it's been a long time, hasn't it?

GUSTAV: Yes, a long time.

TEKLA: You've changed a lot.

GUSTAV: And you're just as lovely and charming as ever. Even more youthful. I'm sorry to break in on you like this. Don't worry; I don't intend to sour your happiness by hanging around. If I had known you were here, I would never have—

TEKLA: Stay, by all means—that is, if you don't find it too awkward. Please.

GUSTAV: For my part, there's no reason why I shouldn't. However, I was thinking of—. Oh, dear, whatever I say, it's going to hurt someone.

TEKLA: Sit down for a while. You won't hurt me. You have that rare gift, Gustav—you've always had it—of being tactful and discreet.

GUSTAV: You're too kind, Tekla. Nevertheless, whatever you may say, your husband isn't likely to regard my qualities as indulgently as you do.

TEKLA: On the contrary. Just now he was telling me how much sympathy he had for you.

GUSTAV: Is that so? Well, we all grow and change. Like initials carved on a tree. Not even dislike can make a permanent place for itself in our hearts.

TEKLA: How could he feel dislike for you when he's never seen you? . . . As far as I'm concerned, I've always entertained a dream—seeing the two of you for a moment as friends—or at least seeing you meet in my presence—greeting each other as friends—and then going your separate ways.

GUSTAV: I, too . . . have had a secret desire . . . of seeing you—whom I have loved more than life itself—of seeing you in good hands, well cared for. I've heard nothing but good things about him, and I've kept up with his work. However, before I grow old, I'd like to clasp his hand in mine, look him in the eye, and ask him to guard well that treasure that providence left in his possession. By that very act I would also be ridding myself of the hatred that one instinctively and inevitably feels, here inside. I'd find the peace of mind I need, the humility of spirit, that would enable me to live out the rest of my sad days.

TEKLA: My very thoughts. You've understood me perfectly. Thank you, Gustav.

GUSTAV: Dear me, I cut such a poor figure, I'm so insignificant, I could never stand in your light. My simple, monotonous daily routine, my dull work, my small circle of friends could never have satisfied you. You wanted freedom, broad horizons, fast company. I admit it now. But you must understand – you've studied human nature enough – how difficult it has been for me to face up to it.

TEKLA: It's noble of you, Gustav; it shows a magnanimous soul to be able to admit one's failings. Not everyone is capable of it. (*Sighs.*) However, you were always honest, loyal, and dependable. That's what I valued in you. But –

GUSTAV: No, no. I wasn't that at all. Not *then*. But suffering purifies and sorrow ennobles. And *I* have suffered.

TEKLA: My poor Gustav. Can you ever forgive me? Can you? . . . Say you can, Gustav.

GUSTAV: Forgive you? What kind of talk is that? It is I who beg forgiveness of you.

TEKLA (*suddenly warm and intimate*): I think we're both about to cry. A couple of sentimental old fools.

GUSTAV (*adjusting to her changed tone, but warily*): Old? *I* am, but not you. You grow younger with each passing day.

> *Unobtrusively, he sits down on the chair, right; whereupon Tekla seats herself on the sofa.*

TEKLA: How sweet of you.

GUSTAV: And you know how to dress.

TEKLA: You taught me how. Remember? You showed me what colors were most becoming to me.

GUSTAV: No.

TEKLA: Of course you do. Don't you remember? You even got mad at me whenever I didn't wear something poppy-red.

GUSTAV: Come, come. Not mad. I never got mad at you.

TEKLA: Yes, you did—when you tried to teach me to think logically. Remember? I couldn't think at all.

GUSTAV: Of course you could. Everybody can think. Look at you now—you've got a sharp mind. At least when you write.

TEKLA (*rushing ahead, unhappy with this turn in the conversation*): Well, dear Gustav, it is delightful to see you again—and in such quiet circumstances too.

GUSTAV: You really can't accuse me of kicking up a row, you know. Things were rather quiet when you were with me.

TEKLA: Yes, a little too quiet.

GUSTAV: Indeed! Odd, I thought that's how you wanted me—quiet. That's the impression I got when we were engaged.

TEKLA: Who knows what they want when they're engaged? As Momma told me: to get a man a girl has to make a bit of an ass of herself.

GUSTAV: Now look at you! Always on the go, riding the merry-go-round of success. Never a dull moment in the life of an artist, and I gather your husband isn't the retiring sort.

TEKLA: Sometimes you can have too much of a good thing.

GUSTAV (*suddenly taking note of her earrings*): Look at that! You're still wearing the earrings I bought you.

TEKLA (*embarrassed*): Why shouldn't I wear them? We've never been enemies, you and I. Besides, I thought I should wear them as a kind of symbol—as a memento, I mean, since we always got along. Anyway, you can't buy this kind anymore, you know that? (*She takes off one of the earrings.*)

GUSTAV: None of my business, of course. But what does your husband think of it?

TEKLA: Why should I care what he thinks?

GUSTAV: You don't care, maybe, but what about him? Puts him in a bad light. Makes him look like a fool.

TEKLA (*curtly, as though to herself*): He was that to begin with.

> *She has been having trouble putting the earring back on. Gustav goes over to help her.*

GUSTAV: Mind if I lend a helping hand?

TEKLA: Thanks.

GUSTAV (*pinches her ear*): That sweet, lovely ear. . . . Suppose the man of the house saw us like this!

TEKLA: He'd bawl like a baby.

GUSTAV: Jealous, is he?

TEKLA: That man jealous? Ha! You can't imagine.

> *A noise in the room offstage right.*

GUSTAV: Who's in there?

TEKLA: I don't know. . . . Why don't you tell me about yourself? How things are—what you're working on.

GUSTAV: You tell me how things are with you.

> *Tekla is preoccupied and troubled. Moves about and absentmindedly removes the cloth from the figure on the stand.*

GUSTAV: My, my! Who is it? —What do you know, it's you!

TEKLA: Not very likely.

GUSTAV: Oh, but very like you.

TEKLA (*impudently*): How would you know?

GUSTAV: Reminds me of the old joke. Two men skinny-dipping. They come out of the water; see two ladies walking toward them. They put their towels over their heads so they won't be recognized. One lady says to the other, "That looks like Horace."

TEKLA (*guffaws*): You're too much! —Do you know any new jokes?

GUSTAV: No. But I bet you do.

TEKLA: Afraid not. Nowadays I never get to hear anything funny.

GUSTAV: Bashful, is he?

TEKLA: You might say—when he talks.

GUSTAV: Not otherwise?

TEKLA: Well, he's sick now.

GUSTAV: Oh, the poor thing. Well, Little Brother shouldn't go sticking his nose into somebody else's honey pot.

TEKLA (*laughing*): You're too awful, you really are!

GUSTAV: How about that time when we were just married? And we lived in this very room. It wasn't the lounge then, and it was furnished differently. There was a washbasin, wasn't there?—over there, between the windows. And—over there—was the bed . . .

TEKLA: Better stop now.

GUSTAV: Look at me.

TEKLA: All right, I'm looking at you. So . . . ?

They look intensely at each other.

GUSTAV: You don't really think I can forget? Forget the things that affected me most?

TEKLA: No. Memories have a terrible power. Especially the memories of our youth.

GUSTAV: Remember when I first met you? You were a small, lovable child. Your mind was pure and simple, like one of those little slates that children write on. There was nothing on it except some scribblings by your parents and your nanny. I wiped the slate clean and wrote my own words on it, and kept on writing until you felt there wasn't room for more. That's the real reason, you know, why I wouldn't want to be in your husband's shoes. However, that's his affair. It's also the reason why it's such a joy to see you again. Our thoughts dovetail, always have. When I sit here like this, talking to you, it's as if I were opening a bottle of my favorite wine, from my own vineyard. My own wine comes back to me, only improved with age. And now, when I'm thinking about getting married again, I have deliberately chosen a young girl whom I can raise to suit myself. Woman is supposed to be the child of man, you know; and if she isn't, *he* becomes *her* child; and that turns the world upside down.

TEKLA: You're going to get married again?

GUSTAV: Yes; tempting fortune once again. This time, however, I'm going to hold the reins tight. No running wild.

TEKLA: Is she pretty?

GUSTAV: To me she is. Maybe I'm getting old. The strange thing is that now—when chance has brought me close to you again—now I have my doubts about it—about playing the hand over again.

TEKLA: Meaning what?

GUSTAV: My roots are still imbedded in you. I feel it. I'm part of you, and the old wounds are opening up again. You're a dangerous woman, Tekla.

TEKLA: Am I now? How nice! And my young fellow says I'm past the age of making any more conquests.

GUSTAV: That means he no longer loves you.

TEKLA: What he means by love—that's what I don't understand.

GUSTAV: Your trouble is that the two of you have been playing hide-and-seek too long without finding each other. Happens sometimes. You had to pretend to be innocent—remote and pure—to please yourself—and consequently he could never be brash and bold. Oh, yes, changing the game creates problems. It does create problems.

TEKLA: You reproach me—

GUSTAV: Not at all. Whatever happens happens out of some kind of necessity. If that hadn't happened, something else would have. This happened to us, and it happened to turn out this way.

TEKLA: That's what I like about you, Gustav. You're broadminded and understanding. I can't talk intelligently with anyone else the way I can with you. No sermons, no exhortations. You don't make demands on people. I feel free and relaxed in your company. You know, I think I'm beginning to feel jealous of your wife-to-be.

GUSTAV: You know, I feel jealous of your husband.

TEKLA (*getting up*): And now we must part. Forever.

GUSTAV: Yes, we must part. But not without a fond farewell. What do you say?

TEKLA (*uneasy*): No.

GUSTAV (*pursuing her across the floor*): I say yes! A fond farewell, a last fling! We'll drown the past in drink. We'll get so drunk that when we wake, all our memories will have vanished. It's possible, you know: a binge to end all binges. (*Puts his arm around her waist.*) You've caught some disease from that sick soul. He's infected you with spiritual anemia. Let me breathe new life into you. Perhaps it is autumn for us, but I'll make your talent burst into bloom again—like a remontant rose. I'll—

> *Two ladies pass by outside on the veranda. Catching sight of Gustav and Tekla, they look surprised. Point their fingers, giggle, and move on.*

TEKLA (*freeing herself from Gustav's embrace*): Who was that?

GUSTAV (*indifferently*): A couple of tourists.

TEKLA: Get away from me. You scare me.

GUSTAV: How so?

TEKLA: You're taking my heart and soul.

GUSTAV: And giving you mine in their place. —What do you mean, your soul? You don't have any. It's a mirage.

TEKLA: You have a wonderful way of saying unkind things without making me mad.

GUSTAV: That's because you owe me. I hold the first mortgage on you. —Now tell me: when? And where?

TEKLA: I can't. I feel too sorry for him. He still loves me, I'm sure. I don't want to hurt him anymore.

GUSTAV: He doesn't love you. Want me to prove it? Do you want evidence?

TEKLA: How can you give me evidence?

> *Gustav picks up the pieces of the torn photograph from the floor.*

GUSTAV: Here it is! See for yourself.

TEKLA: Oh! It's scandalous! Outrageous!

GUSTAV: What more proof do you want? —So . . . when? And where?

TEKLA: The dirty little cheat!

GUSTAV: When?

TEKLA: He's sailing tonight on the eight o'clock boat.

GUSTAV: So—?

TEKLA: Nine. All right?

> *Noise is heard offstage in the room to the right.*

Who the devil is making all that noise? Who's in there?

GUSTAV (*goes to the door and peeps through the keyhole*): Let's take a look. . . . There's an end table that's been knocked over. . . . And a broken water carafe. That's all. Maybe they locked in a dog. —All right. Nine o'clock. Agreed.

TEKLA: Agreed. He's got no one to blame but himself. —What a cunning little wretch. He was always preaching frankness and honesty. Always telling me to be above board. —Now, wait a minute! There's something strange about this. . . . Let me think. . . . He didn't greet me the way he used to. Wasn't very friendly. Didn't come down to the dock. And . . . he said something about the boys on the steamboat, which I pretended not to understand. How could he have known about that? Now just a minute—he began to talk about women—analyzing them. . . . Then—he couldn't stop talking about you, thinking about you. . . . Said something about taking up sculpture because that was the art form of the modern age. Carried on about art exactly as you used to do.

GUSTAV: Not really!

TEKLA: "Not really!" —Ah, ha! I get it! I see it now. Oh, what an awful bastard you are! —You were here. You tore him into little pieces. It was you who had been sitting on that sofa. You got him to believe that he had epilepsy. You told him he had to—to—abstain from sex. Told him he should act like a man and rise up in revolt against his wife. You—you—it was you! —How long have you been here?

GUSTAV: A week.

TEKLA: So it was you I saw on the steamboat!

GUSTAV: I'm afraid it was.

TEKLA: And you really thought you could trap me?

GUSTAV: I already have.

TEKLA: Not yet, you haven't!

GUSTAV: Oh, yes, my dear, I have.

TEKLA: The big bad wolf sneaking up on my little lamb. Coming here with some dastardly plot to destroy my happiness—and you even put it in operation. Until I caught on to what you were up to, and put a spoke in your wheels.

GUSTAV: You haven't got it quite right. Let me fill in the details. . . . Of course I wanted to see you fall flat on your face. That was the wish I nourished secretly in my heart. However, I didn't really believe I would have to take any action. I was pretty sure things would go wrong without my intervention. Besides, I had so many other things that demanded my attention, there was no time left over for laying elaborate plots. But one day when I went out for a stroll, and by chance saw you with the boys on the boat, I thought the time was ripe for me to drop in on you. . . . I came here, and your little lambkin immediately threw himself into the arms of the big bad wolf. I won his sympathy because we were rather like mirrors reflecting each other. I'm afraid it would be very rude of me to explain. At first it was I who couldn't help sympathizing with him. After all, he was now in the same predicament I had once been in. Then, alas, he had to go and pick the scab off my old sores: the book you wrote about me, "the idiot," all that. That's when I could not resist the temptation to knock Humpty-Dumpty off the wall and make sure no one could ever put him together again. And it worked—thanks to you who had so conscientiously done all the preliminary work. . . . That left you. You were the mainspring in the works. All I had to do was wind you up till the spring broke, and all the wheels started spinning and whirring. . . . When I came to you here, I honestly didn't know what I was going to say. I suppose I had a number of alternatives in mind, like a good chess player; but it was your moves that determined my strategy. One thing led to another; Lady Luck played her part; and at last you were trapped, finished, kaput.

TEKLA: I am not kaput.

GUSTAV: Oh, but you are! What you least wanted has happened. The world—represented in this instance by two tourists (I assure you I never arranged it; I don't connive with others)—the world has seen you, the famous novelist, reconciled with your former husband—seen you, the repentant wife, crawling back into his ever faithful arms. What more could I wish for?

TEKLA: Nothing, if revenge is what you want. But then tell me—if you're so enlightened and fair-minded—how it happens that you, who believe that everything happens out of necessity, and that all our actions are predetermined—

GUSTAV (*correcting her*): *To a certain extent* predetermined.

TEKLA: It's the same thing.

GUSTAV: No, it isn't!

TEKLA: —How can it be that you, who regard me as innocent—and you have to, since it was my temperament and circumstances that compelled me to act the way I did—how can you imagine that you have the right to take revenge?

GUSTAV: On the same basis that you've argued—the basis being that my *temperament* and *my* circumstances compelled me to seek revenge. . . . Same rules for both sides. The two of you happened to draw the low cards. And do you know why?

Tekla sneers.

GUSTAV: —Why the two of you were so easy to fool? Because I was stronger than either of you, and cleverer. You, Tekla, you were the idiot. So was he. Understand? A person isn't an idiot just because he doesn't write novels or paint pictures. Keep that in mind for next time.

TEKLA: You are utterly devoid of feeling, aren't you?

GUSTAV: Utterly. That's why nothing gets in the way of my brains. Which means I can think—you knew that from before. And act—as you've just found out.

TEKLA: And all this merely because I hurt your little ego!

GUSTAV: Not the only reason. And why hurt other people's egos? It's their most sensitive spot.

TEKLA: Vengeful bastard! You disgust me!

GUSTAV: Frivolous bitch! You nauseate me!

TEKLA: It's my nature to be a frivolous bitch. Like it or lump it.

GUSTAV: It's my nature to be a vengeful bastard. Where does that leave us? You don't give a damn about other natures as long as your nature can take its course. But somebody gets hurt that way. Then comes judgment day and a wailing and a gnashing of teeth.

TEKLA: You can never forgive what was—

GUSTAV: Yes, I can. I've forgiven you, haven't I?

TEKLA: Forgiven me?

GUSTAV: Certainly. Have I ever raised my hand against you in all these years? Not once. All I did was come here to have a look at the two of you. One look and you split apart like a ship on the rocks. Have I ever reproached you, or lectured you, ever judged you? No. All I did was have a little fun with your spouse. That's all it took to make him crumble. —What am I doing? Why am I defending myself? I'm the plaintiff, not you. Tekla: have you nothing to reproach yourself with?

TEKLA: Nothing, nothing whatsoever! It's providence that determines our actions; that's what Christians say. Others call it fate. Either way, it makes us innocent.

GUSTAV: You think that fits all the facts, covers everything. It doesn't. Something more is needed—for the seams. You need some extra material for them—for our debts, which have to be forgiven. Sooner or later the bill collectors show up. Innocent? Yes, before God—who no longer exists. But still responsible to oneself and to one's fellow creatures.

TEKLA: So you've come to collect.

GUSTAV: I've come to take back what you stole, not what I gave you as a gift. You stole my honor, my reputation. How could I get it back without taking yours? Wasn't I right?

TEKLA: Honor! Ha! —Are you satisfied now?

GUSTAV: Yes! Now I'm satisfied.

He rings for a Waiter.

TEKLA: Running off to your girlfriend? Your fiancée?

GUSTAV: I haven't got one; and will never have one. And not running home. Because I haven't got a home; and don't want one.

The Waiter enters.

GUSTAV: Could you let me have my bill, please? I'm taking the eight o'clock boat.

The Waiter bows and leaves.

TEKLA: No reconciliation?

GUSTAV: Reconciliation? Your vocabulary is full of words that no longer have any meaning. How can we be reconciled? Should we arrange a cozy little threesome? You're the one who should reconcile us by making up for the harm you've done. But that you cannot do. Because you have only taken, and what you've taken, you've consumed, so there's nothing left to give back. . . . Would it satisfy you if I said: forgive me for allowing you to tear my heart and soul to pieces? Forgive me that you dishonored me. Forgive me for being made fun of by my students every day for seven years. Forgive me for liberating you from the tyranny of your parents, for educating you and freeing your mind from old superstitions and silly old ideas. For making you mistress of my house, for giving you friends and a social position. For making the child I first met into a woman. Forgive me my debts as I forgive you yours! —All right? I tear up all the IOU's; cancel all our debts. Now you settle your account with the other man.

TEKLA: What have you done with him? My God! You've done something, haven't you? Something terrible.

GUSTAV: With him? Do you still love him?

TEKLA: Yes.

GUSTAV: And a moment ago you said you loved me. Didn't you mean that?

TEKLA: I meant it, yes!

GUSTAV: You know what that makes you?

TEKLA: You despise me?

GUSTAV: I feel sorry for you. —Loving as you do—I don't say it's wrong, simply disadvantageous. It leads to the wrong things. —Poor Tekla! I almost regret what I've done, although I'm innocent. Like you. Perhaps you can learn something from going through what I had to go through. −Do you know where your husband is?

TEKLA: I . . . think I do. He's there−in the next room, isn't he? He's heard everything, hasn't he? And seen everything. And the man who sees his own double, he dies.

> *Adolph appears at the veranda door, deathly pale, a streak of blood on his cheek. His eyes are blank and expressionless, and he is frothing at the mouth.*

GUSTAV (*recoils at the sight of him*): No, he's here! −Settle up with him. Let's see if he's as generous as I have been. −Goodbye, Tekla. (*He moves toward the door at the left, but stops.*)

> *Tekla approaches Adolph, her arms outstretched toward him.*

TEKLA: Adolph!

> *Adolph sinks to the floor against the doorjamb. Tekla throws herself on his body, caressing him.*

TEKLA: Adolph! My sweet child! Don't die, don't die! Speak to me, Adolph. Forgive Tekla who was so mean to you. Forgive me, forgive me! Forgive me. Little Brother mustn't be mean. He must answer when he's being spoken to, do you hear?! Oh, God, he doesn't hear me. He's dead. Oh, God in heaven, my dear God, help us, help us!

GUSTAV: She really does love him, too! Poor fool!*

---

* In Strindberg's original manuscript (1888) the last line reads simply, "She loves him!" Strindberg expanded it in the French translation that he prepared and in the printed Swedish text.

Introduction
to
The Stronger

The critical success of Antoine's Théâtre-Libre in Paris inspired Strindberg to organize his own experimental theater in Scandinavia. His wife, Siri, was to be the star, and three or four amateurs would be recruited to form the company. For economic reasons the plays had to have small casts and simple sets, if the company was to tour. *Miss Julie* and *Creditors* were to be the show pieces in the repertoire, and Strindberg would furnish new plays as the venture prospered. Regrettably and predictably, it proved to be a fiasco. The Experimental Theater was to open in Copenhagen with a performance of *Miss Julie*, but the Danish censor forbade the public performance of that shocking play, even though Siri appealed directly to him. A newspaper demanded that its scurrilous author be made to leave the country. *Creditors* had to be substituted at the last moment, and the first performance of *Miss Julie* took place five days later, on 14 March 1889, when Strindberg rented a hall and invited theatergoers to a "private" presentation. A few days later the Experimental Theater performed in southern Sweden, and that was the end of it. Strindberg's dreams of having his own theater were broken by bad notices, poor actors, and unyielding censors.

One of the plays Strindberg wrote with the touring company in mind was *The Stronger* (written December 1888–January 1889), which was probably intended to be performed with either *Miss Julie* or *Creditors* to make a full evening in the theater. The short, serious sketch, called *quart d'heure*, had just come into vogue in Paris at the Théâtre-Libre.

The unusual feature of Strindberg's sketch was that one of the two actresses remains silent throughout. It is a clever tour-de-force, popular in acting classes, and another example of Strindberg's ability to concentrate dramatic action.

Inevitably the question arises: who is the stronger: the married talkative actress or the silent single one? Strindberg's own remarks, with one possible exception, indicate that the married woman is stronger because she has learned to be adaptable. The exception is that Strindberg told a Danish newspaper that the heroine of the skit does not say a word. But what did he mean by heroine? A scholar who has gathered all the material, pro and con, that bears on the question has concluded that Strindberg has neatly balanced one role against the other.* In the theater the question is settled by the way in which the parts are cast.

Strindberg's advice (letter of March 1889) to his wife when she was about to take the role of the married actress is clear and sensible.

Play the part
(1) bearing in mind she's an actress; in other words, not your conventional proper family wife.
(2) as the stronger, that is, the more pliant. The cataleptic one snaps, but the supple one bends under pressure – and rises again.
(3) elegantly dressed – use your dress from *Miss Julie*, or get a new one.
(4) If you get a new coat, beware of smooth surfaces, smooth pleats – and buy a new hat. Something in fur, bonnet shape, not English style.
(5) Study the part awfully carefully, but play it simply – that is, not simply. Make 50% of it phoney profound, like Mrs. Hwasser [as Nora in *A Doll's House*] and Ibsen, and hint at deep profundities that don't exist.
(6) Change phrases if they don't feel natural – and fix up your exit to get applause (but don't hiss at Y).

* Egil Törnqvist, *Strindbergian Drama* (Stockholm and Atlantic Highlands, N.J., 1982), pp. 64–70.

The Stronger

(Den starkare)

A Sketch

CHARACTERS

MRS. X, actress
MISS Y, actress
[A WAITRESS]

Time: 1888

*A ladies' café, only one corner of it visible. Two small wrought-iron bistro tables; a red shag sofa; some chairs.**

Mrs. X enters, wearing a hat and a winter overcoat, with a handsome Japanese basket on her arm.

Miss Y is sitting at one of the tables, a glass of beer, half-empty, in front of her, reading an illustrated magazine, which she exchanges for others as the scene progresses.

MRS. X: Well, hello, Amelia! Darling, what *are* you doing here —alone on Christmas Eve? Like some poor bachelor.

Miss Y looks up from her magazine, nods, and goes on reading.

Mrs. X takes off her coat. Her dress is tasteful and modish.

MRS. X: Oh, Amelia, dearest Amelia! This is distressing. You mustn't sit here all by yourself, alone on Christmas Eve, in a restaurant. I won't have it. Reminds me of when I was in Paris and saw a wedding party in a restaurant, and the bride sat there looking at the comics in a magazine, while the groom played billiards with the best man and the ushers. My God, I said to myself, if it's like this on the wedding night, how will it be in the morning, how will it all end? . . . Playing billiards on his wedding day!

---

* In a letter to Siri von Essen, March 1889, Strindberg suggested how the set could be quickly improvised. " 'Erect' onstage the corner of the café, a cave-like section, a booth . . . using flats from other plays in rehearsal. Hang up scenic vistas, travel posters, theater posters on the walls, so it looks like a café, with the counter and cases offstage. Set out an umbrella stand, coat rack, and so on."

—Well, she was reading the comics—that's what you're thinking. Not quite the same thing, though, is it?

> *The Waitress enters, brings in the cup of hot chocolate that Mrs. X had ordered, and exits.*

MRS. X: You know what, Amelia? Whatever I may have thought *then, now* I think you should have held on to him. I know I was the first to tell you to forgive and forget. You do remember that, don't you? Why, you'd be married now, and have a home for yourself. Remember last Christmas, how happy you felt out there on the farm, visiting your fiancé's parents? How you went on about the joys of family life—how you wanted to get away from the theater? . . . It's true, Amelia; having a home is still the best—after the theater. —And children, of course. Darling, you wouldn't understand that.

> *Miss Y gives her a contemptuous glance.*
>
> *Mrs. X takes a few sips of chocolate, using her teaspoon. Opens her basket and displays Christmas presents.*

MRS. X: Let me show you what I've bought for the kiddies. (*Shows a doll*). Isn't it cute? It's for Lisa. Look—it can roll its eyes, and its neck turns. What do you think, hmm? —And this is for Maia: a toy gun.

> *Mrs. X loads the popgun, aims it as Miss Y, and shoots. Miss Y gestures in fear.*

Mrs. X: Afraid?! You didn't really believe I'd shoot you, did you? Really! Bless my soul, I didn't think you'd harbor such nasty thoughts, darling. Now, if *you* had wanted to shoot *me*, that wouldn't surprise me. After all, I did get that part you had your heart set on, didn't I? You'll never get over it, I know. But I assure you I had absolutely nothing to do with it. You still believe, don't you, that I plotted to get you out of the City Theater. Well, I didn't. No matter what you believe, I didn't. . . . What's the use of talking. No matter what I say, you still believe I was behind it all. (*Takes out a pair of embroidered slippers.*) And here's what I got for the old man. Tulips! I embroidered them myself. I simply abominate tulips, really I do, but he has to have tulips on everything.

> *Miss Y raises her eyes from her magazine, suddenly interested, a sardonic expression on her face.*

MRS. X (*putting a hand in each slipper*): He's got such tiny feet, Bob has. Don't you think? —And he walks so elegantly. Well, you've never seen him in his slippers, so you wouldn't know.

> *Miss Y laughs aloud.*

MRS. X: Then when he gets mad—look—he stamps on the floor —like this. "That damned cook! Can't she ever learn how to make a decent cup of coffee?"—"Those aren't maids; they're cretins! They can't even trim a wick!" . . . Now there's a cold draft blowing across the floor, and his feet are cold. "Damn! It's freezing in here. Those blockheads, can't they keep a fire going in the stove?" (*She rubs the slippers together, the sole of one against the toe of the other.*)

> *Miss Y guffaws.*

MRS. X: Now he's just come home, and he's looking for his slippers, which Marie has put under the bureau. . . . Oh, I shouldn't be making fun of him like this. He's such a sweet man, really, my dear little hubby. You should have one just like him, Amelia. Do you a world of good. —What are you laughing at? Hm? Hm? What's so funny? —Listen, darling, one thing I know for sure: that he's faithful, true to me. Absolutely. He's told me all about it. —Now what are you grinning at? —That time when I was touring the provinces and along came that disgusting ogress Frederika and tried to seduce him. Can you imagine anything quite so infamous? (*Pause.*) I would have scratched her pink little eyes out if she tried anything like that while I was home. I would have. (*Pause.*) Fortunately, Bob told me all about it, so I didn't have to hear it via the grapevine. (*Pause.*) Of course, Frederika wasn't the only one. Believe me, she wasn't! I don't know why, but the women go gaga over him. He's *my* husband, but they want him. Evidently they think he's got something to say about

their contracts because he works in the administration. . . . I
suppose you've been on the prowl after him, too. . . . I've never
really trusted you, but there's one thing I do know: he was never
interested in you. And you always bore him some sort of a
grudge. Well, that's how it struck me.

> *Pause. They glance at each other, both a little tense and
> edgy.*

MRS. X: Oh, come on, Amelia; spend Christmas Eve with us.
Just to show that you're not mad at us – not at me, at any rate.
I don't know why, but it's so unpleasant – our not being friends,
I mean. I don't mind the others, but you –. I suppose it's because
I got that part you wanted. (*Rallentando.*) Or because –. I haven't
the foggiest idea. . . . Why? . . . I mean, why?

> *Pause. Miss Y stares probingly at Mrs. X.*

MRS. X (*thoughtfully*): It was so odd – our friendship. When I
met you for the first time, I was afraid of you. So scared I didn't
dare let you out of my sight. No matter where I went, I always
found myself near you. I didn't dare have you for an enemy, so
I made friends with you. Still, there was a wall between us, even
when you visited us at home. I could see that Bob couldn't stand
you. I could tell that something was out of kilter, just wasn't
right. Like a dress that doesn't fit properly. I did everything I
could to make him like you. But no luck. Not until you got yourself engaged. Than all of a sudden you became great friends. It
was as if the two of you couldn't let down your defenses until *you*
had found some security. And then –? What *did* happen? I didn't
get jealous, no. . . . So strange! . . . I remember the christening, when you were there as godmother, and I made him kiss you.
And he did kiss you, and you got so flustered. Funny, I didn't
think of it then. Didn't think of it till later. Never thought about
it till – *this moment*! (*Stands up abruptly.*) Why don't you say
something? You haven't said a single word all this time. You've
just let me sit here prattling on and on. Sitting looking at me,
dragging out my thoughts. Like raveling out silk from the
cocoon, where they've been lying all this time. Sleeping thoughts.
Things I suspected but didn't dare –. Let me think. . . . Why

did you break off your engagement? Why did you never come to
our house after that time? Why won't you come home to us
tonight?

Miss Y looks as if she is about to speak.

MRS. X: No, don't say it! You don't have to say anything. I can
see it all now. The whole thing. Why that was. −And that.
−And that. Oh, yes. It all adds up. That's it, all right. −How
disgusting! I refuse to sit at the same table with you.

She moves her things to the other table.

That was why I had to embroider tulips on his slippers. I detest
tulips. It was you who liked tulips. That was why −

Throws the slippers on the floor.

we had to have our summer place up at Lake Mälar: because you
simply couldn't stand the ocean. That was why my boy was
named Eskil. Because that was your father's name. That was why
I had to wear colors that suited you, read books you liked, eat
your favorite dishes, drink your favorite drinks − hot chocolate,
for instance. That was why −.

The enormity of the thought strikes her.

Oh, my God! Oh, God in heaven. How awful! How disgusting!
Everything, even what we did when we made love − everything
comes from you. . . . Your soul crept into mine like a worm
into an apple, bored its way in, ate and burrowed until there was
nothing left but the skin and some black crumbs. I wanted to get
away from you, only I couldn't. You lay there like a serpent, your
black eyes bewitching me. I wanted to run away from you but my
feet were like lead. I felt like I had been thrown into the water
with my legs tied together, and the more I struggled with my
arms, the faster I sank. Down . . . down until I hit bottom.
And there you were, lying in wait, like a gigantic crab, to catch
me in your claws. That's where I am now. . . .

My God, how I hate you, detest you, abhor you! Let me look at you. You just sit there, silent, indifferent, not caring whether it's Christmas or New Year's, new moon or full moon, whether others are happy or sad. Incapable of loving or hating. Quiet and unmoving, like a cat at a rat hole. You don't know how to catch your prey on your own; you don't know how to hunt it down; all you can do is outwait it. So all you do is sit here in your favorite corner. By the way, darling, you know what they call it, don't you?–because of you–"The Crocodile's Den." Reading the papers to find out what show is floundering, who's been thrown overboard, so you can gobble up the part. The crocodile flicks her tail, figures out who'll sink, who'll swim, looks for victims and collects her tributes.

Poor, dear Amelia. You know, darling, I really feel sorry for you. I can't help it. Because I know you're unhappy. Unhappy because you've been hurt; and malicious because it does hurt so. –I can't even get mad at you. I want to, only I can't. Because you're such a little person. So small and helpless. All that hanky-panky with Bob–why should I bother about that? What's it got to do with me? If you hadn't taught me to like hot chocolate, somebody else would have. What difference does it make?

Sips a spoonful of chocolate. Assumes a know-it-all air.

Besides, chocolate is very good for one's health. –Maybe I did learn from you what sort of clothes to wear. So what? *Tant mieux.* Now he's more mine than ever before. Where you lost, I won. In fact, to judge by certain indications, I believe you've already lost him. –Of course, I know what you thought would happen: I'd leave him. That's what you thought. Because that's what *you* did. Now you're sitting here regretting it. But, Amelia dearest, I have no intention of leaving him. Now we mustn't be small-minded, right? And if nobody else wanted him, why would I want him?

Maybe after all is said and done, maybe at this moment I really am the stronger of us. You never got anything from me. You only gave things–ideas. I feel almost like a thief in the night. You woke up, and I had everything you'd lost.

How else can you explain it? Everything you touched became worthless. You had the touch of sterility. You couldn't keep his love – any man's love, for that matter – with your tulips and your lovemaking. But I could. You couldn't learn the art of living, not for all those books. But I did. You didn't have a baby you could name Eskil. You only had a father named Eskil.

And why do you never say anything? Always, eternally not saying anything? I thought it was your strength; I did. But I guess I was wrong. You just didn't have anything to say. Because you don't have a thought in your head.

Rises and picks up the slippers.

Well, I'm going home. And taking the tulips with me. *Your* tulips. . . . You couldn't learn from others; you couldn't bend and adapt. So you broke like a dry stick. Well, darling, I didn't!

Thanks, dear Amelia, for all your help, your how-to-do-it lessons. Thanks for teaching my husband how to be a good lover. – Now I'm going home, to love him.

Exits.

Introduction

to

Playing with Fire

In 1891 and 1892 when Strindberg was separated from his wife, Siri, and involved in divorce proceedings, he wrote a series of one-act plays that he later characterized as "scenes from the cynical life." The series concluded with two longish plays that Strindberg wanted published together: *Playing with Fire* and *The Bond*, the first about erotic passion, sex and marriage; the second about sexual hatred and divorce.

Strindberg wrote *Playing with Fire* in August 1892, when, like Axel in the play, he was waiting for his divorce to become final. The situation in the comedy reproduced a factual episode from the previous year, the characters in the play being so unmistakably identifiable that publishers hesitated to print the play. Axel, however, is only twenty-six years old, not forty-two as Strindberg was at the time, and it has been persuasively argued (by Hans-Görman Ekman) that Strindberg chose to dramatize this episode because it so closely resembled one that had occurred in the 1870s when the twenty-six-year-old Strindberg had met and fallen in love with Siri. At that time she was married to Baron Carl Gustaf Wrangel. The baron eased Strindberg into Siri's arms. The three of them played with fire and they eventually suffered the consequences. Thus, Strindberg's 1892 play is a cautionary tale.

Both in its subject matter and in its tone it lies midway between sprightly French boulevard comedy of the nineteenth century and Chekhov's richly atmospheric and understated drama, which was still to be written. As in French erotic comedy, the plot takes shape around a few contretemps and ill-timed intrusions. As in Chekhov's plays, there are long, meaningful pauses and silences; the characters seem to be obsessed by love and have all the time in the world to play at it.

In *Creditors*, Gustav says that the lovers did not have the courage to tell the husband that they love each other. In *Playing with Fire* the lovers do exactly that. *Creditors* ends tragically; *Playing with Fire* ends comically. But hardly with any great inevitability. Strindberg wrote three endings for the play. As first written, the play ended with Axel discovering that Kerstin is two months pregnant. For the German translation, Strindberg provided another ending in which Axel learns from a letter that his divorce is not final. In both these versions, external reasons prompt Axel's sudden departure. In the final version, printed in 1897, Strindberg avoided any last-minute revelations and let Axel himself realize how intolerable his situation is.

Playing with Fire
(Leka med elden)

A Comedy in One Act

CHARACTERS

THE FATHER, 60, of independent means
THE MOTHER, 58
KNUT, their son, 27, a painter
KERSTIN, his wife, 24
AXEL, Knut's friend, 26
ADELE, Knut's cousin, about 20

Time and place: a seaside resort on a summer morning in the 1890s.

The set: a glassed-in veranda used as a living room. Doors at both ends of the veranda, and a door at the back leading to the garden.

[1]

Knut is at his easel, painting.

His wife, Kerstin, enters, wearing a dressing gown.

KNUT: Has he gotten up yet?

KERSTIN: Axel? How would I know?

KNUT: I thought you had your eyes on him.

KERSTIN: Shame on you. If I didn't know you don't have a jealous bone in your body, I'd think the green-eyed monster had got you.

KNUT: And if I didn't know that you could never be unfaithful to me, I'd never let you out of my sight.

KERSTIN: What brought this on? And why now?

KNUT: You heard me say "if" – "if I didn't know." You know how I feel about Axel. He's our best friend and good to have around. I think it's wonderful that you share my sympathy for that poor troubled soul. It's fine with me.

KERSTIN: Yes, I can see he's unhappy. But I must say he does act strangely at times. Last summer, for instance. Dashing off in such a hurry, without even saying goodbye, and leaving all his stuff behind. Why?

KNUT: Bizarre, wasn't it? I thought he left because he was in love with cousin Adele.

KERSTIN: Oh, did you?

KNUT: I did; but not anymore. Mamma's theory is that he went back to his wife and child.

KERSTIN: How could he? Weren't they divorced?

343

KNUT: Not definitely. And still aren't. He's expecting the final papers any day now.

KERSTIN: So you thought he was in love with Adele, did you? Interesting. Funny you never said anything before. Not a bad idea, the two of them getting together. Not bad at all.

KNUT: I wonder. Adele is such a wet blanket.

KERSTIN: Adele! Ha! A lot you know.

KNUT: She may have a marvelous figure, but I'll bet she's about as passionate as a fish.

KERSTIN: What do you want to bet?

KNUT: What do you know about it?

KERSTIN: I know that if she ever lets down her hair — well!!!

KNUT: Really?

KERSTIN: You seem interested.

KNUT: In a way.

KERSTIN: Which way?

KNUT: She posed for me, you know. When I painted the swimmer coming out of the water.

KERSTIN: Yes, I know she posed for you. But who hasn't? — Which reminds me, Knut: you shouldn't show your sketches to every Tom, Dick, and Harry who comes along. — Ah, here's Mommykins!

[2]

> *The Mother enters, unkempt, frowsily dressed, a wide-brimmed, showy Japanese hat on her head, a wicker basket on her arm.*

KNUT: Mama! You look like something the cat dragged in.

MOTHER: Such a sweet boy!

KERSTIN: Knut likes to be shocking. Find anything tempting in the shops this morning?

MOTHER: I saw these delicious flounder, and couldn't resist.

KNUT (*poking around in the basket*): What the hell! What are these? — Ducklings!

KERSTIN: Not very plump, are they? Feel the breasts.

KNUT: Oooh, I'd love to! May I?

KERSTIN: Naughty!

MOTHER: Well, he's back, isn't he? Your friend, Axel. I saw him come in last night.

KNUT: My friend! Ha! Kerstin's friend. She's nuts about him. They went for each other like lovers last night when he came through the door.

MOTHER: You shouldn't joke about it, Knut. You know what happens when you play with fire.

KNUT: I know, I know. But you can't teach an old dog. — Anyway, look at me. Why should such a handsome dog need to be jealous?

MOTHER: It's not what shows, Knut. Is it, Kerstin?

KERSTIN: I haven't the faintest idea what you mean.

MOTHER (*tapping her lightly on the cheek*): Don't overdo it, little girl.

KNUT: Kerstin is incredibly innocent — and an old hen like you shouldn't go around wising her up.

KERSTIN: You have a nasty way of joking. I can never tell whether you're serious or not.

KNUT: I'm always serious.

KERSTIN: It looks like it. You keep a straight face when you make your disgusting remarks.

MOTHER: I can see the two of you are just itching for a quarrel. Didn't you sleep well?

KNUT: We didn't sleep at all.

MOTHER (*clucking her tongue*): Shame on you. — Well, I can't waste the day standing here. Papa will be cursing a blue streak.

KNUT: Where is the old man? I haven't seen him.

MOTHER: I suppose he's out taking his constitutional with Adele.

KNUT: Aren't you jealous—a little bit?

MOTHER: Pooh!

KNUT: I am.

MOTHER: Jealous of whom?—if I may ask.

KNUT: Of the old man, of course.

MOTHER: Do you hear that, Kerstin? You see what a fine family you've married into.

KERSTIN: If I didn't know what Knut is really like—and if I hadn't known when I married him that artists are a tribe apart, I honestly wouldn't know what to make of you all.

KNUT: Just a minute! I'm the artist, the bohemian. Mom and Pop are philistines.

MOTHER (*no anger in her voice*): Nonsense. You're the philistine. Typical middle-class son, you are. You've never worked a day in your life—and how old are you now? And your father was no profiteering capitalist when he built this house for a good-for-nothing like you.

KNUT: Oh, it isn't easy to be the only son. It's hard, hard, hard. Come on, off you go. Otherwise the old man will be cursing you *here*—and I don't want to have my delicate ears singed. —I can see him. Hurry!

MOTHER: I'll slip out the other way. (*She exits.*)

KNUT: There's a hell of a draft in this house. Blows right through. Might as well be out in the open.

KERSTIN: Yes. Why can't your parents leave us alone a bit? Why do we have to eat at their table? Why can't we have our own maid?

KNUT: Why do you put crumbs on the windowsill for the birds? To have the pleasure of watching them eat.

KERSTIN (*listening to footsteps outside*): Shhh! Try to be a little more pleasant to your old man. I hate these morning tiffs.

KNUT: If only I could. It's not entirely my fault. He's never in the mood for my brilliant wit.

[3]

The Father enters, wearing a white vest and a black velvet jacket with a rose in the lapel.

Cousin Adele comes in a little later. At first she walks around rather aimlessly, then begins to dust and clean.

FATHER (*has kept his hat on*): It's chilly in the morning.

KNUT: So I see.

FATHER: Do I look cold?

KNUT: Evidently your head is freezing.

The Father looks at him disdainfully.

KERSTIN: You shouldn't talk to your father like that, Knut.

FATHER: "A fool's mouth is his destruction" – "and the father of a fool has no joy."

KNUT: Without the Bible, you'd be tongue-tied.

KERSTIN (*to Adele*): The room's already been dusted, Adele.

FATHER: "Every wise woman buildeth her house: but the foolish plucketh it down with her hands." Proverbs 14.

KNUT: Did you hear that, Adele?

ADELE: Me?

KNUT: Yes. Here's another one for you: "A fair woman who is without discretion is like a gold ring in a swine's snout."

KERSTIN: That's enough, Knut!

FATHER: I see you had a visitor last night. Late.

KNUT: *Too* late, you mean.

FATHER: I don't mean anything. However . . . why can't a young man choose a more convenient time to drop in?

KNUT: So you do think it was late.

FATHER: Was he invited?

KNUT: What is this? The inquisition? Have you brought the thumbscrews?

FATHER: No, that's your department. —If I ask you the simplest question, you threaten to leave. I built this house for you so I could spend some time with you, at least in the summer. When you get to be my age, you have a desire to live for others.

KNUT: Come off it! You're not old. Look at you! You look like you've been courting. A rose in your lapel! Who's the lucky girl?

FATHER: There are limits, Knut—even for your jokes. Wouldn't you agree, Kerstin?

KERSTIN: Knut *is* dreadful. But he doesn't mean anything. If he did—!

FATHER: If he doesn't mean anything when he says something, he's an idiot. (*He studies the portrait of Axel, which Knut has started on.*)

FATHER: Who's that supposed to be?

KNUT: Don't you recognize him? My friend, Kerstin's friend, our friend in common.

FATHER: Looks common. A bad sort, if you ask me—in this portrait.

KNUT: Well, he's not.

FATHER: A man without religion is a bad sort. And a man who breaks his marriage vows is a bad sort. So say I.

KERSTIN: But he hasn't broken his marriage vows. He's letting the courts dissolve the marriage.

FATHER: There was a time when Knut did nothing but revile your friend. Now it seems he can do nothing wrong. What happened?

KNUT: I didn't know him before. I've learned what he's really like. —Are you going to take any more pot shots? Or have you used up your morning supply?

FATHER: How about another proverb. I don't believe you've heard this one.

KNUT: I've heard all your proverbs and all your stories.

FATHER: There's "a time to love—and a time to hate." Ecclesiastes 3:8. —Good morning. (*He leaves.*)

[4]

Adele has started to water the flowers.

KERSTIN: They've already been watered, dear girl.

ADELE: I'd prefer it if you didn't call me that. I'm not your dear girl. You hate me.

KERSTIN: I don't hate you. Perhaps I should. It's because of you there's all this quarreling in the family.

KNUT: And now the two of you are at it.

KERSTIN: Well, why does she always have to be dusting and cleaning and watering in *my* house? You think she's helping me out. She's not. It's her way of criticizing me and showing me up.

ADELE: You take it that way because you know you're neglecting your house and your child. But I don't have any designs on you. I do these chores because I want to be useful. That's all. I don't want to live on charity. But you! You! What do you do?

KNUT (*going to Adele and taking a long look at her*): So you've got a temper, have you? Hot and excitable, hmm? Hot and passionate, too? Hmm?

KERSTIN: Forget it, Knut. Her passions have nothing to do with you.

ADELE: That's true. I'm poor. I can't afford to have any moods, any opinions, any desires, any passions. But if you get yourself a rich man and marry him, then you can do what you like—be waited on at table, have your bed made for you, do just what you want—*even at night!*

KERSTIN: You watch your tongue!

ADELE: You watch it! I could say plenty. I've got a good pair of eyes in my head! And ears, too! (*She leaves.*)

[5]

KNUT: All hell is breaking loose.

KERSTIN: Not yet, but it will. The day isn't over. I'm warning you, Knut: watch out for that girl. . . . Do you realize what would happen if your mother should die?

KNUT: No. What would?

KERSTIN: Your father could remarry.

KNUT: Ah ha! Adele?

KERSTIN: Exactly!

KNUT: Damn! —But we could put a stop to that. (*Thinking out the situation.*) She'd become my stepmother, and her children would share in the inheritance.

KERSTIN: I've already heard rumors that your father has changed his will to include Adele.

KNUT: It's not serious, is it? How far have they gone?

KERSTIN: Nowhere—all the way—who knows? One thing is sure: he's very fond of her.

KNUT: Fond, yes. That's all.

KERSTIN: Over head and ears, I'd say. Even last year he was jealous of Axel.

KNUT: Good! Let's pair them off. If they married each other—

KERSTIN: Put a bridle on Axel?? Not so easy.

KNUT: Why not? He's always in heat—like all ex-husbands.

KERSTIN: I'm beginning to feel sorry for him. He's too good for that she-devil.

KNUT: For some reason, the air is getting awfully heavy in here. Feels like a storm coming on. Oh, to get away from it all—go abroad.

KERSTIN: On what? You haven't sold any of your paintings. And if we leave here, your father will cut off your allowance. . . . Let's talk to Axel—tell him the whole story. He's good at arranging other people's lives—even if he made a mess of his own.

KNUT: Do you think it's prudent to ask a stranger to wash our dirty linen?

KERSTIN: He's our only friend, you said so yourself. How can you call him a stranger?

KNUT: It still bothers me for some reason. Blood is thicker than water. . . . Anyway, I don't like it. . . . As the old man likes to say, quoting the Seven Sages, "Always treat friends like future enemies."

KERSTIN: Now he's got you quoting his aphorisms. He has another one, just as awful: "The one to fear is the one you love."

KNUT: Oh, he's a hard man when he puts his mind to it.

KERSTIN (*seeing Axel offstage*): Well, good morning! Rip van Winkle is finally awake! (*Going to meet him.*) Did you sleep well?

[6]

Axel enters. He has on a light summer jacket, a blue necktie, and white tennis shoes.

KNUT: Top of the morning, Axel.

AXEL: Good morning, good morning! You haven't been waiting for me, I hope?

KERSTIN: We certainly have.

KNUT: Kerstin here has been worrying herself sick thinking you didn't get any sleep last night.

AXEL (*puzzled and embarrassed*): How so? Why wouldn't I?

KNUT (*to Kerstin*): Look at him! He's so bashful.

Kerstin studies Axel carefully, her curiosity aroused.

AXEL: Glorious morning, isn't it? What a delight to wake up in a house with happy people in it. Makes one feel that life is worth living.

KNUT: You think Kerstin and I are happy people?

AXEL: Of course! And your father is doubly happy. He's got his children and his grandchildren. With them around, he can live the best days of his life all over again. I tell you, fate allots few men such a happy old age.

KNUT: Never envy anyone!

AXEL: Oh, I don't. Quite the contrary. What makes me happy is seeing how beautiful life can be – for some people. Leads me to hope that life will smile on me sometime. Especially when I consider what your father has gone through: bankruptcy, ostracism, disowned by his parents . . .

KNUT: And now he has his own house – and property – a son well married. Or don't you think so?

AXEL: Of course I do. Absolutely.

KNUT: But what about last summer? Don't tell me you weren't in love with my wife?

AXEL: I wouldn't say that. Oh, I was mad about her for a while. . . . That's all over now.

KERSTIN: Aren't you the fickle one!

AXEL: Only when I'm infatuated. Fortunately – for me.

KNUT: So why did you run away last year? You dashed out of here as if the house were on fire. Was it because of another lady? . . . Or because of Adele?

AXEL (*embarrassed*): Now you're prying.

KNUT: Ah ha! It was Adele! I told you so, Kerstin.

KERSTIN: Why on earth would you be afraid of her? Unless you're afraid of girls.

AXEL: I'm not afraid of girls, only of my feelings for them.

KNUT: You're wriggling, Axel; and you're good at it. Never know where you're at.

AXEL: Why this particular interest in me?

KNUT: Do you know what my father said when he saw that portrait of you?

KERSTIN: Knut, don't!

KNUT: He said you looked like a bad sort.

AXEL: It must be a striking likeness. I am a bad sort—at least for the time being.

KERSTIN: You're always bragging about how bad you are.

AXEL: Maybe it's my way of hiding the fact that I am.

KERSTIN: You don't fool me. You're a good person, much better than you let on. But the way you act scares your friends away.

AXEL: Are you scared?

KERSTIN: Yes, sometimes—when I don't know what's going on in your head.

KNUT: You have to get married again. That's all there's to it.

AXEL: That's all, huh? And whom have you in mind for me?

KNUT: Ohhh . . . Adele, for example.

AXEL: Let's change the subject, if you don't mind.

KNUT: Ah ha! That's where the shoe pinches. You see, I was right all along. It's Adele.

AXEL: Enough of this chit-chat. I think it's time I changed. Into something darker.

KERSTIN: You'll do nothing of the sort. That outfit is perfectly charming. Adele will adore you in it.

KNUT: Listen to that, Axel! My wife thinks you're perfectly charming.

KERSTIN: What's so terrible about saying he looks nice?

KNUT: Women don't ordinarily go around publicly flattering the men they meet. Of course, we're not ordinary people, are we?

AXEL: After I've changed, perhaps you can help me find a room in town.

KERSTIN: What do you mean? You're staying here with us.

AXEL: No, I never intended to do that.

KNUT: Well how about that!

KERSTIN: Why won't you stay here with us? I want to know.

AXEL: I don't know. . . . Maybe you should be left alone. —Who knows, we might get bored with one another.

KERSTIN: Are you already bored with us? —Now, Axel, it just won't do, your staying in town. Tongues would start wagging.

AXEL: Wagging about what?

KERSTIN: Oh, come on, you know how people make up stories. You arrive one night, you move out the next day . . .

KNUT: It's settled: you're staying here. Let them talk all they want. If you stay here, they'll say you're my wife's lover — obviously. If you move into town, they'll say the lovers have split up — obviously. Or that I kicked you out. Given those alternatives, I think your reputation suffers less if you are taken to be my wife's lover. What say you?

AXEL: Phrased with admirable clarity. But if you don't mind, under the circumstances, I'd prefer to consider *your* reputation.

KERSTIN: There's something behind this — something you haven't told us.

AXEL: Quite frankly, I don't dare stay. . . . Listen, you know —. I mean . . . it's so easy to live someone else's life. . . . Enjoying their happiness. Your feelings merge with theirs. And after that, it's very difficult to separate.

KNUT: Why separate?! Now look, you're going to move in here with us. —Come on, give my wife your arm, and we'll go for a stroll.

Abashed and uneasy, Axel offers his arm to Kerstin.

KERSTIN: I think you're trembling. —Knut, the poor boy's shaking.

KNUT: You look so handsome, the two of you, arm in arm. —He really is all atremble. All right, stay here if you're shivering.

AXEL: Yes, if you don't mind, I'd prefer to sit here and read the paper.

KERSTIN: Of course, Axel, by all means. You do just what you like. And I'll send Adele in to keep you company. Knut and I will do a little shopping, won't we? (*Calling and waving offstage.*) Yoo-hoo, Adele! I've got something for you!

[7]

Adele enters.

AXEL: Would you mind keeping me company while Knut and Kerstin go shopping?

ADELE: Are you afraid of being alone?

AXEL: Terrified.

Knut and Kerstin leave.

AXEL (*checking to see that they are alone*): This may be my only chance to speak to you in confidence, as a member of the family. May I?

ADELE: Of course.

AXEL: You know how much I like Knut and Kerstin. —You're smiling. I know what you're thinking. It's more than a liking. It's true: Kerstin, being a young woman, exerts a certain attraction on me. But I assure you that, as far as her attractions are concerned, I keep my feelings reined in. Only for one moment was I afraid they had run away with me.

ADELE: Well, I am not surprised that you're a little taken with

Kerstin. She can be captivating, I know. What I don't understand is what you see in Knut. He seems to exercise some power over you. But he's a nonentity, far beneath you in talent and experience.

AXEL: A child, that's what you mean, a little boy. But that's what I like about him. After spending a whole winter among academics and intellectuals, I find his company gives me peace of mind.

ADELE: So can playing with children, but it's boring. Yet you never get bored with Knut. Explain that if you can.

AXEL: I haven't thought about it. However, I can see that you have. What's your explanation?

ADELE: I think that, without knowing it, you're in love with Kerstin.

AXEL: I don't think that's it. I like them best when they're together. Each one separately isn't as good company as the two of them together. If I saw them apart from each other, they'd both fade away. Anyway, even if what you say is true, if I were in love with Kerstin, what difference would that make, as long as I hide my feelings?

ADELE: The peculiar thing about feelings is that they spread — like fire.

AXEL: Possibly. I still don't see any danger in it. I've just gone through all the torments of a divorce. Rest assured I have no desire to see anyone else go through them — and much less would I want to be the cause of them. — Besides . . . Kerstin is in love with her husband.

ADELE: In love? She's never loved him. Unless you think being in love means having the same routines and habits. But Knut has very strong appetites. And one day he's going to get bored with the same old strawberries and sweet cream for dessert.

AXEL: Listen to you! You must have had a long engagement.

ADELE: Why do you say that?

AXEL: You seem so familiar with the territory. Let's go a bit deeper into it. I get the impression that there have been a lot of changes here since last year.

ADELE: For instance?

AXEL: There's a different atmosphere, a different way of talking, of thinking. – There's something that makes me uncomfortable.

ADELE: So you've noticed? Well, it is a strange family. The father hasn't done a thing for ten years except collect dividends. His son hasn't done a thing since the day he was born except clip coupons. They eat, they sleep, and await their going hence by passing their time on earth in the most agreeable fashion. Nothing to live for, no ambitions, no genuine passions. Just a general dismissive indifference to what's going on in the world. "He's a bad sort" – that fits everybody, explains everything. It's served up every day with our daily bread and a bit of the Bible, especially Ecclesiastes: "All is vanity."

AXEL: You're remarkably eloquent. And very penetrating.

ADELE: Like hate.

AXEL: Anyone who hates as you do must also be able to love.

ADELE: Pooh!

AXEL: Adele, now that we've thoroughly abused our friends, we have to be friends to each other, whether we want to or not.

ADELE: Whether we want to or not.

AXEL: Give me your hand on it. Promise not to hate – me. (*He offers his hand to her, and she takes it.*)

ADELE: My, but your hand is cold.

Kerstin can be seen in the doorway.

AXEL: Makes you seem all the warmer.

ADELE: Shh! There's Kerstin!

AXEL: We'll have to continue our little chat some other time.

[8]

Silence.

KERSTIN: So quiet all of a sudden. I hope I'm not intruding?

ADELE: Not at all. Perhaps I'm the intruder.

KERSTIN (*handing a letter to Axel*): This is for you. From a lady, I see.

Axel looks at it and turns noticeably paler.

KERSTIN: You're white as a ghost. If you're still freezing, I can loan you my shawl. (*She takes off her shawl and puts it over Axel's shoulders.*)

AXEL: Thanks. At least that's warm.

ADELE: Perhaps you'd like a cushion under your feet?

KERSTIN: It might be better to have a fire laid in your room. After a couple of days of rain everything down here by the ocean gets so damp and clammy.

ADELE: Yes, that's very true.

AXEL: All this trouble for my sake. Please don't bother.

ADELE: Bother? It's no bother at all. (*She leaves.*)

[9]

Silence.

AXEL: So quiet all of a sudden.

KERSTIN: Just like a moment ago. You two looked like you were exchanging secrets.

AXEL: I was getting a load off my chest. An old habit that I haven't outgrown.

KERSTIN: Unload some of it on me. . . . You're unhappy . . .

AXEL: Mainly because I can't seem to do any work.

KERSTIN: And you can't work because – ?

AXEL: Yes? Because?

KERSTIN: Are you still clinging to your wife?

AXEL: Not to *her*—only to the memory of her.

KERSTIN: Then why not relive the memories?

AXEL: Not on your life!

KERSTIN: Was she the one you ran off to last summer?

AXEL: No, she wasn't. I ran to other women. Since you ask.

KERSTIN: I think that's disgusting.

AXEL: Maybe. But they say that if you've been stung badly, the best remedy is a roll in the mud. Toughens the skin.

KERSTIN: I think that's awful. You, of all people!

AXEL: Bear in mind: there's good clean mud—and there's dirty mud.

KERSTIN: What's that supposed to mean?

AXEL: You know. You're a married woman. And we're both past puberty. Within marriage is consecrated earth; outside marriage is profane earth. But it's all dirt, all of it.

KERSTIN: You don't mean to compare—!

AXEL: Oh, but I do mean to.

KERSTIN: What sort of woman was she, the one you married?

AXEL: A virtuous woman, from the best of families.

KERSTIN: And you loved her?

AXEL: Much too deeply.

KERSTIN: And what happened?

AXEL: We got to hate each other.

KERSTIN: But why? . . . Why?

AXEL: There are a lot of unanswered questions in life, and that's one of them.

KERSTIN: There has to be a reason.

AXEL: I thought so too. However, it turned out that the causes of our hate were actually the consequences of it. We just didn't get along. It wasn't our differences that caused the breakup. Our love did. When love ended, the breakup began. That's how it is. And that's why the so-called loveless marriages are the happiest.

KERSTIN (*innocently*): I guess Knut and I have never had any serious difficulties that way.

AXEL: Now you're being a little too candid, Kerstin.

KERSTIN: How so? What did I say?

AXEL: You said that you've never loved your husband.

KERSTIN: Loved? Yes, what does it mean to love?

AXEL (*rising*): What a question! And from a married woman. What is it to love? I'll tell you: it's something you do but can't explain.

KERSTIN: Was your wife pretty?

AXEL: I thought so. In a way she was much like you.

KERSTIN: Does that mean that you think I'm pretty?

AXEL: Yes.

KERSTIN: Knut didn't think I was, until you told him so. It's remarkable how attractive he finds me when you're around. You seem to light a fire under him. He becomes so passionate.

AXEL: Does he now? That explains why he's so eager to have me hanging around. What about you?

KERSTIN: Me?

AXEL: I guess we'd better call a halt—before we go too far.

KERSTIN (*bristling*): What do you mean? What do you take me for?

AXEL: Nothing bad, Kerstin. Nothing at all. Forgive me if I offended you.

KERSTIN: You offended terribly. Even though I know you have a low opinion of women.

AXEL: Not all women. For me you are—

KERSTIN: Yes, what am I?

AXEL: My friend's wife—and therefore—

KERSTIN: And if I weren't?

AXEL: Time again to stop. Kerstin, you strike me as a girl who isn't accustomed to being flattered by men and played up to.

KERSTIN: It's true, I'm not. That's why being liked by someone just a little means a lot to me. Just a little.

AXEL: Just a little? Lucky you! You can't help but be happy in this life if you expect so little from it.

KERSTIN: What do you know about my expectations?

AXEL: You're not ambitious. You don't want to remake the world, climb to the top, become *somebody*.

KERSTIN: No. None of that means much to me. But I can't stand this monotony—no work, no emotional excitement, every day the same. You know, I get so bored I think the most awful things. Anything, even a great sorrow, is better than nothing. Sometimes I find myself yearning for—an epidemic—or hoping the house will burn down— (*Whispers.*) or wishing that my child would die. —Or that I would die.

AXEL: You know what's behind this, don't you? Idleness. Too many of the good things the earth offers. . . . Perhaps something else.

KERSTIN: What?

AXEL: What you need is sex—and you need it bad.

KERSTIN: What did you say?

AXEL: I'd rather not repeat it. You heard it, and you know what I mean. —And I didn't mean anything ugly or demeaning, so don't say I offended you.

KERSTIN: I'll say one thing: I don't know anybody like you. You slap your friends in the face and they don't really feel it.

AXEL: Could be. I've heard tell of women who love to be struck.

KERSTIN: You sound dangerous.

AXEL: I am.

KERSTIN: Who are you anyway? What do you want? What are you really up to?

AXEL: Don't be too inquisitive, Kerstin. You'll get your nose bent.

KERSTIN: Another insult.

AXEL: No, just friendly advice. —Why are we always quarreling when your husband isn't around? Have you noticed? It's not a good sign.

KERSTIN: Of what?

AXEL: Of a lasting friendship. We need a third party—a lightning rod.

KERSTIN: There are times when I think I could hate you. This is one of them.

AXEL: Now there's a good sign. . . . Tell me, haven't you ever felt that you could love me?

KERSTIN: Yes, once in a while.

AXEL: For instance?

KERSTIN: You've been pretty frank with me. I feel like being equally frank.

AXEL: So? When do you feel you could?

KERSTIN: When I see you talking to Adele.

AXEL: You seem to have the same heating system as your husband. He gets hot and amorous when I'm around. Adele and I seem to have the same function: we turn on the heat.

KERSTIN (*laughs*): That sounds so funny I can't help laughing. I can't even get mad at you.

AXEL: You should never get mad. It becomes you even less than others. —To change the subject: where's the man of the house?

> *Axel rises, walks over to the window, and looks out. Kerstin follows and also looks out. She is upset by what she sees.*

AXEL: I'm sorry. I had no idea he was there in the garden with Adele.

KERSTIN: So what! It's not the first time I've seen him kissing Adele.

AXEL: Too bad that Adele can't poke up your husband's fire enough to make you glow too. Very unfortunate. You know, there's a lot going on in this house that bothers me this year. I'm sure there's something rotting beneath the floorboards.

KERSTIN: I haven't noticed. Anyway, it's only a game.

AXEL: A game! With lighted matches, hunting knives, sticks of dynamite? That's no game!

[10]

The Father comes in, wearing his hat.

FATHER: Is Knut here?

KERSTIN: No, he went out shopping. Did you want to speak to him?

FATHER: Why else would I ask for him? What about Adele? Have you seen her?

KERSTIN: Not for quite a while.

The Father notices Axel.

FATHER: I'm sorry. Didn't see you. How are you?

AXEL: Fine, thank you. And how are you, Mr. Anderson?

KERSTIN: Perhaps I can be of help.

FATHER: Yes, you might at that, thank you. But if this is an inconvenient moment, I can come back.

KERSTIN: Inconvenient? Of course not.

FATHER: I have a little problem. There are mosquitoes in my bedroom, and I was wondering if I might sleep in your attic room.

KERSTIN: How awkward! We've just arranged for Axel to stay there.

FATHER: Ah! So he has settled in here, has he? Well, of course, if I had known that, I would never have ventured to suggest—

AXEL: I would never have considered the invitation to stay here, sir, if I had known that you—

FATHER: Now, now, now. I don't want to get in the way. There's an old saying: Put not your hand between the bark and the tree. Or between a lover and his lass.

Embarrassed silence.

Has Knut started painting?

KERSTIN: No, he doesn't feel inclined to.

FATHER: He has never felt inclined to work—now less than ever.

KERSTIN: Anything else you wanted?

FATHER: No, no. It doesn't matter. —Oh, yes: no need to speak to Knut about the room, if you don't mind.

KERSTIN: Mind? I'd be happy not to.

FATHER: Yes. No point in making a fuss if nothing can be done about it. Just embarrassing. If I could have had the room, that would be different. But if it's taken—! Well, see you later. (*He leaves.*)

[11]

AXEL: Excuse me, Kerstin. I'll be back in a minute or two.

KERSTIN: Where are you going in such a hurry?

AXEL: I'd . . . rather not say.

KERSTIN: You're going to look for a room in town, aren't you?

AXEL (*has his hat in his hand*): You can't think I'd want to stay here after being shown the door like that? I know when I'm not wanted.

KERSTIN (*attempting to take his hat from him*): No, you mustn't go! We didn't show you the door; he did. Besides —

[12]

Knut enters.

KNUT: What's this? Fighting? Or making love?

KERSTIN: Call it a lovers' tiff. Knut, can you imagine that this poor restless soul wants to leave us again and get himself a room in town? And all because Daddy came in and asked if he could have the attic room.

KNUT: Don't be silly. Why would he want the attic room? That was an excuse. He wanted to see what the two of you were up to. Don't tell me you wanted to go your way because of him! Axel! Axel! Down on your knees and beg Kerstin's pardon.

Axel kneels.

Now kiss her foot. She's got such beautiful feet, believe me.

Axel gives her shoe a fleeting kiss; then stands up.

AXEL: All right? I've begged forgiveness for going out to get a room. Satisfied? Goodbye for now. (*Exits hastily.*)

KERSTIN (*riled*): Axel! Axel!

[13]

KERSTIN: Why did the old man have to stick his nose in here like that? Absolutely indecent of him, if you ask me. Disturbing our domestic bliss! Now we'll never have a moment's peace — night or day.

KNUT: We'll have to make do somehow. I still think you could make a little effort to hide your true feelings. A wee little effort.

KERSTIN: What feelings? What *are* you talking about? Don't tell me you're . . . jealous?

KNUT: Jealous! Me? What's going on here! I was talking about your bad feelings toward my father.

KERSTIN (*suddenly sweet*): Knut, don't let's talk anymore about feelings. (*She takes a package from her purse and opens it.*) Here! Put on this necktie. It'll make you look more like a human being.

KNUT: What? Another tie! And blue again!

KERSTIN (*as she puts the tie on Knut and knots it*): We should do something about your clothes, too. You shouldn't go around looking so shabby. And you should comb your moustache.

KNUT: All right, Kerstin. Cut it out! You're so obvious. I can see right through you.

KERSTIN: What?

KNUT: Shouldn't I have a white linen jacket, too? And tennis shoes?

KERSTIN: Not a bad idea. It would suit you, now that you're getting a bit thick in the middle.

KNUT: And I should lose a little weight, too, hm? Look haggard and worn? Only one thing would be lacking: a divorce.

KERSTIN: Oh, my, Knut! Oh, my! Now you *are* jealous.

KNUT: I think you've gone the limit. Maybe. I don't know. It's strange. I'm in the grip of the green-eyed monster, but I don't feel envy or anger. I'm so fond of this guy that I can deny him nothing. I mean nothing.

KERSTIN: Nothing! Do you know what you're saying?

KNUT: Yes, I know what I'm saying. It's crazy, it's criminal, it's base, but if he asked me if he could sleep with you, I'd say, "Sure, go ahead."

KERSTIN: You're terrible! Talk about the limit! I've heard you say some awful things; I've taken a lot from you, but this—!

KNUT: It's not my fault. I can't do anything about it. You know, sometimes I'm haunted by a vision . . . when I'm awake . . . when I'm asleep. I seem to see the two of you together—I mean *together* . . . and I don't suffer any pain or anguish. Instead I sort of revel in it, as at the sight of something very beautiful.

KERSTIN: You really have gone the limit!

KNUT: An unusual case, perhaps. But, come on now, isn't it devilishly interesting?

KERSTIN: There are times, Knut, when I believe you want to get rid of me.

KNUT: You don't believe that for a moment.

KERSTIN: Yes, I do. Sometimes I have the distinct impression that you're nudging him, pushing him into my arms, so that you can make a case for a divorce.

KNUT: Hardly likely. Tell me, Kerstin, have the two of you ever made love?

KERSTIN: No, I swear it—on my mother's grave.

KNUT: Promise me, Kerstin, when it does happen, you'll be perfectly frank with me, and say, "It's happened."

KERSTIN: Knut, you're losing your mind.

KNUT: Yes. To prevent which I have to *know*. Either I give you up to him or I hold onto you and wonder if you're being unfaithful. I'd rather give you up and know where I stand.

KERSTIN: I've had just about enough of your soul-searchings. What about mine? What's going on between you and Adele?

KNUT: Nothing that you don't know and approve of.

KERSTIN: I have *never* approved of adultery!

KNUT: Ah ha! Changing your tune! It was harmless a moment ago. Now it's a crime.

KERSTIN: There's no change. A moment ago my relationship with Axel was perfectly harmless. It still is.

KNUT: Harmless and innocent today, but who knows what the morrow will bring?

KERSTIN: Wait till tomorrow and find out.

KNUT: Might be too late.

KERSTIN: Well, what *do* you want?

KNUT: I don't know. —Yes. An end to this business. If there is an end. We have woven our own net and trapped ourselves in it. God, how I hate him when he's out of my sight. But when I see him, and he looks at me with those big sad eyes, I love him like a brother, like a sister. . . . I can understand the effect he has on you. What I don't understand is what's going on with me. Evidently I've been living for such a long time alone with you and your skirts and petticoats that my senses have been infected—womanized—as if I had caught from you your affection for him. . . . Your love for him must be as wide as the ocean, although you don't know it.

KERSTIN: It's true. And now you're trying to put the blame on me! Of all the nerve!

KNUT: No, that's what you're trying to do!

KERSTIN: I am not! You are!

KNUT: You are! —I'm going stark raving mad!

KERSTIN: That's obvious.

KNUT: And you don't feel a bit of pity for me!

KERSTIN: Why should I pity *you* when you're torturing *me*!

KNUT: You have never loved me!

KERSTIN: You have never loved me!

KNUT: Here it is! The ultimate squabble—the one that will last till the day we die.

KERSTIN: Let's give it a rest—before it's too late. . . . Go take a swim. It will cool you off.

KNUT: I see. You want to be alone.

[14]

Axel enters, in high spirits.

AXEL: Well, I was in luck. Just as I was leaving I ran into Adele who had a room—

KERSTIN: Don't tell me that working girl rents rooms, too?

AXEL: She knew *of* a room.

KERSTIN: I'll just bet she did. She knows a lot, that girl.

AXEL (*taking out his cigarette case*): Cigarette?

KNUT (*pettishly*): No, thanks.

AXEL: That's a handsome tie. Who gave it to you?

KNUT: Like it? I'll bet you do!

AXEL: You've been saying nasty things about me in my absence. It's written all over you.

KNUT (*agitated*): Excuse me. I have to go for a swim. (*He leaves quickly.*)

[15]

AXEL: What's the matter with him?

KERSTIN: Jealousy.

AXEL: Really? But there's no reason for it.

KERSTIN: Knut believes there is. Where does Adele have that room you mentioned?

AXEL (*his thoughts elsewhere*): Room? Oh, over there, right across from the pilot's house.

KERSTIN: Isn't that cleverly arranged! From there you can look right into her room. What a little schemer she is!

AXEL: I don't think Addy ever gave it a thought.

KERSTIN: Addy! You call her Addy now? You must be very chummy with each other.

AXEL: Kerstin, you're making a mountain out of a molehill. You're letting your imagination run riot. Leave it alone, I say, or else—

KERSTIN: I know. Or else you'll run away, as usual. But this time I won't let you. You have no right to.

AXEL (*lighting a cigarette*): Maybe I have an obligation.

KERSTIN: If you're a true friend, Axel, you won't leave me here alone and unprotected. My honor is at stake, don't you see? In this house Knut is uncontrollable. His parents protect him. He can do whatever he feels like, no matter how indecent. You won't believe it. He even sank so low as to say he would, if he had to, give me up . . . to you.

AXEL: I thought you said he was jealous. I call that a most endearing form of jealousy. What was your response?

KERSTIN: How could I answer such a suggestion?

AXEL: Why ask me?

KERSTIN (*hysterically*): You're playing cat and mouse with me! I'm in your power. You see how I suffer, how I twist and turn to escape from this net you've trapped me in. Axel, look at me! Give me one pitying glance, but don't sit there like a stone statue, waiting for adoration and sacrifice. (*She goes to her knees before him.*) You're so strong; you can control your feelings. You're so proud, so honorable. Because you've never known what it is to love, to love as I love you!

AXEL: A lot you know about it! —Oh, for God's sake, get up, Kerstin! —Now go over there. —No, way over there! Sit in the easy chair. . . . That's better. . . . Now let me speak my piece. (*He remains sitting, smoking his cigarette.*) I have loved you—I guess that's the word for it—from the first moment I saw you. Remember an evening at sunset last year when we got to know each other? Your husband was at his easel, down in the dale, painting, when I happened to walk by. I was introduced to you, and we stood there talking to each other until we got tired standing. You sat down on the grass, asked me to join you. But there was a heavy evening dew, and I hesitated to sit on the wet grass. Then you unbuttoned your coat, spread out one of the tails, and offered it to me to sit on. You can't possibly imagine how I felt. It was as if you had opened your arms to me and asked me to lay my head in your lap. There I was, so unhappy, tired to death, all alone, and within that coat of yours was warmth, comfort, softness. I wanted to creep into it, physically, and hide myself in your young, virginal bosom. But I felt ashamed and ridiculous when I suddenly glimpsed in your innocent eyes a flickering smile. You were laughing at me, of course, seeing that a man like me could be overcome and flustered by your charms. . . . We saw each other time and again. Knut seemed to get some sort of pleasure out of the adoring attention I paid you. It was as if I discovered you for him. So I became your captive, and you played your little games with me. Knut felt no embarrassment in teasing me openly, even at parties. He was so cocksure, so confident, I felt insulted. Sometimes I could hardly resist the temptation to knock him right out of his shoes—and step into them. Remember that afternoon when I invited you both to celebrate my birthday? You told me you would arrive a little late. And after we had waited—for an hour—you made your entrance, dressed in a pansy-colored skirt and a bright, flowery bodice. And you had on a large straw hat, trimmed with yellow lawn, which filtered the light and showered your whole figure with golden rays. And when you handed me a bouquet of roses, with the shy impudence of a fourteen-year-old girl, I found you so overpoweringly beautiful that I lost my tongue, could say neither hello nor thanks. Tears welled up in my eyes, and I had to leave the room.

KERSTIN: I'll say one thing for you: you certainly know how to hide your feelings.

AXEL: Later that night, after the midnight supper, remember how for hours we talked, trading stories about our lives, letting our souls embrace? How Knut solemnly—and evidently with your consent—invited me to come live with you in town that winter? Do you remember what I replied?

KERSTIN: You replied—I remember the exact words—"I dare not."

AXEL: And the next morning I was gone.

KERSTIN: And I was in tears the whole day. So was Knut.

AXEL: Think how many tears there will be now!

KERSTIN: Now? —Now?

AXEL: Sit still!! —Now that everything is out in the open, nothing remains but for us to part.

KERSTIN: No, no! We mustn't part! Why can't things remain as they are? You're taking it calmly, and I'm not at all worried. What does Knut have to do with our feelings, as long as we control them? Look at us: we're sitting here, calm and collected, examining what has happened like an old married couple reminiscing about the time they fell in love.

AXEL: You're talking like a child. After you've said you love each other, you can never be just friends again. Don't you know that? If you don't, I wonder what sort of married life you've had. And me! I'm about as cool as a bursting boiler. As collected as a keg of dynamite with a lighted fuse! I—! I've agonized; I've fought against myself; but I can't answer for myself.

KERSTIN: I can. I can answer for myself.

AXEL: Yes, I'm sure you can. You can put out the fire as soon as it flares up. You've got a fireman in the house. But I live alone. —God, what an infernal idea! To live here after all that's been said! Feeding on crumbs from the rich man's table, filling my lungs with the air you breathe, drinking in the heady perfume of your flowers, my senses reeling, my blood boiling— and my mind burdened with a bad conscience.

KERSTIN: Why should you have a bad conscience? He doesn't make any bones about having a mistress whom he kisses in full view of everybody.

AXEL: Don't try that, Kerstin! Don't try shifting the blame. That shows how desperate you are. Dancing along the precipice, with nothing left but the final, fatal fall. Let's be different; let's be original for once. Let's show the world what it means to behave honorably. We'll make a clean breast of it. The instant he walks in we'll tell Knut, "This is it. We love each other. We want your advice. Tell us what we should do."

KERSTIN: Oh, Axel, Axel! That's magnificent! That's noble. Yes, that's what we must do. And whatever happens afterward, let it happen! And we can do this with our heads held high, because our hands are clean.

AXEL: And afterward? Of course, he'll tell me to leave.

KERSTIN: Or he might ask you to stay.

AXEL: On what conditions? That everything remains as it was? No, I couldn't accept that. Do you really think that after all this I could endure to see the two of you cuddling each other, hear the door to your bedroom close at night? No! There's no way out. Still, he has to be told, otherwise I could never look him in the eye again, never shake his hand. We have to tell him everything, and see what happens.

KERSTIN: Oh, how I wish the next hour were already over. Tell me you love me. I 've got to hear it, otherwise I'll never have the courage to plunge the knife into his heart. Tell me you love me!

> *Both Axel and Kerstin stay seated, far apart from each other.*

AXEL: I love you body and soul. I love your little feet, peeping out from beneath the hem of your dress. I love your pretty white teeth—that mouth made for kisses—your ears—your sexy, inviting eyes. I love every bit of your lighter-than-air body. I want to throw it on my shoulders and carry if off to the woods. Once when I was young I met a girl in the street, lifted her in my arms, and carried her up four flights of stairs. I was a kid then; imagine what I could do now!

KERSTIN: Is that all you see in me—just a body? I've got a soul, too.

AXEL: I love that too. Because it's frailer than mine, combustible like mine, faithless like mine!

KERSTIN: Won't you let me get up now and come to you?

AXEL: No! Absolutely not!

KERSTIN: Knut is coming! I can hear his footsteps. I won't be able to say anything unless you let me kiss you . . . on the forehead.

AXEL: You hear him coming?

KERSTIN: Shhhh!

[16]

The Father enters, hat on head. He crosses directly to Axel, who, startled, stands up.

FATHER (*picking up a newspaper from a table behind Axel's chair*): Pardon the intrusion. I was looking for something to read. (*To Kerstin.*) Have you seen Adele?

KERSTIN: That's the fifth time you've asked after Adele.

FATHER: Didn't know you were counting. Aren't you going for a swim before lunch?

KERSTIN: No, not today.

FATHER: Not wise of you to neglect your daily swim, when your health is so delicate.

Silence.

The Father leaves.

[17]

AXEL: This is too much! I can't stay here a moment longer!

KERSTIN (*approaches him and looks at him passionately, her eyes like glowing coals*): Shall we run away?

AXEL: Not "we." *I* shall run away.

KERSTIN: Then I'll run away too! We can die together!

AXEL (*taking her in his arms and kissing her*): We're lost, you know. Why did I do this? Why? It's the end. The end of honor and faith. The end of friendship. The end of peace. Talk about the fires of hell! Here they are—burning and searing all that was green and blooming. Oh, God!

They separate, move off in opposite directions, and sit down.

[18]

Knut enters on the run. His Father has obviously spoken to him.

KNUT: Why are you continents apart from each other?

KERSTIN: Because we . . .

KNUT: Why these troubled looks?

KERSTIN: Because we . . . (*Long pause.*) love each other.

KNUT (*studying them both for a while. To Axel*): Is that true?

AXEL: It's true.

KNUT (*somewhat crushed, slumps into a chair*): Why did you have to tell me?

KERSTIN: This is the thanks we get for being upright and honest!

KNUT: It's very original, but it's also shameless.

KERSTIN: You said yourself that when the time came we—

KNUT: True, true! And the time has come. It strikes me that I've known all along what was going to happen. And yet it's so strange to me that I can't take it all in. Whose fault was it? No one's. Everyone's. —Well now what do we do? What's next?

AXEL: Do you have anything to reproach me with?

KNUT: No. You fled when you saw the danger. You rejected our invitation to come live with us. You concealed your true feelings so well that Kerstin thought you hated her. Still, why did you come back to us?

AXEL: Because I thought my feelings were dead.

KNUT: Very plausible. I believe you. In the meantime we have to deal with a situation that we neither asked for nor could put a stop to. We tried to avert the peril by being ever so sophisticated and frank—joked about it—and all the good that did was to bring the danger ever closer. And now we're in over our heads. . . . What should we do? . . . I suggest we have a calm

discussion and remain friends right through to the end. . . .
What do you say? . . . What do we do?

> *Silence.*

No one answers. . . . Come, come, we can't just sit here while
the house is on fire. (*He gets to his feet.*) Let's begin by considering
the consequences.

AXEL: The most sensible thing would be for me to withdraw,
wouldn't it?

KNUT: I'm inclined to agree.

KERSTIN (*wildly*): No! No! You mustn't go! If you do, I'll
follow you!

KNUT: Is this your idea of a calm discussion?

KERSTIN: Love is not calm! (*She goes over to Axel.*)

KNUT: At least spare me the sight of your unbridled lust. Have
some consideration for my feelings. I am the innocent party—
comparatively—and I always end up suffering the most.

KERSTIN (*hanging on Axel's neck*): You mustn't go away, do you
hear! I won't have it!

> *Knut takes Kerstin's arm and pulls her away from
> Axel.*

KNUT: You might at least behave like decent people and wait
until I have left the premises. (*To Axel.*) Listen, old friend: we
have to come to some sort of arrangement, and as quickly as possible. They'll be calling us to lunch at any moment now. It's
obvious to me that you can't conquer your love for Kerstin, while
mine for her, on the other hand, can be vanquished—with a bit
of effort. Furthermore, for me to continue to live intimately with
a woman who loves someone else would always be unfulfilling.
It would always seem like polygamy to me. Consequently, I shall
depart. But—but not until I have some guarantee from you that
you will marry Kerstin.

AXEL: For some odd reason, your magnanimous offer is more

humiliating than any guilt I might have felt if I had stolen her from you.

KNUT: I can see that. I find it less humiliating to give a wife away than to be robbed of one. Now, you've got five minutes to make up your mind. I'll be right back. (*Knut leaves.*)

[19]

KERSTIN: Now what?

AXEL: Don't you see how ridiculous I've become?

KERSTIN: It isn't ridiculous to be honorable.

AXEL: Not always, maybe. But in this case it strikes me that the husband is less ridiculous. And one day you will despise me.

KERSTIN: Is that all you can say at a moment like this? Now, when nothing stands between us, and you can open your arms to me with a clear conscience, now you hesitate.

AXEL: Yes, I hesitate! Because I'm beginning to see my frank and honorable Kerstin for what she is. You don't hold anything back because you have no sense of decency. And you love to talk about honor because you have no heart.

KERSTIN: Well, of all the—!

AXEL: And that rotten smell I noticed in this house—I have a pretty good idea where it comes from.

KERSTIN: And so do I! It was you who seduced me! Pretending to be cold and indifferent, giving me those innocent little-boy looks, treating me brutally, getting me all excited, standing over me with a whip in your hands. Oooh! And now the clever seducer plays the virtuous prig! God!

AXEL: There's another version. It was you who—

KERSTIN: No! No! No! It was you! You! You! (*She throws herself full-length on the sofa and shrieks.*) Help me! Please help me! I'm dying! I'm dying!

Axel does not move.

Why don't you help me? Have you no pity, no compassion?
You're a beast! Don't you see I'm sick? Help me, help me!

Axel still does not move.

Send for a doctor! You might at least do for me what any man
would do for a stranger! —Call Adele!

Axel walks out.

[20]

Knut comes in.

KNUT: What's this? What's going on? (*To Kerstin.*) Don't tell
me you didn't come to an agreement?

KERSTIN: Shut up! I don't want to hear one word from you!

KNUT: Why did he dash through the garden like that? Ran as
if his pants were on fire. A human tornado uprooting bushes and
trees!

[21]

The Mother and Adele enter.

MOTHER: Well, children, do you feel like a bit of lunch?

KNUT: Lovely idea! Just the thing!

MOTHER: Now where's Axel? Shall we wait for him, or not?

KNUT: We certainly won't wait for him. He has fled the field.

MOTHER: A bizarre fellow, I must say! Dear me! I fried the
flounder for his sake.

The Father enters.

KNUT (*to his Father*): That attic room's available now, if you're
still interested.

FATHER: No, thanks. I no longer have a need for it.

KNUT: You're remarkably changeable.

FATHER: Not the only one around here. However, "He that is slow to anger is better than the mighty; and he that ruleth his spirit than he that taketh a city." Proverbs 16:32.

KNUT: I have one for you. Say not to a friend, "Get thee hence and come again."

FATHER: Not bad. Where did you pick that up?

KNUT: I got that from Kerstin.

FATHER: Ah, Kerstin, my child! Have you had your swim yet?

KNUT: No, she hasn't. She settled for a cold shower.

The luncheon bell is heard.

MOTHER: There! Come to lunch!

KNUT (*to his Father*): You take Kerstin in, and I'll take Adele.

FATHER: Nothing doing, my boy! You keep Kerstin for yourself!

CURTAIN

Strindberg's Plays

Strindberg's Plays

Fritänkaren (The Freethinker), 1869*
Hermione, 1869–70
I Rom (In Rome), 1870
Den fredlöse (The Outlaw), 1871
Mäster Olof (Master Olof), prose version, summer 1872
Mäster Olof, in verse, 1875–76. Epilogue probably written
   1877
Anno fyrtioåtta (1848), 1876–77
Gillets hemlighet (The Secret of the Guild), 1879–80
Lycko-Pers resa (The Travels of Lucky Peter), 1882
Herr Bengts hustru (Sir Bengt's Wife), summer 1882
Marodörer (Marauders), 1886. Revised in collaboration with
   Axel Lundegård as *Kamraterna (Comrades)*, 1887
Fadren (The Father), January–February 1887
Fröken Julie (Miss Julie), summer 1888
Fordringsägare (Creditors), summer 1888
Den starkare (The Stronger), December 1888–January 1889
Paria (Pariah), January 1889
Hemsöborna (The People of Hemsö), January–February 1889.
   Adapted by Strindberg from his novel of the same name.
Samum (Simoom), February–March 1889
Himmelrikets nycklar (Keys to the Kingdom of Heaven), autumn
   1891–February 1892
Första varningen (The First Warning), February–March 1892
Debet och kredit (Debit and Credit), February–March 1892
Inför döden (Facing Death), March–April 1892
Moderskärlek (A Mother's Love), April–May 1892
Leka med elden (Playing with Fire), August–September, 1892
Bandet (The Bond), August–September 1892
Till Damaskus, Part I *(To Damascus)*, January–March 1898
Till Damaskus, Part II, summer 1898
Advent, November–December 1898
Brott och brott (Crimes and Crimes), January–February 1899

*Dates correspond to year of composition.

Folkungasagan (Saga of the Folkungs), January–April 1899
Gustav Vasa, April–June 1899
Erik XIV, summer 1899
Gustav Adolf, September 1899–March 1900
Midsommar (Midsummer), summer 1900
Kaspers fet-tisdag (Punch's Shrove Tuesday), September 1900
Påsk (Easter), autumn 1900
Dödsdansen, Part I *(The Dance of Death)*, October 1900
Dödsdansen, Part II, December 1900
Kronbruden (The Bridal Crown), August 1900–January 1901
Svanevit (Swanwhite), February–March 1901
Karl XII (Charles XII), spring 1901
Till Damaskus, Part III, February–September 1901
Engelbrekt, August–September 1901
Kristina (Queen Christina), September 1901
Ett drömspel (A Dream Play), September–November 1901
Gustav III, February–March 1902
Holländarn (The Flying Dutchman), not completed, July 1902
Näktergalen i Wittenberg (The Nightingale in Wittenberg),
    August–September 1903
*Genom öknar till arvland, eller Moses (Through the Wilderness
    to the Land of Their Fathers, or Moses)*, September 1903
Hellas, eller Sokrates (Hellas, or Socrates), October 1903
*Lammet och vilddjuret, eller Kristus (The Lion and the Lamb,
    or Christ)*, October–November 1903
Oväder (Storm Weather), January–February 1907
Brända tomten (The Burned House), February 1907
Spöksonaten (The Ghost Sonata), February–March 1907
Toten-Insel (The Isle of the Dead), a fragment, April 1907
Pelikanen (The Pelican), May–June 1907
Siste riddaren (The Last Knight), August 1908
Abu Cassems tofflor (Abu Cassem's Slippers), August–September
    1908
Riksföreståndaren (The Regent), September 1908
Bjälbo-Jarlen (The Earl of Bjälbo), autumn 1908
Svarta handsken (The Black Glove), November–December 1908
Stora landsvägen (The Highway), spring 1909

Selected Readings

Selected Readings

SURVEYS OF THE LIFE AND WORKS

Campbell, G. A. *Strindberg*. London, 1933.

Gustafson, Alrik. *A History of Swedish Literature*. Minneapolis, 1961.

Johnson, Walter. *August Strindberg*. Boston, 1978.

Lagercrantz, Olof. *August Strindberg*. Translated by Anselm Hollo. New York, 1984.

Lamm, Martin. *August Strindberg*. Translated and edited by Harry G. Carlson. New York, 1971.

Lind-af-Hageby, L. *August Strindberg*. London, n.d.

McGill, V. J. *August Strindberg, the Bedeviled Viking*. New York, 1930.

Meyer, Michael. *Strindberg*. New York, 1985.

Mortensen, Brita M. E. and Downs, Brian W. *Strindberg: An Introduction*. Cambridge, 1949.

Ollén, Gunnar. *August Strindberg*. Translated by Peter Tirner. New York, 1972.

Sprigge, Elizabeth. *The Strange Life of August Strindberg*. New York, 1949.

Steene, Birgitta. *August Strindberg: An Introduction to His Major Works*. Atlantic Highlands, N.J., 1982. (A revised edition of *The Greatest Fire: A Study of August Strindberg*. Carbondale, 1973.)

Uddgren, Gustaf. *Strindberg the Man*. Translated by Axel Johan Uppvall. Boston, 1920.

ON STRINDBERG'S DRAMATIC WORKS

Bentley, Eric. *The Playwright as Thinker*. New York, 1946. Paperback edition, revised: New York, 1955.

Blackwell, Marilyn Johns, editor. *Structures of Influence: A Comparative Approach to August Strindberg*. Chapel Hill, 1981.

Brustein, Robert. *The Theatre of Revolt*. Boston, 1964.

Carlson, Harry G. *Strindberg and the Poetry of Myth*. Berkeley, 1982.

Huneker, James. *Iconoclasts: A Book of Dramatists*. New York, 1905.

Reinert, Otto, editor. *Strindberg: A Collection of Critical Essays*. Englewood Cliffs, N.J., 1971.

Smedmark, Carl Reinhold, editor. *Essays on Strindberg*. Stockholm, 1966.

Sprinchorn, Evert. *Strindberg as Dramatist*. New Haven, 1982.

Törnqvist, Egil. *Strindbergian Drama*. Atlantic Highlands, N.J., 1982.

Valency, Maurice. *The Flower and the Castle*. New York, 1963.

Ward, John. *The Social and Religious Plays of Strindberg*. London, 1980.

Williams, Raymond. *The Drama from Ibsen to Eliot*. London, 1953.

SPECIALIZED STUDIES

Andersson, Hans. *Strindberg's Master Olof and Shakespeare*. Uppsala, 1952.

Bergman, G. M. "Strindberg and the Intima Teatern," *Theatre Research/ Recherches Théâtrales*, vol. 9, no. 1 (1967), pp. 14–47.

Berman, Greta. "Strindberg: Painter, Critic, Modernist," *Gazette des Beaux-Arts*, vol. 86 (1975), pp. 113–22.

Borland, Harold H. *Nietzsche's Influence on Swedish Literature with Special Reference to Strindberg, Ola Hansson, Heidenstam and Fröding*. Göteborg, 1956.

Brandell, Gunnar. *Strindberg in Inferno*. Translated by Barry Jacobs. Cambridge, Mass., 1974.

Bulman, Joan. *Strindberg and Shakespeare*. London, 1933.

Dahlström, Carl Enoch William Leonard. *Strindberg's Dramatic Expressionism*. Ann Arbor, 1930.

Dittmar, Reidar. *Eros and Psyche: Strindberg and Munch in the 1890s*. Ann Arbor, 1982.

Johannesson, Eric O. *The Novels of August Strindberg*. Berkeley, 1968.

Johnson, Walter. *Strindberg and the Historical Drama*. Seattle, 1963.

Kauffman, George B. "August Strindberg's Chemical and Alchemical Studies," *Journal of Chemical Education*, vol. 60, no. 7 (July 1983), pp. 584–90.

Madsen, Børge Gedsø. *Strindberg's Naturalistic Theatre: Its Relation to French Naturalism*. Seattle, 1962.

Marker, Frederick J. and Marker, Lise-Lone. *The Scandinavian Theatre*. Oxford, 1975.

Meidal, Björn. *Från profet till folktribun. Strindberg och Strindbergsfejden 1910–12*. Stockholm, 1982. (English summary, pp. 390–403). On Strindberg's last years.

Palmblad, Harry V. E. *Strindberg's Conception of History*. New York, 1927.

Sprinchorn, Evert. "Strindberg and the Psychiatrists," *Literature and Psychology*, vol. 14, nos. 3–4 (1964), pp. 128–37. (Comment and reply by Theodore Lidz and Harry Bergholz in the following issue.)

Sprinchorn, Evert. Introduction to Strindberg, *Inferno, Alone, and Other Writings*. New York, 1968.

Stockenström, Göran. *Ismael i öknen. Strindberg som mystiker*. Uppsala, 1972. (English summary pp. 451–82.) On the religious and mystical thought in the post-Inferno works.

Uhl, Frida. *Marriage with Genius*. London, 1937. On Strindberg's second marriage.

FURTHER READING

Bryer, Jackson R. "Strindberg 1951–1962: A Bibliography," *Modern Drama*, vol. 5, no. 3 (December 1962), pp. 269–75.

Gustafson, Alrik. Bibliographical guide in his *History of Swedish Literature*, pp. 601–9.

Lindström, Göran. "Strindberg Studies 1915–1962," *Scandinavica*, vol. 2, no. 1 (May 1963), pp. 27–50.

Steene, Birgitta. "August Strindberg in America, 1963–1979: A Bibliographical Assessment," in *Structures of Influence. A Comparative Approach to August Strindberg*, edited by Marilyn Johns Blackwell, pp. 256–75.

Evert Sprinchorn, professor of drama at Vassar College, is the author of *Strindberg as Dramatist,* editor and co-translator of Strindberg's *Chamber Plays* (revised edition, Minnesota, 1981), and translator of several of the dramatist's autobiographical works. He has also edited Ibsen's letters and Wagner's writings on music and drama.